Sexual Violence and American Slavery

Sexual Violence and American Slavery

The Making of a Rape Culture in the Antebellum South

Shannon C. Eaves

The University of North Carolina Press CHAPEL HILL

This book was published with the assistance of the Anniversary Fund of the University of North Carolina Press.

Set in Merope Basic by Westchester Publishing Services
Manufactured in the United States of America

Library of Congress Cataloging-in-Publication Data
Names: Eaves, Shannon, author.
Title: Sexual violence and American slavery : the making of a rape culture in the antebellum South / Shannon Eaves.
Other titles: Making of a rape culture in the antebellum South
Description: Chapel Hill : The University of North Carolina Press, [2024] | Includes bibliographical references and index.
Identifiers: LCCN 2023047025 | ISBN 9781469678801 (cloth ; alk. paper) | ISBN 9781469678818 (pbk. ; alk. paper) | ISBN 9781469678825 (epub) | ISBN 9798890887139 (pdf)
Subjects: LCSH: Enslaved women—Crimes against—Southern States—History—19th century. | African American women—Crimes against—Southern States—History—19th century. | Sexual assault—Southern States—History—19th century. | Rape—Southern States—History—19th century. | Slavery—Southern States—History—19th century. | BISAC: HISTORY / African American & Black | HISTORY / United States / State & Local / South (AL, AR, FL, GA, KY, LA, MS, NC, SC, TN, VA, WV)
Classification: LCC E443 .E28 2024 | DDC 975.00496/073003—dc23/eng/20231025
LC record available at https://lccn.loc.gov/2023047025

Cover art by feisty/stock.adobe.com.

For Pearl and Clay

Contents

List of Illustrations ix

Acknowledgments xi

Introduction 1

CHAPTER ONE
Navigating the South's Rape Culture 16

CHAPTER TWO
She Would Rather Die a Thousand Deaths 48

CHAPTER THREE
The Men Had No Comfort with Their Wives 71

CHAPTER FOUR
The Greater Part of Slaveholders Are Licentious Men 96

CHAPTER FIVE
A Licentious Master and a Jealous Mistress 113

CHAPTER SIX
Petitions from Jealous and Discontented Wives 139

Epilogue 169

Notes 175

Bibliography 201

Index 217

Illustrations

Virginia Boyd letter 61

Laura Gresham letter 126

Acknowledgments

"'To whom much is given, much is required." My father spoke these words to me frequently throughout my childhood. This scripture has become a great source of strength, motivation, and light in my life and certainly helped me bring this book to fruition. I could not have completed this work without the advisement, financial support, guidance, prayers, and encouragement of many people. My prayer is that this book honors these words and my ancestors upon whose shoulders I stand.

I graciously thank Heather A. Williams, my dissertation adviser at the University of North Carolina at Chapel Hill, who took a chance on me and believed that I could do this work from the very beginning. My dissertation committee members, Kathleen DuVal, Thavolia Glymph, Jacquelyn Dowd Hall, and John Wood Sweet, mentored me, encouraged me, and provided guidance that helped me shape this project.

I am grateful to all the organizations that funded my research and writing of this book. I received yearlong fellowships from the American Association of University Women and the Department of History at Rutgers University, under the direction of Deborah Gray White. I am especially grateful to Dr. White for not only paving the way for Black women's history and Black women scholars like me but also affording me the opportunity of a lifetime. I also received generous funding from the Office of the Dean of the School of Humanities and Social Sciences, the Department of History, and the Office of Institutional Diversity at the College of Charleston; the Office of Academic and Student Affairs at the University of North Florida; the Graduate School, the Department of History, and the Center for the Study of the American South at the University of North Carolina at Chapel Hill; and the Virginia Museum of History and Culture.

Thank you to the archivists and staff members at the National Archives and Records Administration, the Virginia Museum of History and Culture, the Library of Virginia, the State Archives of North Carolina, the Southern Historical Collection, the South Carolina Department of Archives and History, the South Carolina Historical Society, the South Caroliniana Library, the Special Collections Archive at the College of Charleston, and the State

Library and Archives of Florida. I would especially like to thank archivists Holly Smith and Mary Jo Fairchild for lighting pathways in the archive.

To my colleagues and students—past and present—at the College of Charleston and the University of North Florida, I thank you for your collegiality and inspiration. My graduate assistant Lauren Wingate was especially helpful as I prepared this manuscript. She was an excellent fact-checker and source of encouragement.

Thank you to Debbie Gershenowitz at the University of North Carolina Press for your enthusiastic support of this book. Your confidence never wavered, and I appreciate you beyond measure. I also thank JessieAnne D'Amico and the entire UNC Press team.

So many scholars blazed the trail and inspired my research of slavery, race, and gender. I am especially grateful to Deborah Gray White, Darlene Clark Hine, Saidiya Hartman, Thelma Jennings, Wilma King, Nell Irvin Painter, Brenda Stevenson, Jacqueline Jones, Tera Hunter, Thavolia Glymph, Jennifer Morgan, Daina Ramey Berry, Erica Armstrong Dunbar, Amrita Chakrabarti Myers, Jessica Millward, Stephanie M. H. Camp, Marisa Fuentes, Deirdre Cooper Owens, Sasha Turner, Stephanie E. Jones-Rogers, and Tamika Nunley.

There are numerous scholars who took time to talk with me about my project, read chapter drafts, and offer helpful comments at conferences and seminars. These scholars include Thavolia Glymph, Tera Hunter, Richard Godbeer, Catherine Clinton, Hannah Rosen, Marisa Fuentes, Deirdre Cooper Owens, Tamika Nunley, Mari N. Crabtree, Alexis Broderick, Jessica Wilkerson, Elizabeth Lundeen, Anna Krome-Lukens, Sarah McNamara, Joey Fink, and my colleagues in the Department of History at the College of Charleston. I owe a tremendous debt of gratitude to Sasha Turner and Danielle McGuire, who read the entire manuscript and offered keen insight for making the book better. Thank you also to the participants of the Black Bodies Seminar convened by Marisa Fuentes and Bayo Holsey and sponsored by the Rutgers Center for Historical Analysis. I received mentoring and valuable feedback from so many, including Marisa Fuentes, Bayo Holsey, Deborah Gray White, Kim Butler, Kali Gross, Brittney Cooper, Nikol Alexander-Floyd, Savannah Shange, and Poe Johnson.

Without Sasha Turner, this book might have remained a series of files on my desktop. Sasha, thank you so much for your mentorship. You extended yourself to me at a time when I needed it most. You gave me the confidence and tools to start the publication process, and I cannot thank you enough.

Mari N. Crabtree, Tara Bynum, and Lisa Young—my writing group crew—you gave me the motivation, accountability, and sisterhood that I needed to revise this manuscript. You provided much-needed light during the height of the COVID-19 pandemic and a soundtrack to which I could write, survive, and thrive.

People say that friends are the family you get to choose. I can attest that this is true. Thank you Candice Coleman, Sharee Smith, Stephanie Lykes, Curtrell Rhodan, Kimberly Jenkins, Shadonna Richardson, Sylvia G. Brown, Marcia R. Mensah, Tonya D. Registre, Jessie Wilkerson, Liz Lundeen, Sarah McNamara, Alexis Broderick, and my many special sisters of Alpha Kappa Alpha Sorority, Inc. To Danielle Duvall Adams, my dearest friend and sister, this book is as much yours as it is mine. Thank you for everything.

My family has been my rock throughout this process. I give thanks to my foremothers and forefathers, Lemuel and Edna Eaves and Hawley and Pearl Newsome. To my parents, Robert and Lil Eaves, thank you for encouraging me to pursue my dreams, for nurturing my talents and interests, and for supporting my education. Most importantly, thank you for your unconditional love, your prayers, and teaching me to place my faith in God. I am grateful for my brother, Bradford Eaves. Thank you, Brad, for always being my biggest cheerleader. I admire your compassion, vast knowledge of the world, and cool style. Thank you to Tracy Wells, who is not just my sister-in-law but my sister. To my precious niece and nephew, Pearl and Clay: This book is dedicated to you. May you never forget that you are your ancestors' wildest dream.

Family means everything to me, and I am who I am because of my amazing extended families. The Eaves, Newsome, and Parker-Dance families are my foundation. I especially want to acknowledge Bettie and Jimmy George, my godparents, as well as Hawletta Newsome, Lee Askew, Jeanna (my sister-cousin) and Jay Hawkins, Harlow Hawkins, Kylin Hawkins, Alex Askew, Wesley Newsome, Cynthia Quarles, Meshia Eaves, Brittney Eaves, Tanisha Malcom, Justin Eaves, and the entire Eaves Connection. I know my uncle Leon Newsome continues to look down on me. I hope I have made him proud. Lastly, I give all honor and glory to God. This book is evidence that I can do all things through Christ who strengthens me. Thanks be to God.

Sexual Violence and
American Slavery

Introduction

As a young boy, Frederick Douglass felt great admiration for his aunt Hester. He described her as a young woman of noble form and graceful proportions who had personal charms few could match. It was no surprise that the fifteen-year-old Hester caught the eye of a young enslaved man named Edward Roberts, who, according to Douglass, was "as fine looking a young man, as she was a woman." The two developed an intense romance, much to her owner's displeasure. Aaron Anthony had a long history of sexually assaulting and harassing enslaved women, and now Hester was the focus of his attention. He made it his mission "to break up the growing intimacy between Hester and Edward," said Douglass. Because he wanted access to Hester, whenever and wherever, he ordered her not to go out in the evenings and "warned her that she must never let him catch her in the company" of Edward.[1]

Hester was determined, however, to have some control over her sexual and romantic life. She continued to see Edward when she could, and she did so at grave risk. Anthony had threatened to "punish her severely if he ever found her again in Edward's company." Yet Hester was strong willed, and "it was impossible to keep Edward and Esther [Hester] apart. Meet they would, and meet they did," said Douglass. Hester likely found comfort, in addition to pleasure, in being intimate with a man of her choosing, despite how dire the consequences would be if she were ever caught.[2]

One night, Anthony went looking for Hester, as he had done on many nights before, because he "desired her presence." After conducting an extensive search, he found her, but she was not alone. She was with Edward, the young man Anthony had forbidden her to see. Infuriated, Anthony seemed determined to crush once and for all Hester's resolve to resist his sexual demands and explore her sexuality on her own terms. Because he had the authority to do so, he "very easily took revenge," said Douglass. Anthony dragged Hester into the very kitchen where she worked and slept. From there, he tore off her clothes, tied her hands together, and hung her from a hook in the ceiling. Next, Anthony yelled, "I'll learn you how to disobey my orders," and started flogging her with a cowhide whip. With each strike, she screamed out. A seven-year-old Frederick Douglass, who had been asleep in a makeshift closet in the kitchen, was awakened by her "heart-rending

1

shrieks," a sound that became grossly familiar to him over time. Through the boards of the makeshift closet, Douglass witnessed Anthony wage this vicious attack on Hester.[3]

This was the first time Douglass witnessed Anthony bind and whip his aunt. Anthony staged these brutal acts, as Douglass came to understand, to rebuke Hester for evading his attempts to sexually assault her and pursuing a romantic partnership of her own choosing. Recounting the whip, blood, and thickness of the air, Douglass likened the first assault he witnessed to a "blood-stained gate." He described this moment as his personal entryway into the "hell of slavery." It was the foundational moment when he became acutely conscious of the "gross features of slavery."[4]

Douglass wrote that though he had heard of floggings before, something transformative occurred when he first bore witness to this sexual assault. Though indirectly, he shared in this experience of sexual violence with Hester. He was shaken by the sordid mixture of crudeness and pleasure that appeared in Anthony's eyes and the way in which he fixated on Hester's limp body. Douglass cared for and admired his Aunt Hester. He spoke fondly of her outer beauty and inner tenacity. Seeing her in pain and later learning that she was being tortured for resisting sexual assault and trying to carve out space for love and joy caused him distress. Though a child, he quickly learned how grotesque and sexually charged Anthony's displays of ownership and power were.[5]

Hester experienced unimaginable pain as a result of Aaron Anthony's brutality. The victim of sexual violence, she suffered unquestionable physical and psychological trauma. Douglass, in his retelling of Hester's abuse, gave voice to the trauma he incurred as a witness to this brutality. His trauma did not mirror Hester's, of course, but the impressions were intense and lasting. "I was so terrified and horror-stricken at the sight, that I hid myself in a closet and dared not venture out till long after the bloody transaction was over," he said. Douglass thought that if he left his small, makeshift closet, making his presence known, "it would be [his] turn next."[6]

Hester's sexual assault became permanently etched in Douglass's consciousness. "I was quite a child, but I well remember it. I never shall forget it whilst I remember any thing," said Douglass. "It was the first of a long series of such outrages, of which I was doomed to be a witness and a participant." It was Douglass's fate of knowing—knowing the dreadful possibilities and knowing the enslaved person's constraints in escaping such fates—that stood before Douglass, this metaphorical "blood-stained gate." Passage through the gate was not voluntary. The sight of his aunt "struck me with awful force," Douglass said, hurling him across the threshold to the other side.[7]

It was in my quest to better understand the emotional toll that rape, sexual violence, and reproductive exploitation took on enslaved women that I first encountered Douglass's accounts of his aunt Hester. Initially, all I could absorb were the descriptions of the brutality. As I read and reread Douglass's accounts of Hester's abuse, I began to pay more attention to how he described his own relationship to the "long series of such outrages" Anthony inflicted on Hester. It is intuitive to focus one's attention on Hester. Enslaved women and girls *were* the primary victims of systematic rape and sexual assault under chattel slavery. What is less visible is the trauma suffered by those like Douglass, who bore witness through sight or sound or who learned of these events secondhand. Douglass's words were begging for me to pay attention to the collective impact of the systematic rape and sexual exploitation of enslaved women like Hester. Accounts of sexual violence are brutally difficult and can also be traumatic to read; to look away might be tempting. But the systematic rape and sexual exploitation of enslaved women and girls like Hester was and remains a painful truth of American slavery. I could not shield myself (or the reader) from these accounts of sexual violence because the reality is that the physical, emotional, and psychological impact of the systematic rape and sexual exploitation of enslaved women on enslaved people was too great to ignore or downplay.[8]

Rape, sexual harassment, coercion, and sexual reproductive exploitation were not simply ill-fated by-products or unintended evils of the construction and maintenance of chattel slavery in the antebellum South. Rather, the antebellum South was deeply rooted in a rape culture. Within Southern plantation communities, both urban and rural, white male slave owners, overseers, patrollers, and others consciously used rape and sexual violence against enslaved women in particular to demonstrate and reinforce their authority. By subjecting enslaved women to both random and routine acts of sexual violence and prohibiting enslaved mothers, fathers, lovers, children, and communities from mounting formidable measures of defense, they communicated their dominance over not only enslaved women but enslaved communities at large. They also made it clear that those who determined to challenge these conditions would do so at grave risk.[9]

At its core, *Sexual Violence and American Slavery: The Making of a Rape Culture in the Antebellum South* is about knowing. It explores how the enslaved and enslavers alike came to know about the systematic rape and sexual exploitation of enslaved women and what living within this rape culture meant for their lives and the lives of others. Through sight, sound, and lessons taught by parents to children, the enslaved and the enslavers learned how to survive and sustain this rape culture. In this study, I examine the ways in which the enslaved and the enslavers, as well as their agents, challenged the boundaries of power that the rape and sexual exploitation of enslaved women were intended to hold firm in the antebellum South. I also examine how this shared consciousness between enslavers *and* the enslaved manifested in their day-to-day navigation of space, interpersonal relationships, and negotiations for power and autonomy within the slaveholding South.[10]

Scholar Susan Griffin has likened rape to a form of mass terrorism. In the South's slave regime, the terrorism of rape was "beneficial to the ruling class of white males," fortifying their claims of absolute authority over enslaved people's bodies. It severely restricted, though to varying degrees, the rights to self-determination for all who were living in bondage. For Frederick Douglass, he came to understand that Aaron Anthony's brutal attacks against Hester—these performances of mastery—were designed to terrorize him as well. Douglass said that his vantage point from the utility closet in Anthony's kitchen doomed him not only to witness but also to *experience* her suffering. He did not receive strikes on his back or have blood pooling at his feet. Neither did he crack the whip that tore into his aunt's skin. Yet as a witness to these horrors, he felt consumed with fear, helplessness, and guilt.[11]

Slave owners perpetrated rape, sexual violence, and exploitation in spaces like Aaron Anthony's kitchen across the slaveholding South, the same spaces where enslaved people labored, slept, shared stories, listened, and observed. As these spaces were where enslaved people formed families and extended kinship networks, sexual violence became inseparable from the everydayness of life for those like Hester, her lover Edward, Douglass, and the other enslaved people who lived within earshot of Hester's cries. In addition to Douglass and Hester, Anthony enslaved ten other people in and around his household. Though their experience of and proximity to these moments of violence and exploitation varied, they shared in a collective understanding of what was possible and who was vulnerable within this culture that was constructed over years of experience, witnessing, and teaching. Having been stalked, ripped from the arms of her lover, hung from a ceiling by her hands, and lacerated by Anthony's whip, Hester suffered greatly as a result of her experiences. When Douglass saw Anthony brandish his lash and heard his aunt's cries of despair, he felt trapped inside his makeshift closet by the violence occurring on the other side of the door. Seeing as none of Anthony's other enslaved people intervened on

Hester's behalf, they likely felt hindered to disrupt the cycle of violence and trauma as well.

The South's rape culture had an even longer physical and metaphorical reach. Slave owners like Aaron Anthony and their family members navigated these spaces as well. While they were not the targeted victims of this systematic rape and exploitation, they also shared in the knowledge of slave-owning men's common engagement in interracial sex and sexual violence against enslaved women. By witnessing and through instruction from one generation to the next, they learned the violent forms that slave-owning power could take. They also learned that interracial sex and unfettered sexual violence against the enslaved could result in consequences for their own families and communities.

Of record, the white occupants of Anthony's household—which included his son, Andrew, and daughter, Lucretia, along with Lucretia's husband, Thomas Auld—made no meaningful attempts to impede their father's actions or protect Hester from his abuses. They conducted their lives in the brick house that was a few feet away from the detached kitchen where Hester received her brutal lashings with the understanding that cries from enslaved people were no cause for alarm but merely the daily sights and sounds of enslavement. Among these were the sights and sounds of the South's rape culture as well. Lucretia and Andrew likely noticed that their father paid particular attention to Hester. They would have seen him frantically searching for her after the sun went down. If they did not hear him forbid Hester from seeing Edward, perhaps they heard his angry tirades whenever he found the young couple together. Though two walls separated them from Hester when she was being brutalized with Anthony's whip, they most likely heard the same shrieks of resistance and pain that Douglass heard. They were expected to ignore Hester's cries in observance of their father's prerogative to discipline as well as sexually assault enslaved people as he saw fit.[12]

Douglass provided us with only a snapshot of life under Aaron Anthony's roof. This glimpse, however, reveals how rape and sexual violence culturally situated slave owners and the enslaved. Though white Southerners decried sexual relations with the enslaved as taboo and distasteful, men like Anthony assumed the privilege to engage in these acts with little resistance. Anthony's enslaved people and his children were expected to play their respective roles in his performance of domination. Yet one was not born knowing this script of rape and sexual exploitation; there was a process by which enslaved people and those who owned them came to know their roles. Members of these communities also learned ways to subvert these roles to resist, protect others from, and protest interracial sex and sexual violence. Learning, knowing, and navigating these roles were crucial elements for the making and survival of the rape culture that fortified the political, social, and economic foundations of the antebellum South.

The Making of a Rape Culture

In her groundbreaking work *Black Sexual Politics*, Patricia Collins argues that lynching and rape of African American men and women, respectively, from the late nineteenth century onward bound Black communities politically, economically, and socially. Collins uses the term "rape culture" to describe Black people's physical and psychological landscape. She places special emphasis on Black women's experiences, stating that the terms "*institutionalized rape* and *rape culture* encompass the constellation of sexual assaults on Black womanhood." *Sexual Violence and American Slavery* builds on Collins's framework. I take the term "rape culture" and apply this framework to the very establishment of the colonies that would become the United States of America to articulate how critical the systematic rape of Black women especially and the sexual exploitation of Black people more broadly were to the founding of the nation. Collins also draws attention to the ways that the rape of enslaved Black women resulted in political and economic consequences for African American society at large.[13] I contend that as slavery became ever more indispensable in the rapidly expanding South, it cultivated a rape culture that had implications for more than just enslaved populations but would be consequential for the political, social, and economic lives of everyone— Black and white, enslaved and free—living within the South's plantation complex.[14]

By definition, a rape culture exists when a set of societal beliefs and ideals normalize sexual violence and thus foster environments conducive to rape. Anthropologists David Jordan and Marc Swartz put forth that while a culture is not "timeless and changeless" and is "incompletely shared in every group," its existence is evidenced through shared understandings and predictability. In fact, "social life is impossible if people cannot predict each other's behavior with a rather high probability of success." In the case of Frederick Douglass's aunt Hester, she, along with Douglass; her lover, Edward; her abuser, Aaron Anthony; and most likely the entire Anthony family, shared an understanding that enslaved women like Hester were vulnerable to being raped and sexually exploited by men like Anthony and that this was one way in which enslavers demonstrated their authority. They understood that rape, sexual harassment, and reproductive exploitation were intended to reinforce Black subjugation in this slave society.[15]

In many ways, enslaved women's bodies served as an ideological and physical landscape upon which the slaveholding South was built. From the early colonists to the nation's founders, African women's sexuality was as the center of public discourse on racial difference and Black inferiority. As historian Jennifer Morgan notes, the development of racialist discourse was deeply linked to gendered notions of difference and human hierarchy. European travelers and early colonial settlers assigned meaning to the Blackness of African women's skin, their unabashed nakedness, and their perceived ability to labor like men and give birth without pain. This served to fortify their demarcations between whiteness and Blackness. Ideas regarding Black women's savagery, hypersexuality, and suitability for hard labor and sexual reproduction were central to the process of codifying a racialized system of perpetual slavery. In 1643, the Virginia General Assembly passed a statute that distinguished Black women's labor from that of white women by defining it as taxable, making them "tithables" along with white and Black men. In 1662, the assembly determined that children born to white fathers and Black bondwomen would inherit the status of their mothers rather than that of their fathers, which was custom per English common law. Into perpetuity, enslaved women were to be imagined as conduits for economic production and security. They could also be raped and coerced to gratify white men's sexual desires without legal consequence. Enslaved women, indeed, had the least formal power of any group in antebellum America.[16]

From Maryland's eastern shore to the piedmont of North Carolina to the coastal sea islands of South Carolina and Georgia to the sprawling Mississippi delta, planters, merchants, slave traders, and legislators in no small part amassed their economic and political power through systematic rape and reproductive exploitation. The ability of white men to rape and brutalize enslaved women and cause these women's wombs to swell with a new generation of enslaved laborers with impunity reflected and reinforced their power and identity in public and private spaces. As an instrument of power, sexual violence bolstered patriarchal authority, secured Black subjugation, and sustained chattel slavery.

While all Southerners were touched on some level by the rape culture that pervaded the antebellum South, enslaved women were the most vulnerable to its perils. Historian Deborah Gray White argues that "black in a white society, slave in a free society, woman in a society ruled by men, female slaves had the least formal power and were perhaps the most vulnerable group of antebellum Americans." However, sexual violence could befall any member of enslaved communities. Enslaved men and boys, too, experienced rape and other forms of sexual violence. Alongside enslaved women, enslaved men were systematically exploited for their reproductive labor. If past is prologue, the rape and molestation of enslaved men and boys were more likely to linger in the shadows of slavery's other atrocities, generating fewer discussions and going grossly unreported. Yet scholars—most notably Martha Hodes and Thomas Foster—remind us that despite these silences, the sexual assault of enslaved men and boys "lurked as a possibility regardless of how frequently it came to pass."[17]

The invisibility of sexual assaults against enslaved men and boys in the archives can also be attributed to the failures of colonists and would-be statesmen from the seventeenth century onward to criminalize sexual assaults on Black bodies. From the beginning, colonists tactically crafted and refined legal systems that refused to acknowledge the rape and sexual assault of enslaved people at the hands of white perpetrators. As the South's political and economic cache became more contingent on the profitability and expansion of enslavement in the early decades of the nineteenth century, there became an even greater need to continue to decriminalize the sexual exploitation of enslaved people in legal, political, and social discourses.[18] Any such restrictions would fundamentally erode the absoluteness of an owner's power, which was deemed necessary to "render the submission of the slave perfect."[19] This created vulnerabilities for all members of enslaved communities, but enslaved women had an expressly hostile terrain to chart. According to the formerly enslaved Fannie Berry, the white man's attitude toward enslaved women was this: "What I can't do by fair means I'll do by foul."[20]

For these reasons, *Sexual Violence and American Slavery* explicitly foregrounds the rape and sexual exploitation of enslaved women as the hallmark feature of the South's rape culture. It is important to acknowledge that the South's rape culture—built on the ideological intersection of white supremacy and patriarchy—produced many victims and many perpetrators. In addition to enslaved men and boys, white women and girls as well as Indigenous people were also vulnerable to sexual violence. White slaveowning women also sexually assaulted, coerced, and exploited enslaved men and women as an expression of their racial power. This book, however, is not a broad examination of rape and sexual violence in the antebellum South. Rather, it hones in on enslaved women as the primary victims of sexual violence in the South to illustrate that the systematic rape and sexual exploitation of enslaved women was so pervasive as to shape the consciousness of an entire society.

The South's rape culture thrived because in many ways white men were incentivized to have sex with enslaved women. If a man impregnated one of his own enslaved women, he expanded his slave coffers and, by extension, his overall wealth, even if it came at the expense of community gossip and marital strife. Young white men were also encouraged by fathers, brothers, and friends to gain sexual experience within the slave quarters, reinforcing the trope of the disposable, hypersexual female slave, who lay in contrast to the chaste and virtuous white woman. The rape, sexual coercion, harassment, and reproductive exploitation of enslaved women was so indistinguishable from so many facets of chattel slavery that for all intents and purposes, the enslaved woman was cast as virtually "unrapable."[21]

Because of the everyday threats that enslaved women had to navigate and anticipate as a matter of survival, they, along with enslaved communities at large, looked at most white men with suspicion. Former bondman James Pennington proclaimed that it was nearly impossible for any man or woman to be unaware that white men were having sex with Black women. "Who does not know, that in three-fourths of the colored race, there runs the blood of the white master—the breeder of his own chattels!" he declared. Formerly enslaved in North Carolina, Jacob Manson said, "At dat time it wus a hard job to find a marster dat didn't have women 'mong his slaves. Dat was a ginerel thing 'mong de slave owners." The most elite members of the South's slave-owning class also acknowledged the pervasive nature of white men's sexual relations with enslaved women. Ella Gertrude Clanton Thomas, a wealthy slave-owning woman from Georgia, said, "I know that this is a view of the subject that is thought best for women to ignore," but how can we "when we see so many cases of mulattoes commanding higher prices, advertised as 'Fancy girls.'" Other prominent slave-owning women, like Mary Boykin Chesnut, said, "Our men live all in one house with their wives & their concubines, & the mulattoes one sees in every family exactly resemble the white children." The rate with which white men sexually exploited enslaved women would be an impossible statistic to calculate. However, the aforementioned testimony solidifies that it occurred enough to put people—white and Black—on notice. For this reason, enslaved people determined that they must approach most white men with caution.[22]

A culture is made not only when people have a collective understanding of "the ways things are or ideas about ways things can be done." Culture also entails a "prescriptive element." In other words, there must be shared understandings that also tell people "what things *should* be like and how things *ought* to be done."[23] The South's white, patriarchal, slave-owning power brokers cultivated social and cultural prescriptions for themselves and for the free and enslaved people who fell under their control. This is why *Sexual Violence and American Slavery* juxtaposes the lived experiences of the cultivators, perpetrators, victims, resisters, and witnesses of the South's rape culture. Through the law, enforcing the economic and social dependency of white women and children and inflicting violence to subjugate Black bodies, white men cultivated physical and cultural space to engage in interracial sex and perpetrate acts of sexual violence. Many expected to be excused for illicit sexual behavior or curry the favor of a blind eye, especially if they exercised discretion. For example, the enslaved and white society writ large were expected to feign ignorance in the presence of white men's mixed-race enslaved children and ignore the sights and sounds of sexual violence. Under the South's rape culture, Southern patriarchs' expectations were clear: this was not only how things *were* but how things *should* and *ought* to be done.[24]

Knowing the South's Rape Culture

The historical record of slavery in the South is composed of texts as well as silences and is marred by the erasure of enslaved people's voices and experiences, including their traumas and triumphs. For enslavers and the enslaved, shame, fear, jealousy, and rage lurk within the silences. Historian Marisa Fuentes draws our attention to the ways in which the archive itself is a construct, its fabrication a reflection and by-product of the commodification, subjugation, and exploitation of Black bodies. Here lies the challenge in doing this kind of work. We are often tasked with reading against the grain and sitting with the silences, having to use white people's words to illuminate enslaved people's experiences. It is with these snapshots of enslaved people's lives that we strive to illustrate how significant the threat of rape and sexual exploitation was in their lives with as much care and respect as we can offer. So many factors, the least of which were laws prohibiting enslaved people to read and write, restrained their voices in everyday life and in the historical record. Yet amid the silences are powerful and invaluable accounts of family life in urban and rural enslaved spaces, religious conversions and prayers for liberation, heart-wrenching tales of families torn apart by sale or death, and violence.[25]

In crafting this book, I drew heavily from enslaved people's autobiographies, Works Progress Administration interviews, and court and government documents to illuminate enslaved people's voices and have them articulate their experiences and emotions regarding systematic rape and sexual exploitation whenever possible. They testified to how their experiences with rape and the threat of sexual exploitation occupied their thoughts, and they expressed the fervor with which they tried to prepare and protect their families and communities as well as resist. To capture the voices of enslavers, I used diaries, plantation records, personal correspondence, and court and government documents. My research revealed how the enslaved and slave owners, often along gender lines, assessed their physical and emotional capacity to rebuke, reshape, and exploit the South's violent and sexually charged landscape. At times, I experienced immense frustration due to silences around sexual relations between white men and enslaved women from the enslaved and their enslavers. References were few and many were quite subtle, consistent with nineteenth-century sensibilities that called for modesty and discretion where sexual relations were concerned. The subtlety and even hesitancy in some people's testimony, their inability to speak directly about their experiences of rape and sexual exploitation, reveal that some horrors were unspeakable or were intended to be unknown. Some testimony was resounding, intent on exposing the horrors of slavery and sexual exploitation especially to audiences in the North and across the Atlantic. On a few occasions, I found myself surprised by the candor with which some people spoke about interracial sex, especially white women and those who espoused moral authority, such as ministers and politicians. Whether implicitly or explicitly, however, enslaved communities and white Southerners laid bare the evidence of the South's rape culture, such as the racial and gender prescriptions to which they were expected to adhere to make this system of power and domination work.

In their testimonies, enslaved women and men characterized the sexual assault of enslaved women and girls as one of the greatest ills of slavery. Their documents reveal that the specter of rape was always there and speak to the fear and anxiety that permeated enslaved communities. These sources illustrate how tales of caution were passed from parent to child that warned against coming into close contact with certain men and being alone in remote spaces. They also unmask the pain, fear, and trauma caused by violence and how impactful the threat of violence was on everyday life.

While enslaved people were speaking about caution, fear, and horror, white women were expressing different concerns. Their own words, in addition to testimony from enslaved people, reveal slave-owning women's frustrations over white men's sexual behavior and lack of discretion. They expose their tendency to harbor jealousy and contempt for the enslaved women with whom white men had sexual relations and reveal their coping mechanisms, which ranged from violence to gossip to willful ignorance. In her diary, Mary Boykin Chesnut detailed the moment when her mother-in-law explained to her the steps women in their position had to take to prevent their husbands from being "seduced" by enslaved women. Like enslaved girls, white girls, too, learned lessons from their mothers. They were frequently taught the art of willful ignorance and the virtue in remaining silent.[26]

Within documents of contention, such as divorce petitions, criminal court records, and slave owners' and enslaved people's writings, is evidence of both enslaved and slave-owning people's efforts to cast off their prescriptive roles and reject the power dynamics the South's rape culture helped curate. What we see are battles for power—power to protect oneself or one's community, power to avenge hurt and humiliation, and power to punish and eliminate future threats. For the enslaved, threats of death, rape, flogging, and separation from loved ones kept most enslaved people preoccupied with staying alive and holding their families and communities together. During it all, they continued to form partnerships and birth new generations of enslaved children as mandated. At times, however, they expressed hesitancy and regret over bringing children into such a dangerous and depraved world, especially baby girls who would one day have to contend with the threat of sexual violence. Enslaved people engaged in acts of resistance and used strategies to mitigate threats of rape and sexual exploitation. Avoiding intimate relationships and devising schemes to escape slavery are just a couple of the ways enslaved people sought autonomy and refuge from exploitation. In exceptional instances, enslaved women petitioned courts and government agencies for their freedom and financial compensation, to which they felt they were due because of their sexual ties to white men. And some enslaved men and women took up arms and injured or killed white men who assaulted or made threats against themselves or women to whom they were intimately connected.

As for enslavers, their power struggles sometimes spilled into the public sphere at slave markets and in local courts. Slave-owning women went to court to seek divorces from men on grounds of adultery and licentiousness, asserting that these men's sexual relations with enslaved women threatened the integrity of the plantation household and the white patriarchal power structure upon which Southern society was built. Though most marriages survived and most households stayed intact, there were no guarantees that tensions would dissolve quickly or at all.

Sexual Violence and American Slavery synthesizes these scant narrative pieces, as well as the silences, around enslavement, rape, sexual exploitation, and power into a study of the ways in which sexual violence as a mode of power served as a tie that bound *all* inhabitants of the slaveholding South. It illustrates that, as a consequence, the South's rape culture marked the rapists and the victims of rape. Within the imaginations of slaves and slave owners, victims and perpetrators existed within each community. In reality, a victim and perpetrator could be one and the same. In addition to concrete instances of violence, one's consciousness of enslaved women's vulnerability to sexual violence generated its own kind of lived experience for both the enslaved and the enslavers. Building on Stephanie Camp's framework of rival geographies, this study forces readers to rethink the ways in which those in the antebellum South navigated the terrain of urban and rural plantations, moved past one another in city streets and within the plantation household, and helped their children understand their position of power in these patriarchal slave societies. It illustrates that in the midst of exploitation, slaves and slave owners made informed decisions regarding their intimate and familial relationships with the hopes of maximizing or gaining some semblance of autonomy and security. In the process, they contested or, at the very least, pushed the bounds of the racial and gender prescriptions that governed the antebellum South. Most importantly, by placing slave owners and the enslaved side by side within the context of enslaved women's sexual exploitation, we see that this horrifying expression of slavery did not always create a one-directional flow of power and violence from white slave-owning patriarchs to white women and the enslaved but generated a multidirectional and constantly negotiated flow of power. The consequences of domination, violence, and oppression were vast and wreaked havoc on all of them. Untangling oneself from this web was an arduous undertaking.[27]

Sexual Violence and American Slavery contends that the normalization of rape and sexual exploitation of enslaved communities facilitated and sustained one of the most enduring open secrets in American history. The South's rape culture *is* inseparable from our historic and contemporary understandings of Southern honor and patriarchy. The South's rape culture did not contradict the edicts or fundamentality of Southern honor; rather, it worked alongside these cultural prescriptions to bolster Southern white patriarchy. In addition to serving white men's economic interests, being sexually violent and exploiting the sexuality of enslaved women *and* men was also a privilege of mastery. As such, behind the thin veil of Southern honor lay dishonor, deviance, and shame. Now is the time to consider sexual relations across the color line—forced, coerced, and consensual—as not so much an open secret but a hallmark of the South's slave society.

Organization

This book is organized to allow the reader to encounter the antebellum South's rape culture and enslaved women's vulnerability to sexual violence from the differing vantage points of enslaved and slave-owning men and women. While this study contends that these groups were tethered together by shared cultural understandings of rape and sexual exploitation, it acknowledges that each group's experiences and perspectives were unique. The first three chapters focus on enslaved people's experiences, while chapters 4–6 are devoted to the experiences of white Southerners.

Chapter 1 explores how enslaved people learned to navigate a culture of rape. It shows how enslaved women and girls, specifically, navigated both a geographical and a psychological landscape marked by sexual violence in the antebellum South and how their desires to avoid fraught spaces and individuals often had implications for the most intimate aspects of their lives, notably marriage, sexual relations, and childbearing. Chapter 2 takes up the long-standing historiographical debates on how to best characterize long-term sexual relationships between enslaved women and white men. Through a series of case studies, it explores how enslaved women themselves perceived their ability to shape the terms and conditions of sexual servitude and long-term sexual liaisons with white men to improve the quality of life for themselves and their families. Chapter 3 explores how enslaved men grappled with white men's assertion of patriarchal authority and their own inability to freely claim authority and responsibility within enslaved communities. Though they frequently expressed feelings of powerlessness, their status rarely eroded their desires to protect, provide for, and exercise power within their communities. The chapter highlights cases in which enslaved men lashed out against sexual abusers, stepping far outside the bounds set for them within the South's white patriarchal culture.

Chapter 4 reveals that just as the enslaved came to know the threat white men could pose, slave-owning men learned how to use sex as a tool of power and pleasure against enslaved communities. It illustrates how slave-owning men reconciled their illicit behavior with public and private condemnation of interracial sex and how some attempted to draw stark distinctions between their true selves—honorable Southern patriarchs—and their flawed and sinful nature. Chapter 5 takes stock of slave-owning women's responses to white men's sexual relations with enslaved women, especially the ways in which they used their authority to seek retaliation against enslaved women through violence and the slave marketplace. This chapter explores these moments of contention in order to provide a more nuanced understanding of white women's power and agency within the South's patriarchal structure. Chapter 6 explores what happened when marital conflict caused by white men's sexual relations with enslaved women spilled over into the public sphere. Through the lens of divorce, it reveals what Southern society via the court system could and could not tolerate, especially in instances in which sex across the color line ran the risk of disrupting the South's patriarchal and racial hierarchies.

FREDERICK DOUGLASS'S ACCOUNT of his aunt Hester's brutal sexual assault has been the subject of much debate on the ethics of retelling violence. I offer that examining Hester's assault and trauma, along with the experiences of other enslaved women and girls, results in a necessary—though painful—archival record of the everydayness of sexual violence under America's brand of slavery. Any effort to understand and deconstruct the founding of our nation as well as contemporary rape culture is futile without first looking to racialized slavery. This challenges scholars who, in their analysis of the relationship between sexual violence and patriarchy in American culture, have often failed to incorporate the experiences of Black women seriously and completely. Such a gross oversight erases the ways in which the systematic rape and sexual exploitation of Black women has been used historically to reinforce white supremacy and patriarchy, key ingredients in the cultivation of American culture. Enslaved people's voices need to be heard louder than ever before. As this book is about knowing, I pray that I have honored our enslaved ancestors in my attempt to make more of their stories known.

Sankofa—*"Go back to the past and bring forward that which is useful."*
—West African proverb

CHAPTER ONE

Navigating the South's Rape Culture

At the age of twenty-one, a young and enslaved Elizabeth Keckley gave birth to her only child, a son she named George. Due to the circumstances surrounding George's conception, Keckley wished she had never given him life. George's father was a white man named Alexander Kirkland. He was the son of a prominent merchant in the small town of Hillsborough, North Carolina, where Keckley lived with her owners, Robert and Anna Burwell. Robert had moved his family and Keckley from Virginia to Hillsborough four years prior (1835), when he took the job as pastor of Hillsborough Presbyterian Church. Kirkland lived on his family's sizable Ayr Mount plantation, which was near the Burwells' parsonage where Keckley labored as a household servant. He and his family were parishioners at Robert's church. At some point, Kirkland, nine years her senior, raped Keckley or coerced her to have sex, piecing together a string of assaults that would occur over the course of four years and result in the birth of one child. "He persecuted me for four years," said Keckley, "and I—I—became a mother."[1]

In writing her autobiography, Keckley faced the challenge of naming abuses that many in her position found to be unspeakable. Although there were visual clues that she had been sexually assaulted by a white enslaver— most notably her mixed-race child—Keckley made the choice to disclose painful and traumatic experiences for the public to consume. Her choice of words—stating that Kirkland had "persecuted" her—and the way she used dashes to force the reader to pause before she revealed that she had become a mother as a result suggest that her revelation was what Toni Morrison called "an unspeakable thing spoken at last."[2] Her reticence exposes not only how silencing the trauma of rape and sexual exploitation could be but how white Southern society chose to reckon with enslaved women's systematic abuse. The enslaved understood that Southern society and the law did not recognize their sexual assault as heinous or even criminal, which meant that their pain and pleas were largely marked as irrelevant outside their own enslaved communities. Keckley declared the South a place whose edicts "deemed it no crime to undermine the virtue of girls in my then position."[3]

Rape was defined as "carnal knowledge of a woman forcibly and against her will." Keckley knew that, per Southern laws and sensibilities, enslaved women like herself were not entitled to personal will. In the words of a former bondman, "A slave shall have no higher appeal than the mere will of her master, she cannot escape, unless it be by flight or death." For practical and legal purposes, rape statutes did not protect enslaved women, men, boys, or girls. Beginning in the colonial period, the race, age, gender, and enslaved status of both the victim and the accused determined whether a crime had been committed. Most Southern states had statutes prohibiting the rape of a white woman by an enslaved man, but none had statutes prohibiting the rape of an enslaved woman by any man—white, Black, enslaved, or free. This legal and cultural denial of protection against rape for enslaved women reinforced a foundational principle that the Black woman's body was "fair game." White men could and did rape enslaved women without legal repercussions.[4]

For the enslaved, embedded in the South's rice and tobacco fields, cotton plantations, and bustling urban centers was a cultural and physical landscape that was carved out by the systematic rape and sexual exploitation of enslaved women. Enslaved women like Elizabeth Keckley were acutely aware of the legal and social frameworks that created this fraught terrain that they were forced to mentally chart and physically navigate. They understood that rape and the threat thereof, coupled with the lack of legal protection, served to reinforce their objectification within the South's economic and social regime. According to philosophers and feminist theoreticians Marilyn Frye and Carolyn Shafer, rape leads victims to see themselves as "a being within someone's domain and not as a being which has domain." In other words, rape conveys that the victim is a "being without respect, that she is not a person." What Keckley and so many other enslaved people knew was that rape served to erode enslaved people's sense of personhood.[5]

The South's rape culture is laid bare by the testimony of victims like Keckley, who understood their everyday existence as maneuvering through a time and place where it was deemed no crime to undermine their minds, bodies, and space through rape, sexual coercion, harassment, and reproductive exploitation. In addition to the enslaved, slave owners and outside observers confirmed that the slaveholding South was distinguishable for the frequent rape and sexual exploitation of enslaved women, as well as a collective consciousness of enslaved women's vulnerability to rape and sexual exploitation.

This chapter explores how enslaved people learned to navigate this rape culture. Through personal experience and witnessing, enslaved people developed a collective understanding of enslaved women's vulnerability to rape and other forms of sexual violence and exploitation and the social conditions and spaces that bred such dangers. It also examines how enslaved women, specifically, used this knowledge to navigate a physical and cultural terrain marked by sexual violence and how their desires to avoid fraught spaces and individuals shaped the most intimate aspects of their lives, notably marriage, sexual relations, and childbearing.

IN 1848, MARY WALKER accompanied her owner, Duncan Cameron, to Philadelphia to provide care for his sick daughter Mildred. While there, Walker ran away in hopes of becoming free. Walker's quest for freedom was not without sacrifice. She left behind her mother and her three children, Frank, Agnes, and Bryant, who remained enslaved by the Cameron family in Raleigh, North Carolina. Mary Walker's early life consisted of laboring in the Cameron's Fairntosh plantation household, where she attended to the needs of the Cameron daughters. Their father, Duncan, moved about the most elite circles in North Carolina. During his lifetime, he served as a superior court judge, state senator, and trustee of the University of North Carolina. Owning thousands of acres of land in central North Carolina, Alabama, and Mississippi, the Camerons were one of the wealthiest slave-owning families in the antebellum South. After becoming president of the State Bank of North Carolina, Cameron moved his family and his household servants to their new residence in the state's capital of Raleigh. This was where Mary's children remained when she seized the opportunity to be free.[6]

When Walker escaped Duncan Cameron in Philadelphia, she found refuge with Peter and Susan Lesley, a Philadelphia couple with antislavery convictions. For more than a decade, the Lesleys strategized alongside Walker and other allies to reunite her with her children. Taking a tremendous risk, Peter Lesley finally wrote a letter directly to Mildred Cameron in 1859. Walker's children had fallen under her guardianship when her father, Duncan, died in 1853. Ironically, it was Walker's role as Mildred's caregiver that brought her to Philadelphia over a decade before and precipitated her escape from bondage. Now, Lesley was tasked with convincing Mildred, on Walker's behalf, to reunite her with her two younger children, Agnes and Bryant. He wrote, "I have been lately touched to the heart with a case of heartbreaking distress which you have it entirely in your power I find to cure." He wrote of Walker's enduring pain and that she had been "fearing night and day some terrible calamity befalling either or both of her children." Walker was especially fearful for her daughter, whose "blooming womanhood exposes her more terribly than the worst adventures happening to a young man," wrote Lesley.[7]

According to Lesley, Walker consciously expressed that an enslaved girl's entrance into adulthood presented unique challenges and dangers that far surpassed those of any young man. By blooming womanhood, she was referring to the phase in most girls' lives when their bodies begin to transform into that of a woman. The widening of one's hips, the budding of breasts, and the onset of menses were all indicators of sexual maturation. For Walker, when placed in the context of chattel slavery, the thought and image of a young enslaved girl, blooming into a woman, evoked feelings of terror. She understood that her daughter would become more vulnerable to unwanted attention from the white men under whose control she fell and that she could easily be raped, sexually harassed, or coerced, and would almost certainly be mandated to sexually reproduce.

What Mary Walker described as an enslaved woman's blooming womanhood Harriet Jacobs called the "sad epoch in the life of a slave girl." Jacobs's "sad epoch," what scholar Nazera Sadiq Wright calls a transition from youthful girlhood to prematurely knowing girlhood, began when she was fifteen years old, the point when she, too, likely began to take on the physical characteristics of a sexually mature woman. It was then that her owner, James Norcom, a trusted physician in the town of Edenton, North Carolina, began to "whisper foul words in her ear." These whispers soon escalated to daily reminders that, as his property, he could force her to have sexual relations with him if he wished. Enslaved testimony reveals various coming-of-age stories like that of Jacobs and fears for young girls' safety like that expressed by Mary Walker. Enslaved communities wished to provide all children with what psychologist Joseph Sandler called a "background of safety" to neutralize what is "aggressive, fearful, and anxiety-producing." The many tragedies of slavery—such as being scantily clad, poorly fed, denied adequate rest, severely beaten, and torn from the arms of loved ones who had been sold away—made it very hard for enslaved communities to cultivate and thus experience basic trust, that sense of protection from what is aggressive, fearful, and anxiety producing.[8]

Enslaved women like Walker and Jacobs were not born knowing the ways in which rape and sexual exploitation marred their physical and cultural landscapes, nor were they born knowing how to traverse these landscapes. Rather, culture is transmitted across time through social learning. Anthropologists Marc Swartz and David Jordan explain that each generation must learn from the people they depend on from birth to survive. New generations learn, at least in part, the understandings that constitute the culture of the generations before them. Therefore, people's beliefs and habits are informed by memories of personal experience and what they have heard. Communities transmit expectations about human gratification and frustration, teaching children whom to trust and mistrust. Generations of enslaved people learned about the prevalence of the rape and sexual exploitation of enslaved women through personal experience, witnessing these abuses and then transmitting this knowledge from one generation to the next. The enslaved woman's body was what Kimberly Juanita Brown calls an "archive of time." The images of enslaved women's bodies—whether pregnant with child, bruised from recent assaults, or scarred with marks of resistance—helped the enslaved both "prefigure future slaughter and conquest, and survive it." The enslaved understood that cultivating a collective consciousness of the South's rape culture was crucial to survival. Sharing information, issuing warnings, and maintaining a hypervigilance regarding the various modes of sexual violence and exploitation that an enslaved woman or girl might face was key. Also, knowing the physical spaces where enslaved women would be most vulnerable to attack and coercion and the strategies employed by predators were, in fact, a part of enslaved communities' efforts to establish some semblance of a "background of safety." They understood that it did not serve the interests of enslaved girls not to prepare them for what was likely to come.[9]

Before Walker became the mother of a daughter, she was a daughter herself, just as her own mother was the daughter of an enslaved woman before her. Generations of experience gave her the confidence to make such keen distinctions between boys' and girls' entrances into adulthood. Walker was described as a light-skinned woman "who could scarcely be distinguished from a white woman" and almost certainly had a white father. At least one acquaintance speculated that her owner, Duncan Cameron, was her father. Walker likely grew up hearing chatter among white and Black people regarding her paternity; her mother might have even disclosed the name of her father, putting all speculation to rest. Regardless, Walker did not have to look beyond her own conception to understand the ills to which blooming womanhood exposed enslaved women.[10]

Harriet Jacobs was fifteen years old when she experienced her first sexual assault, victimized by James Norcom's "vile inclinations." However, she was a young child when she learned that "in slavery the very dawn of life is darkened by these shadows." According to Jacobs, enslaved girls became "prematurely knowing" of sexual violation through sight and sound. She said a young girl might see her mistress direct "violent outbreaks of jealous passion" at an enslaved woman who she felt garnered too much of her husband's attention. Even before the slave girl is twelve years old, she "cannot help but understand the cause," said Jacobs. A time will come when the enslaved girl "will learn to tremble when she hears her master's footfall." Jacobs learned from the other enslaved people on Norcom's in-town plantation that he had already fathered eleven children by enslaved women. Though they could not allude to such things beyond whispers among themselves, fearing dire consequences, they made the most of these opportunities and conveyed solidarity, fear, and pity without using words.[11]

Enslaved people developed and cultivated their collective consciousness of enslaved women's vulnerability to rape and sexual exploitation in the moments when they witnessed, coped with the ensuing trauma, and shared collectively in the aftermath. John Brown of Virginia experienced such a moment after being purchased by Starling Finney, a slave trader who made his money by transporting enslaved people to the rapidly expanding deep South and selling them to planters eager to tap into the burgeoning cotton market. When Brown joined Finney's coffle of men, women, and children, he learned that they were bound for Georgia. While on the road in South Carolina, Finney schemed to steal a fellow traveler's female servant, a young woman around twenty years old whom Brown described as being "of smart appearance." After capturing the woman, Finney forced her to get into his wagon, where he then "brutally ill-used her, and permitted his companions to treat her in the same manner," said Brown. According to Brown, they tormented her for several days while he and the other enslaved men, women, and children were forced to hear and see what was occurring in Finney's wagon.[12]

Although Finney sold the young woman once the coffle crossed into Augusta, Georgia, the traumatic experience for the remaining slaves was just beginning. Brown described how the women in their group felt especially tormented. They talked extensively about what had happened, and "many of them cried and said it was a great shame," said Brown. For any woman who had experienced a similar sort of sexual assault, this woman's ordeal opened old wounds and served as a reminder that being raped again was always a possibility. For the children, this might have been their first direct encounter with the sexual violence endemic to enslavement. As the women grieved together, they had an opportunity to reflect on their collective plight. It was a scene that John Brown would never forget.[13]

Through shared knowledge, the enslaved came to know all too well the schemes of sexual predators. Notably, they learned to expect enslavers, overseers, and slave patrollers to use extreme violence and harassment—whipping and threatening enslaved women—in order to commit rape and sexual assault. Shang Harris, formerly enslaved in Georgia, testified that "some de marsters beat de slave women to make 'em give up to 'em." William Anderson said he knew his enslaver to be a violent man. When the man got drunk, he "came out to the field to whip, cut, slash, curse, swear, beat and knock down several, for the smallest offence, or nothing at all," exhibiting all measures of brutality. He was especially brutal to enslaved women and always "kept a colored Miss in the house" with whom he could have sex. Anderson described a time when the enslaver whipped an enslaved woman with a handsaw, "ravished her person, and became the father of a child by her." He characterized these "illegitimate connections" as one of the curses of slavery.[14]

For many, the slave whip or lash itself came to symbolize the threat these men posed to enslaved women. Slave owners, overseers, and patrollers alike would slash their whips across enslaved women's bodies to subdue them, while others threatened to whip women who would not immediately comply with their demands for sex. Ellen Sinclair said that on her owner Bill Anderson's plantation, you could identify the women who tried to resist him or his three sons—Wash, Cliber, and Irvin—who, like their father, raped and impregnated the enslaved women they owned. Sinclair and others could readily see the "cuts 'cross dey back where dey beat 'em to mek 'em do what dey want." She added that although the women tried hard to resist, they had to do what the Anderson men wanted "cose dey slaves and couldn' help deyself." Anyone who stood in between such men and their intended victims could also find themselves on the receiving end of a lash. Samuel Hall recalled how slave patrollers would storm into the slave quarters and "drive and whip the husbands away from their wives and use those same women for their own pleasure." Similarly, Israel Campbell described that "should the colored husband say anything" in order to protect his wife from an impending rape, "he is whipped or sold." For Campbell, these were more "disgraceful and inhuman features of American slavery."[15]

The whip represented the enslavers' power to sexually violate someone, even when it was in someone else's hand. Some slave owners called on enslaved men to whip or physically restrain the enslaved women they intended to abuse. Enslaved men resented being used in this way but understood that their compliance was expected. John Jacobs noted that not only could an enslaved man's wife or daughter "be insulted before his eyes with impunity" but he himself could be "called on to torture them, and dare not refuse." He said that to "raise his hand in their defence is death by the law." John Brown, reflecting on his life as a slave on Jepsey James's Greenville, Mississippi, plantation, described how James's son, Thomas, forced him and other enslaved men to subdue a young, enslaved woman "to whom he made dishonest overtures." Brown said they were required to "hold her whilst he flogged her." He recalled how she screamed "awfully" and "writhed" under the strength of his arms. For a half hour, she was trapped by these men who were forced to "use our united strength to hold her down" while Thomas nearly beat her to death.[16]

For some enslavers and overseers, whipping an enslaved woman or watching her be whipped was its own ritual. Enslaved people came to understand that sometimes the cracking of a whip was its own form of sexual assault. Frederick Douglass recalled the pleasure his owner, Aaron Anthony, took in whipping his aunt Hester. When she resisted his sexual advances and consorted with her enslaved lover, Edward, which he forbade, he wanted not only to admonish her defiance but to torment her for his own gratification, said Douglass. While tying her up, Anthony cursed her with "tantalizing epithets." Next, he paused to roll up his sleeves, signaling his desire to not be impeded. At seven years old, Douglass noticed how "cruelly deliberate" Anthony was. He "protracted the torture, as one who was delighted with the scene," said Douglass. Each lashing was his rebuke of her efforts to find pleasure on her own terms, reinforcing the message that his will and his sexual pleasures superseded her own. Each strike stood in the place of a sexual act and communicated his mastery over her person. For seven-year-old Douglass, the message was clear.[17]

The whip was most effective as an unremitting reminder that the consequences of resisting rape, coercion, and forced sexual reproduction could be horrendous. The physical as well as emotional scars that such violence created were a powerful testimony that resonated among the enslaved. These spoken and unspoken testimonies were a key element in creating generational knowledge regarding enslaved women's vulnerability to sexual exploitation and the consequences of resistance. Minnie Fulkes's mother was left with a body covered in welts and scars caused by a piece of leather that was "bout as wide as my han' fro little finger to thumb," said Fulkes. When she observed the scars and asked her mother why she had been beaten, her mother said she had done nothing "other than she refused to be wife to this man." The man was the overseer who worked for Fulkes's owner, Galespe Graves of Chesterfield County, Virginia. By refusing to be his "wife," Fulkes's mother was refusing to have sex with him. Consequently, he would whip her. "If he didn't treat her dis way a dozen times, it wasn't nary one," said Fulkes. Even though Fulkes was seventy-seven years old in 1937 when she told an interviewer about this conversation between her and her mother, the lessons she learned from her mother's words and scars, both physical and psychological, were still fresh seventy-two years after the end of slavery.[18]

Knowing where danger lurked was essential for the physical safety and emotional health of enslaved communities. In the case of fourteen-year-old Celia, she was first purchased by sixty-year-old Robert Newsom of Callaway County, Missouri, in the neighboring county of Audrain in 1850. On the trip south to Newsom's eight-hundred-acre plantation along the Middle River, Newsom raped Celia for the first time. Although the path between Audrain and Callaway was the initial site of what would become a cycle of rape and sexual coercion, Celia's private cabin on Newsom's plantation would become the epicenter.[19]

The terrain Celia navigated daily was small, but the threat of sexual violence and exploitation was not. Her secluded cabin was sixty steps from Newsom's house, where she labored as a housekeeper. During the day, she fell under his constant gaze. At night, he would walk the sixty steps to her cabin and sexually assault her. As articulated by historian Stephanie Camp, slave owners' sense of mastery rested on their ability to constrict enslaved people's movements through laws, customs, and ideals. As laborers, enslaved women often found themselves bound to the plantation, serving as cooks, domestic servants, nurses, and field laborers. Expected to birth a new baby every one to two years, they also remained close to the plantation homestead, as dictated by their reproductive labor. As a result, women like Celia experienced this constriction of space in an acute way. Their owners were never far removed from the spaces where their lives took place—where they worked, ate, slept, and formed communities. Predatory men like Newsom had proximity, time, and space to sexually assault and exploit enslaved women in a multitude of ways. The plantation amounted to a battleground, and enslaved women needed to be cognizant and suspicious of their surroundings and the white men who moved through them to evade sexual threats to the best of their ability.[20]

Enslaved people exhibited a collective consciousness of the spaces in which enslaved women were most likely to confront rape, sexual coercion, and harassment. Although they could rarely avoid these spaces, their knowledge did influence how they traversed them, whether it be with fear or with an eye of caution. Enslaved people's testimony reveals that cabins, barns, cookhouses, their owners' bedrooms and studies, and even the woods—spaces that provided cover—were frequent sites for acts of sexual violence. According to May Satterfield, her owner would march into the fields and order enslaved women into the woods to assault them. Jermain Loguen recalled how a fellow bondwoman often found herself alone with white men when she labored in their owner's whiskey distillery. One day, when a neighboring planter found her by herself in the distillery, he, "presuming upon the privileges of his position, made insulting advances" and "resorted to a slaveholder's violence and threats," said Loguen. According to Virginia Hayes Shepherd of Churchland, Virginia, her owner expected to have sex with Diana, an enslaved woman, "just the same as if she had been his wife." His scheme was to send Diana to the barn to shell corn, where he could "cage her in the barn so she couldn't get out," said Shepherd.[21]

Slave owners used these spaces to perpetrate rapes, harassment, and coercion because they afforded a sense of privacy, which the enslaved knew. They were intended to immobilize enslaved women by separating them from would-be witnesses, obstructing any avenues of escape, and shielding them from white and Black onlookers who could possibly intervene on their behalves. When James Norcom proposed to build Harriet Jacobs a private cabin four miles outside town, she shuddered. Although he incessantly made threats to physically assault her, she proclaimed, "I had escaped my dreaded fate, by being in the midst of people." Jacobs had developed a profound understanding that being a part of a community provided some semblance of security. For her, isolation was tantamount to death.[22]

When Robert Newsom arrived at his home with fourteen-year-old Celia in tow, creating an isolated space for Celia was exactly what he had in mind. He placed her in a private cabin that was purposefully situated away from his other five bondmen—four men and one boy—but was only sixty steps away from his own door. Newsom shared his home with his adult children and grandsons. The sixty-step walk and the cabin's four walls ensured that it was far enough out of sight of his family but close enough to be easily accessible in the dead of night, which, according to Celia, was when he made his trips to her cabin. Although a slaveowner's prerogative to rape and sexually exploit enslaved women was a central ingredient of their mastery, this kind of covering allowed men to simultaneously engage in what was deemed illicit behavior and retain deniability, as well as respectability, in the eyes of their families and greater Southern society. No matter how thin the veneer, these men typically faced little interference from white or Black onlookers. Even when it became obvious that Celia had given birth to Newsom's child and she made direct appeals to his daughters for protection, Newsom continued to rape her with impunity.[23]

On Moses Mordicia's plantation, he had one set of slave cabins that his enslaved people called the "black quarter." According to Mattie Curtis, he also "had his yaller gals in one quarter ter dereselves." It was known among Curtis and others that "des gals belongs ter de Mordicia men, dere friends an 'de overseers.'" Mordicia created the separate quarters where not only he but also his male family members, friends, and employees could engage in sexual relations with the enslaved women. It does not appear that Mordicia was especially concerned with discretion. All his enslaved people could see that only light-skinned women were sent to live in these separate quarters. Yet he still demonstrated an impulse to keep the spaces separate, to create a hallowed ground where white men could come and go and have unrestricted access to these enslaved women. According to Curtis, when a baby was born, "dey'd sen' hit over ter de black quarter at birth" to be raised so that the mothers could continue to be available to Mordicia and his men. It was said that the female children who were born of these interracial liaisons could expect to be removed from the "black" slave quarters and placed in the other quarter when they came of age, especially if they had light-colored skin. Such a girl's fate was to have "chilluns fer her own daddy or brother," said Curtis.[24]

In other instances, slave owners, overseers, and the like sought no covering and chose to make a spectacle of rape and sexual violence in communal spaces where Black and white people could bear witness, a measure that always served to reinforce their subjugation of enslaved people. An enslaved man, Jesse, testified that his owner, John Francis, made no efforts to hide his preoccupation with an enslaved woman named Peggy. According to Jesse, the tension between Francis and Peggy was unmistakable, and everyone knew the cause. Because Peggy would not willingly have sex with Francis, he regularly kept her chained to a block or locked inside his meat house. Peggy's placement in the meat house, among pieces of cured animal flesh, was a visual reminder for all to see that she was his possession. To Francis, she did not have the right to refuse him, a point that he made clear to everyone when he threatened to "beat her almost to death . . . that he would barely leave the life in her." In addition to hearing Francis's threat, Jessie also heard Peggy testify to why she would never submit to Francis. He was her biological father, and "she could not do a think of that sort with her father," said Jesse. Francis threatened to make Jesse and another bondman Patrick "hold her, to enable him to effect his object," which would have made Jesse and Patrick both witnesses and participants in his sexual assault on Peggy. Due to the spectacular nature of Francis's assault on Peggy, it was no surprise to the people Francis enslaved when Peggy and Patrick conspired to murder him to put a stop to his abuse.[25]

The paradox between white men making a spectacle of sexual violence and their utilization of isolated spaces like the woods, barns, cookhouses, bedrooms, and private studies to carry out sexual assaults meant that no place was truly safe. Although Harriet Jacobs stated that there was some sense of comfort in being among people, the presence of witnesses did not deter all predators. The enslaved learned to always be on guard.[26]

No spaces embodied the troubled nature of both the public and the private more than the slave quarters and plantation household. In the slave quarters, the enslaved ate, slept, formed intimate attachments, nurtured kinship networks, and sought refuge whenever possible. Enslaved people were often the architects of their living quarters; however, they did not have ownership of these dwellings or the materials within. Unlike their enslavers, the enslaved were not entitled to private, independent households. Although enslaved people worked hard to create and re-create safe spaces, enslavers waged sexual assaults within their homes as one way to destroy any sense of autonomy and reinforce the lesson that slave cabins were not intended to be safe spaces.[27] As Harriet Jacobs testified, having a private cabin to herself was no luxury but a vehicle for James Norcom to deny her privacy yet provide himself privacy to demand sex whenever he wanted. The enslaved understood the slave quarters to be the space where white men took their sons to teach them how to rape, how to exercise their mastery over enslaved women and men through sexual violence. Mrs. Bird Walton recalled an enslaved woman named Ethel Mae telling her about their "marsa bringing his son, Levey, down to the cabin." They both raped her, "the father showing the son what it was all about," said Walton, and "she couldn't do nothing about it."[28]

Many enslaved men constructed models of masculinity that placed a high value on their ability to provide for and protect women and children. They understood white men's attacks on slave quarters to sexually assault enslaved women as one way that slavery "violated their ability to protect and provide for family dependents." Henry Bibb said most clearly that "licentious white men can and do, enter at night or day the lodging places of slaves," in order to "break up the bonds of affection in families; destroy all their domestic and social union for life." Ishrael Massie testified that his owner would send the enslaved husband out of the cabin and "den he gits in bed wid slave himself." Jacob Aldrich declared that owners would "tell de man to go outside and wait 'til he do what he want to do" and "her husband had to do it and he couldn't do nothing 'bout it." Whether through witness or experience, the enslaved knew the consequences of trying to protect their dwelling spaces from sexual violence. Lewis Clarke explained that many enslaved men learned the hard way that when a slave owner, overseer, or slave patroller came knocking, "if a slave don't open his door to them at any time of night they break it down . . . and act just as they please with his wives and daughters." He said, "If a husband dares to say a word . . . they tie him up and give him thirty-nine lashes." In this regard, knowledge, swift action to avoid certain spaces, and outright resistance had their limitations. Henry Bibb concluded, "If my wife must be exposed to the insults and licentious passions of wicked slave-drivers and overseers . . . heaven forbid that I should be compelled to witness the sight."[29]

In the plantation household, slave owners ate, slept, entertained, and cultivated their families. Here, the enslaved labored—throughout the night in some cases—placing them in close and constant proximity to their enslavers. They knew that household occupations, such as housekeeping, nursing, and sewing, placed enslaved women at great risk of rape, sexual coercion, and harassment. Sweeping hallways, changing bed linens, serving tea bedside, and taking measurements for tailor-made clothes, these women were under constant surveillance and were highly susceptible to being summoned to or cornered in spaces like bedrooms and closets whose walls provided cover for would-be predators to wage their attacks. Despite how close by their own family members were, male slave owners often seized on this proximity to wage sexual assaults on enslaved women. Victor Duhon's mother, Euripa Dupuis, labored as the hairdresser and barber for the Duhon family of Lafayette Parish, Louisiana. According to Duhon, his mother was attacked while barbering the hair of Lucien Duhon, her owner's son. He grabbed her and said, "He'll shave her head if she won't do what he likes." Duhon added that Lucien forced her to remain "his woman till he marries a white lady." His own conception and birth were the result of this ongoing assault. According to Virginia Hayes Shepherd, her owner made the plantation household a terrifying place for fellow bondwoman Diana. He constantly made sexual demands of her as she moved throughout the household and even ordered her to work in more remote parts of the plantation, where there would be no witnesses to intervene on her behalf. Diana went to her mistress for help, but to no avail. According to Shepherd, though the mistress expressed empathy for Diana, the owner "would beat her if she tried to meddle," making the household a violent space for anyone who attempted to obstruct his predation.[30]

The enslaved also understood how deeply rooted interracial sex was to the sexual economy of the slaveholding South. According to Rosa Maddox, some white men just "had a plumb cravin' for the other color." As a result, "Any man with money (let him be ever such a rough brute), can buy a beautiful and virtuous girl, and force her to live with him in a criminal connexion; and as the law says a slave shall have no higher appeal than the mere will of her master, she cannot escape, unless it be by flight or death," said William Craft. Those who were so inclined could even travel to cities like New Orleans to engage in the "fancy girl" trade, a niche market where enslaved women, frequently of mixed race, were sold at a premium for this purpose. Urban centers offered brothels or bawdy houses filled with enslaved women, where men could exchange money for sex one transaction at a time. These women were forced to engage in sex as a form of labor to satisfy the pleasures and greed of owners, overseers, and even strangers.[31]

Enslaved people had a myriad of ways in which they identified and interpreted long-term sexual liaisons between white men and enslaved women. When interviewed, Jack Maddox spoke of the instance when his owner, Judge Maddox, purchased a pretty enslaved woman ostensibly for the purpose of doing "fine needlework" for his wife. It was clear to Jack and even Judge Maddox's wife that Maddox had purchased this woman for the specific purpose of having sexual relations with her. As Jack's description confirms, enslaved people, through observation and experience, learned to decipher even the most seemingly insignificant details as evidence of a male slave owner's intent to engage in ongoing sexual relations with a specific enslaved woman. For Jack, the first indication of Judge Maddox's intentions with the enslaved woman was her appearance. He described her as a "purty mulatto gal, real bright, and long black hair." Although any enslaved woman, regardless of skin color, hair texture, and stature, could be forced into a long-term liaison, testimony from both white and Black sources reveal that white men had an inclination or fetish for Black women with lighter skin and curly or straight hair—European-like features that were deemed superior to an African aesthetic. These messages trickled down to enslaved communities, and testimony reveals that these communities also came to identify light skin, less coarse hair, and thin noses as symbols of beauty. They also came to see beauty as a liability. In the context of American slavery, beauty was not a prize but a price to be paid. Harriet Jacobs articulated this paradox as follows: "That which commands admiration in the white woman only hastens the degradation of the female slave." Richard Macks concluded as much when he saw a slave trader take an enslaved woman, a "colored girl, a mulatto of fine stature and good looks," into his room to "satisfy his bestial nature." Macks declared, "This attack was the result of being good-looking, for which many a poor girl in Charles County paid the price."[32]

Knowing the characteristics that white men deemed most desirable in enslaved women, enslaved people began to assess the likelihood that any particular enslaved woman would be forced into long-term sexual relations. One former slave said, "Now sometimes, if you was a real pretty young gal, somebody would buy you without knowin' anthin' 'but you, just for yourself." Speaking of his sister Delia, Lewis Clarke said that she "was so unfortunate as to be uncommonly handsome." And when she developed into a mature woman, she "was considered a great prize for the guilty passions of the slaveholders." Once the wife of their owner, Mr. Campbell, died, word of his intentions to "make a mistress of poor Delia" circulated within the slave quarters. On the advice of their mother, Delia exhausted every measure to evade him, even while being "repeatedly and most cruelly whipped," said Clarke. According to Sis Shackelford of Virginia, when a nearby neighbor named Tom Greene offered to buy her mother, her owner, Berry, was amenable to the sale. However, he would agree to sell her only if Greene would purchase her children as well. Greene refused. According to Shackelford, "He was a bachelor you know and he need a woman." It was no surprise to anyone why Greene set his sights on her mother to fill this role. Although she was very young at the time, Shackelford noted, "she was always nice looking and we all knew what Marse Greene want."[33]

As mentioned earlier, enslaved people recognized the plantation household as an unsafe space for enslaved women. An owner's deliberate placement of an enslaved woman within the plantation household was often a clue that he might be intending to sexually exploit her. William Wells Brown's owner, Walker, purchased a woman named Cynthia, whom Brown described as "a quadroon, and one of the most beautiful women I ever saw" in New Orleans. Walker said he purchased her for the purpose of taking her back to his home in St. Louis to "establish her as his housekeeper," but his intentions were much more gruesome. Brown overheard Walker make what he called "base offers" to Cynthia. In other words, he made it clear that being his housekeeper also included having sex with him. When she rejected the idea, he told her she could accept what Brown described as "vile proposals" or he would "sell her as a field hand on the worst plantation on the river." Similarly, a former bondman from Georgia testified that their owner had a "pretty gal he was goin' with," and that "he wouldn't let her work nowhere but in the house, and his wife nor nobody else didn't say nothin' 'bout it; they knowed better." By the time he died, he had fathered three children by her. When Hattie Rogers's owner needed someone to take care of his ailing mother, he not only looked to his enslaved woman Lucy to be a "house girl to wait on his mother" but required that she serve his sexual needs as well. According to Hattie, he eventually fathered eleven children by Lucy, and she became "all the missus" Hattie had ever known to occupy her owner's house.[34]

Slave owners' tendency to sexually exploit those who lived and labored within their households resulted in terms like "housekeeper" and "house maid" becoming interchangeable or heavily correlated with sexualized terms like "concubine," "sweetheart," "kept woman," or "gal" within the enslaved lexicon. Andrew Moss's grandmother gave birth to five children by her owner, George Hopper of Tennessee. According to Moss, the only explanation needed to explain his grandmother's sexual ties to her owner was that "she was his house woman," and "dat's what he call 'er."[35]

Enslaved people understood explicitly that the success and perpetuation of slavery as a labor system rested heavily on enslaved women's capacity to labor in the fields alongside men and give birth to new generations of slaves. At the point of purchase, enslaved women often heard their owners verbalize their desires to capitalize not only on their physical labor but also on the fruits of their wombs. So invested in enslaved women's fecundity, slave owners assessed their bodies at every turn. On the auction block, sellers, buyers, and physicians used their eyes to gaze upon enslaved women's bodies and their hands to touch their breasts, press on their stomachs, and manipulate their genitalia, all to determine whether the woman was fertile or not. One former bondman described the exchange between enslaved women and potential buyers this way: "They would always ask you if you was a good breeder, and if so they would buy you at your word, but if you had already had too many chillum, they would say you warn't much good. If you hadn't ever had any chilun, your marster would tell 'em you was strong, healthy, and a fast worker. You had to have somethin' about you to be sold." Much like with a piece of land, enslavers speculated on how many children an enslaved woman might yield. Their yield, or "increase," continued to be a significant identifying mark throughout their lives. In plantation records, estate inventories, and wills, enslaved women were commonly identified only by their age and their number of offspring.[36]

Enslaved men were also "objectified, eroticized, and dehumanized" in this culturalized context. As noted by historian Thomas Foster, enslaved men's bodies and genitals were "long a site of exploitation and fixation by European American cultures," making men and boys victims of rape and sexual coercion as well. Together, enslaved men and women were poked, prodded, and forced to have sexual intercourse with each other and stamped with a price for generations. The enslaved knew that men and women were likened to livestock in the eyes of sellers and buyers, many of whom had all their money invested in their enslaved labor force. Referred to as "stock," "strong bucks," and "breeders," they were "bought mostly like hosses," said Simon Phillips of Alabama. They sometimes used the nomenclature of animal husbandry that their enslavers employed and could speak to the monetary value placed on their fecundity. "A good young breedin' 'oman brung $2,000 easy, 'cause all de Marsters wanted to see plenty of strong healthy chillum comin' on all de time," said Willis Cofer. According to Rias Body, a good "breeding" woman "would sometimes sell for as high as $1200." John Cole testified that if a man looked as though he could sire "strong black bucks" who could hoe during the hottest part of the day without falter, he may be "sent out as a species of circuit-rider to the other plantations . . . married off again—time and again." Cole said that slave owners considered this method "thrifty," and it "saved actual purchase of new stock." Speaking of slave owners' tactics, Carrie Davis said, "If marster wanted to mix his stock of slaves wid a strong stock on 'nother plantation, dey would do de mens an' women jest lak horses."[37]

Slave owners' desperation to have their enslaved people engaged in sexual relations at all times was directed at the most intimate aspects of enslaved people's lives. They concerned themselves with whether or not their enslaved people were engaging in sexual relations and the frequency with which enslaved women became pregnant and gave birth. While many slave owners were inclined to allow enslaved men and women to form partnerships organically, believing that slave "marriages" provided stability within the slave quarters, the longevity of these relationships almost always rested on the couple's ability to produce children.[38] Enslaved people were reminded of their owners' expectations regarding their sexual reproduction with such frequency that they knew the romantic and intimate connections they desired and sought in one another were of little consequence to those who held them in bondage. In a speech, James Curry declared, "A few masters regard their union as sacred, but where one does, a hundred care nothing about it." According to Marshal Butler, his owner made no fanfare of marriage among his enslaved people: "Boss man would just say: 'don't forget to bring me a little one or two for next year.'" Some owners were quite procedural, bordering on draconian, when it came to ensuring that newly formed couples were engaging in sexual relations. According to Jacob Aldrich, once an enslaved couple was married, the very next morning their owner would ask the woman if the man touched her. "If he didn't, or she wouldn't let him, dat one git fifty lashes."[39]

Despite being encouraged, slave marriages were very fragile. For one, they were not legally recognized. Extending the right to legal marriage to the enslaved would have undermined the entire slave system. Allowing slaves to enter legally binding contracts would contradict the legal claim that enslaved individuals were property, incapable of possessing or executing civil rights. They were also fragile because slave owners had very little financial interest in allowing male and female slaves to maintain sexual and romantic relationships that did not produce offspring. In this vein, owners would have ascribed little monetary value to same-sex romantic attachments, meaning that enslaved men and women who desired same-sex sexual relations or romantic partnerships would have been forced to do so in secret, or suffer the consequences. Although slave owners most frequently relied on the sexual partnering of enslaved males and females to grow their lot, enslaved witnesses reveal that some slave owners took it upon themselves to impregnate their female slaves to increase their slave holdings. One former slave recalled slave traders who "often sleep with the best-looking female slaves among them." In addition to fulfilling their sexual desires, these slave traders aimed to get these women pregnant so as to "make an immense profit of this intercourse, by selling the babe with its mother." According to Henry Box Brown, slave owners and traders who engaged in this practice merely saw their enslaved offspring as "dollars and cents in their pockets."[40]

Enslaved people not only knew their owners' expectations for producing children but also knew the consequences for not meeting those expectations. Where a partnership was not fruitful, enslaved women and men would be forced to take new partners regardless of any emotional bonds they may have formed, or they could be sold and separated from their family and community entirely. Although Berry Clay was never enslaved himself, his family, being poor people of color, hired themselves out to work alongside enslaved people in Macon, Georgia. He recalled that after the slave owner performed marriage ceremonies, "he always requested, or rather demanded, that they be fruitful." If not, "a barren woman was separated from her husband and usually sold." John Brown witnessed an incident when his owner, Hugh Benford, forcefully separated a woman named Critty from her husband because they had failed to conceive any children. On her owner's command, she was "compelled to take a second husband," said Brown. Despite Benford's efforts, Critty and her new husband did not produce any children either. Because she did not reproduce with two different sexual partners, Benford planned to sell her to the highest bidder.[41]

Although forced separation and even forced coupling had become an inescapable part of the enslaved experience, enslaved people never became immune to the distress and disruption this caused. Forcing enslaved people to form new intimate relationships served slave owners' economic agendas, but it failed to acknowledge the physical and emotional ties enslaved people formed to help mitigate the psychological and physical traumas caused by enslavement. While visiting her husband's Georgia plantation, Frances Kemble crossed paths with an enslaved woman named Molly who years later still clung to the memory of her husband, who had been sold away. When she introduced herself to Kemble, she said she "belonged" to an enslaved man named Tony but quickly explained that Tony was not her real husband. Her "real" husband, she told Kemble, had been sold away for attempting to escape. Although her owner "provided her with the above-named Tony, by whom she had had nine children," she had never accepted him as her own. Her owner, Pierce Butler, was the only real beneficiary of Molly and Tony's partnership. Though they had produced nine children together, Molly continued to suffer from the emotional void caused by the loss of her husband. This trauma was compounded by being forced into a sexual relationship with Tony and having to give birth to nine children for someone else's financial gain. Historian Jennifer Morgan argues that for enslaved women, pregnancy and childbirth could stand alongside the "more ubiquitously evoked scenes of violence and brutality at the end of a slave owner's lash or branding iron." Although pained, enslaved women, such as Critty and Molly, had no choice but to forge ahead. Across the antebellum South, enslaved women relied on their individual strength and the fortitude of their communities, applying knowledge born of experience and wisdom to evade and survive the terror of rape and sexual exploitation.[42]

MARY WALKER HAD SUCH a sense of urgency to free her daughter from enslavement in North Carolina because she knew the threats that awaited an enslaved girl entering womanhood. Her own body, with light skin and loosely curled hair—signals to her own mother's sexual exploitation—was an afterimage of the South's rape culture, a testament that fueled Walker's belief that enslaved girls faced dangers that were far greater than those faced by their male counterparts.[43] Yet the distance between them meant that she could neither shield her daughter from rape, sexual coercion, or harassment nor provide her the benefit of her own knowledge and understanding. Walker loved all three of her children. Yet because she could not perform the intimate and critical work of teaching her daughter how to navigate her "blooming womanhood," she became incessantly focused on Agnes's safety. When Walker, the Lesleys, and their network of allies began their campaign to remove the two younger Walker children from the Cameron family in Raleigh, North Carolina, they initially placed priority on rescuing Agnes. When Peter Lesley wrote to Mildred Cameron, he was explicit about Walker's fears for Agnes, conveying her belief that Agnes's risk of sexual assault was imminent. Although this group of allies had previously discussed sending a direct message to the Camerons, they always concluded that the risks for both Walker and her children were too great. Lesley's letter to Cameron signifies the increase in Walker's desperation and her decision to face whatever consequences might result.

Walker would not reunite with her daughter Agnes and son Bryant until 1865, when General William Sherman and the Union Army swept through North Carolina burning any remaining vestiges of Confederate control, paving the way for them, along with thousands of other enslaved people, to escape the confines of the slave plantation. Before war made their freedom possible, Mary prayed and plotted for her children to be emancipated, especially Agnes. When it came to the most intimate aspects of their lives—intimate relations, marriage, child-rearing, and more—enslaved women like Walker exhibited a hypervigilance, spurred by their cultural understanding of their and other women's vulnerability to rape and sexual exploitation, to protect themselves and others from the perils of the South's rape culture.[44]

Although mothers knew there were consequences for evading and resisting enslavers, their faith in the power of preparedness was not squelched. If they could do anything to help their daughters evade sexual violence and exploitation, they were desperate to do so. Mattie Curtis said that before she turned fourteen, she and the other enslaved children went as naked as someone's hand. Yet her owner, a man named Whitfield, thought nothing of keeping his young slaves so scantily clad. Mattie's mother, however, could not afford to ignore the fact that her quickly developing fourteen-year-old daughter had no clothes to cover her body. "I was naked like dat when my nature come to me," said Curtis. With an eye to the future, her mother did not wait for Whitfield to decide it was time to provide Mattie with clothes to conceal her sexually maturing body. "Atter dat mammy tol' him dat I had ter have clothes," said Curtis. Mothers like Curtis's and Mary Walker advocated diligently in their daughters' best interests, thinking proactively about measures, big and small, they could take to protect and prepare their daughters for the dangerous terrain ahead.[45]

From a young age, Minnie Fulkes's mother told her to "let nobody bother yo' principle." Mothers also felt that by indoctrinating their daughters with instructions such as this, they could help them develop a spirit of discernment, a way of sensing when danger was near. The message Fulkes received from her mother was that although men would try, they had no moral right to violate her body. In Fulkes's case, she had been so well indoctrinated to evade unwanted sexual contact that she even applied this test to the enslaved man who had been selected to be her husband. Although a fellow bondman, this man was chosen *for* her, an uninvited stranger with whom the fourteen-year-old girl was told to share a bed. In her testimony, Fulkes shed light on how enslavers' dependency on the sexual reproduction of their enslaved created an environment in which not even enslaved men needed to obtain an enslaved woman's consent to engage in a sexual relationship. Fulkes said that if an enslaved man wanted to marry a particular girl, all he had to do was get permission from her owner and "pulls de gal to him he wants." From there, "dey is pronounced man an' wife," she said. The lesson Fulkes learned from her mother was that enslaved women were vulnerable to the will of all men, white and Black. For three months, Fulkes and her husband shared a bed without touching. Her mother had told her to let *nobody* bother her "principle." For her, this even extended to her new husband. "I 'bey my muma, an' tol' him so," she said. Her mother later told her that—despite her instructions—as a wife, she was obligated to have sex with her husband. Owners punished enslaved couples who abstained from having sex. Only then did she begin to have a sexual relationship with this man.[46]

Under the weight of a rape culture, enslaved mothers battled feelings of guilt, reservation, and even resentment over bringing children, especially little girls, into the world. This pressure made some women feel and do things that belied the prescribed duties of motherhood. In her published autobiography, Betheny Veney addressed the South's elite white women, saying, "You can never understand the slave mother's emotions as she clasps her new-born child, and knows that a master's word can at any moment take it from her embrace." Evoking the universality of motherhood, she urged them to consider the pain an enslaved woman felt when the baby in her arms was a helpless baby girl. An enslaved mother, "from her own experience," knows that a girl's "certain doom is to minister to the unbridled lust of the slave owner, and feels that the law holds over her no protecting arm," wrote Veney. The mother's universal charge was to nurture and protect her children and ensure that they grow healthy and strong. Yet enslavement made meeting that charge seem impossible. Veney argued that the condition of enslavement could induce impulses within mothers that were "rude and uncultured" and even fatal. If it meant delivering her and her daughter from the slave owner's "unbridled lust," she "would have been glad if we could have died together there and then." In his travels to the South, Frederick Olmsted learned of an enslaved woman from Alabama who, in fact, murdered her child to "save it from further suffering." Because the child was of mixed race and had been fathered by its owner, it was tormented by the owner's wife. According to Olmsted, the mother also hoped that killing the child would not only relieve its pain but "remove a provocation to her own ill-treatment."[47]

While some mothers contemplated and even committed infanticide to protect their daughters from abuse, others developed long-lasting and conflicting feelings for their children that shifted between regret and disdain. In an interview, the formerly enslaved Mrs. Thomas Johns told the story of an enslaved woman named Phyllis who worked alongside her mother on a farm owned by a man named Odom. According to Johns, Odom was never married, but he owned a woman called Aunt Phyllis "that he had some children by." Johns said that because Phyllis herself was "half white," the children she had by Odom were "nearly all white." Phyllis gave birth to one son who, according to Johns, "was nigger black" because his father was a Black man. Although all of Phyllis's children were treated as slaves by Odom—even those who shared his blood—Phyllis felt a special affinity for her "black child." She frequently shared her feelings about her favorite child, not afraid of the repercussions of favoring one child over the others. "When she was drunk or mad she'd say she thought more of her black chile than all the others," recounted Johns. A fellow slave had fathered the child that Phyllis favored so much. Finding herself bound to her owner, his household, and his bed, Phyllis had likely found comfort in this man, considering their relationship one of mutual consent and passion. This child, the only one not fathered by her enslaver, was different. As a result, he was saved from his mother's insults and curses and was held in higher regard than the rest.[48]

For Elizabeth Keckley, her outlook on sexual relationships and motherhood was shaped by the pain of sexual assault and knowing that she had limited control over her sexuality and fertility. Keckley experienced "suffering" and "mortification" after being sexually assaulted by Alexander Kirkland and becoming pregnant with his child. In the aftermath, she felt shame and regret. She regretted giving birth to her son George most of all, for he served as the most tangible consequence of her sexual assault by Kirkland. "If my poor boy ever suffered any humiliating pangs on account of birth, he could not blame his mother, for God knows that she did not wish to give him life," Keckley wrote. Keckley associated sex, whether coercive or consensual, with birthing a child into enslavement, something she did not want to do again. Keckley explained that when a man named James proposed marriage to her, she refused to consider his proposal for a long time, "for I could not bear the thought of bringing children into slavery—of adding one single recruit to the millions bound to hopeless servitude, fettered and shackled with chains stronger and heavier than manacles of iron." Although Keckley eventually agreed to marry James, George Kirkland remained her only child. By unknown means, she ensured that she did not birth another child.[49]

When it came to their own fate, some enslaved women preferred death to being raped or trapped in a coerced relationship. Lizzie Beaufort, an enslaved woman from Tennessee, proclaimed that she would rather "die a thousand deaths" than serve as her owner's "concubine." Beaufort was admired for her large black eyes, long black hair, and beautiful oval-shaped face. Attracted to her beauty, her owner "bought her to be his kept woman." When he made his intentions known, she expressed her willingness to work hard and "do anything that was required of her" other than have sexual relations with him. She declared that he would have to kill her before she would submit to his "hateful lust."[50]

For some enslaved women, when the life they desired for themselves or their children and family was endangered by rape or sexual coercion, their resistance knew no bounds. When Fannie Berry was attacked by a white man, she knew that one of them might die because of the fight that ensued. She was determined, however, to be the last one standing. Berry lived her life on guard for sexual predators. "Dese here ol' white men said, 'what I can't do by fair means I'll do by foul,'" recounted Berry. When the man attacked her, he tried to throw her down but couldn't. "We tusseled an' knocked over chairs an' when I got a grip I scratched his face all to pieces," said Berry. As a result of her counterattack, "der wuz no more bothering Fannie from him." Berry knew, however, that fighting back did not always guarantee that outcome: "Some slaves would be beat up so, when dey resisted, an' sometimes if you'll 'belled [rebelled] de overseer would kill yo'." Sexual assault and the risk of death if you resisted were everyday realities, according to Berry. "Us Colored women had to go through a plenty, I tell you," she said. This did not lessen Berry's resolve to inflict physical harm to fight off would-be attackers, no matter the consequence. "I wuz one slave dat de poor white man had his match."[51]

In the case of nineteen-year-old Celia, her owner, Robert Newsom, met his demise in 1855 after years of sexually assaulting Celia. He had purchased her five years prior ostensibly to labor as his housekeeper, though his objective was also sexual in nature. This was made evident when he raped her even before he returned with her to his home in Callaway County, Missouri. By the time of Newsom's death, Celia had already given birth to two children. According to testimony from Newsom's neighbors, he had fathered at least one of her two children. In June 1855, Celia was pregnant once again and in a romantic relationship with George, one of Newsom's enslaved men. Over the course of their relationship, George had begun staying overnight in Celia's cabin, the same space that Newsom relied on to abuse Celia outside his adult children's and grandchildren's physical view. Based on how frequently Celia said Newsom came to her cabin, Newsom and George likely crossed paths. On occasion, Newsom may have even forced George to leave the cabin, asserting his entitlement to Celia's body. George, however, was angered that Celia had sexual relations with Newsom, even if it was by force or coercion. According to Celia, he issued her an ultimatum. He told her "he would have nothing more to do with her if she did not quit the old man." Faced with losing her relationship with George, Celia "threatened him [Newsom] that she would hurt him if he did not quit forcing her while she was sick." Celia told Newsom's neighbor, Jefferson Jones, that during the day of June 23, 1855, Newsom told her that he was planning to come to her cabin that night. In response, she "told him not to come, and that if he came she would hurt him." Knowing he would come regardless, she testified that she prepared herself by getting a stick about the size of a chair leg and putting it in the corner of her cabin. Newsom kept his promise and came to Celia's cabin that night. Before the sun rose the next day, he was dead.[52]

A search party convened on June 24, 1855, to look for Robert Newsom. Neighbors, including William Powell, felt strongly that Newsom's slaves knew something about his disappearance, especially after George told them "he did not believe it was worthwhile to hunt for him anywhere except close around the house." Powell said, "From the statements of George, I believe he had been destroyed in the negro cabin." When the neighbors asked Celia if she knew anything of Newsom's disappearance, she reported that "she knew nothing about him." After further prodding, she "finally acknowledged that she had struck him on the head with a stick and knocked him down and then struck him some after he was down." She confessed that she did not intend to kill Newsom, but when she realized he was dead, she worked quickly to dispose of his body by burning him in her cabin with "one stack of wood and some boards." Although Celia confessed to killing Newsom to the search party and in a subsequent court deposition, there was circumstantial evidence that Celia did not kill Newsom alone. In his trial testimony, Newsom's neighbor, Jefferson Jones, said he went to the jail where Celia was awaiting trial to ask if she had had any accomplices in the crime. He was there representing himself and other members of the Calloway community who had doubts about Celia's guilt. Celia had confessed to striking Newsom on the right side of his head using her dominant right hand as he moved toward her. Jones doubted that Celia could have landed such a substantial blow to Newsom's right side, which was the side farthest away from her right hand. "I asked her if she did not know that she could not have struck him as she said, and if George had not struck the old man from behind," he said. Suspecting that George had administered the fatal blows to Newsom, Jones said, "I told her that George had run off and that she might as well tell it if he had had anything to do with killing the old man." He reported that Celia confirmed that George had threatened to break off their relationship if she did not "quit" Newsom, but when asked if George had advised her to kill Newsom, she maintained that "he never had."[53]

Regardless of whether George committed the murder or not, his ultimatum — that Celia either "quit" Newsom or their relationship was over — certainly placed Newsom's murder into motion. Yet he faced no consequences. Celia refused to implicate him although community members supported her legal defense and maintained their belief that George was somehow involved. Even when she learned that George had told the search party where to look for Newsom's ashes, which made her the key person of interest, and run away to evade suspicion, Celia held fast to her confession. On October 10, 1855, an all-white male jury found Celia guilty of murder and sentenced her to hang until dead. Her conviction and subsequent death guaranteed that she would lose her two children, as well as the fetus she was carrying at the time of the murder and conviction. Still, Celia never wavered from taking responsibility for ending Robert Newsom's life. If she had successfully killed or assisted in killing Newsom and disposed of his body without suspicion, she would have not only ended five years of sexual assault but satisfied George's conditions to continue their relationship. For Celia, the prospect of being free of Robert Newsom and living a life with George and her children appeared to outweigh the risk of being caught as well as the penalty of death. Celia was hanged on December 21, 1855, shortly after giving birth to a stillborn baby.[54]

Although many enslaved women fought hard to resist rape and sexual exploitation, even resorting to murder, some appealed to white men's sexual interests, believing long-term sexual liaisons could lead to privileges, freedom, or simply a more bearable life. Solomon Northup met such a woman on a slaver's boat headed to New Orleans. Maria was "a rather genteel looking colored girl, with a faultless form," who "entertained an extravagantly high opinion of her own attraction," said Northup. She knew that white men liked, even fetishized, enslaved women with light-colored skin and long, straight hair and saw her physical features as an asset to attract the most desirable buyer. According to Northup, Maria had no doubt that "some wealthy single gentleman of good taste would purchase her at once!" Northup had no patience for Maria's strategy. He considered her ignorant and naive. He knew she should be fearful of what these wealthy men might do to her, but she appeared willing to exchange sex for better living and labor conditions. Maria had resolved that her owner would overwhelmingly dictate her quality of life. If she possessed even the slightest bit of leverage to determine who her purchaser would be, she wanted to use it. For Maria, her beauty and sexual appeal were her most powerful tools in shaping the outcome of her sale, and she was unashamed to let onlookers like Northup know it.[55]

Similarly, Willie McCullough spoke of the "beautiful young women who were used by the marster and his men friends or who was the sweetheart of the marster only" and how they received special privileges, including having to work very little. "They had private quarters well fixed up and had great influence over the marster." McCullough claimed that some of these women even tried to break up their owners' families, "getting the marster so enmeshed in their net that his wife, perhaps an older woman, was greatly neglected." Mattie Curtis testified to how privilege and access made these women think very highly of themselves. Her owner, Moses Mordicia, was infamous for the "yaller gals" he kept in separate quarters for the use of him and his friends. "Dem yaller wimen wus highfalutin' too," said Curtis. "Dey thought dey wus better dan de black ones."[56]

Enslaved women taking advantage of sexual relations with their enslavers can be viewed as a power move in what many enslaved people understood to be the psychological and sexualized warfare of enslavement. According to enslaved people's testimony, crafty slave owners tried to disguise their sexual exploitation of enslaved women by promising freedom or giving small trinkets or private cabins in "exchange" for sexual relations. Most understood, however, that promises and trinkets did not signify a true negotiation or exchange between equals. The fact that these men ultimately could rape or retaliate against unrelenting women with violence or sale was never lost on the enslaved. Too many had witnessed enslaved women being raped, harassed, or coerced into long-term sexual liaisons without receiving promises of freedom or special privileges. This was certainly the case for Solomon Northup and explains why he could not see Maria's strategy as anything but naive. Northup had good reason to question that an enslaved woman acquiescing to sexual relations with her owner would result in a more favorable life. He had already witnessed the devastation of an enslaved woman named Eliza, who was her owner Elisha Berry's "concubine." Northup could not deny that for nine years Eliza "enjoyed opportunities such as are afforded to a very few of her oppressed class." And she believed Berry to be "a man of naturally a kind heart" and "had no doubt [he] would grant it [her freedom] to her" due to their sexual relationship and the child they had together. Like Maria, she might have resolved that her long-term sexual liaison with Berry was a means to an end; she was adorned with gold and silk and promised a pathway to freedom. In the end, when Berry encountered financial difficulties, he transferred ownership of Eliza and her children to his daughter, a Mrs. Brooks, who openly expressed disdain over her father's relationship with Eliza. Not long after, her husband, Jacob Brooks, sold Eliza and her children to James Burch, a notable slave trader in Washington, DC. Thus, she was ripped from the home she shared with Berry and its accoutrements and placed in a slave market, where she would be sold and separated from her children. Northup testified that after her sale, she found herself laboring as a field hand. For Northup, these were the harsh realities of slavery, and an enslaved woman could not be saved from them through a sexual relationship. Despite Eliza's hopes for emancipation, her "glorious vision of liberty faded from her sight as they led her away into captivity."[57]

While some women rejected or had little faith in promises of freedom or trinkets, others accepted trinkets and held onto promises of freedom, welcoming the prospect of even nominal improvements to their lives and the lives of their families. Lewis Clarke testified that no one could stop some women from "having genteel ideals." In other words, they valued intimacy and marriage and desired autonomy over who had access to their bodies. For too many, the sad reality was that "they know they must submit to their masters." Clarke felt that enslaved women should not be shamed or feel ashamed for receiving trinkets and privileges for sexual relations. "Their masters, maybe, dress 'em up, make 'em little presents, and give 'em more privileges, while the whim lasts." This was preferable to having sex with "a parcel of low, dirty, swearing, drunk patter-rollers [slave patrollers] let loose among 'em," proclaimed Clarke. If they had to "submit" anyway, they might as well receive some benefit. He felt that the alternative "breaks down their spirits dreadfully, and makes 'em wish they was dead."[58]

Over the course of generations, women like Maria saw or heard the tales of enslaved women who did, in fact, gain freedom for themselves or their children through their sexual ties to white men. The sizable free communities of color that emerged in cities like Charleston, South Carolina; Richmond, Virginia; and New Orleans, Louisiana, served as a testament. Manumission petitions, wills, tax records, and plantation inventories reveal enslaved women and children who not only gained freedom but received land, money, and status within their respective communities. Enslaved people knew, however, that this outcome was exceptional and not the rule. Enslaved people of mixed race like Maria personified the reality that sexual relations with white men rarely resulted in freedom. Still, Maria and others illustrate how some sought to take advantage of any and all opportunities to have the best life possible, no matter the risks.[59]

It is not difficult to understand why enslaved women placed a high value on protection and security. They faced many challenges in addition to sexual exploitation—like keeping their families together and dodging physical and psychological torture. A former bondwoman named Rose, who was born enslaved in Bell County, Texas, told an interviewer that she had reluctantly had sex with an enslaved man named Rufus to avoid being whipped at the stake. When she was about sixteen, her owner informed her that she would be sharing a cabin with Rufus. Rose did not fully understand the implications of her owner's decree. "I thought that he meant for me to tend the cabin for Rufus," Rose said. When Rufus, also having received orders to couple with Rose, attempted to climb in her bunk, she shoved him with her feet and caused him to tumble to the floor. Distressed by the previous night's events, Rose told her female owner of Rufus's attempt to share her bed. According to Rose, the woman said, "You are a portly girl, and Rufus is the portly man. The master wants you to bring forth portly children." Despite this explanation, Rose still greeted Rufus with a fire poker when he tried to enter their cabin that night, mounting resistance to their mutual sexual and reproductive exploitation. The next day, her male owner called for her and made his intentions clear. He said that he had paid a large sum for her and expected her to have lots of children. He further explained that he had "put" her and Rufus together for that purpose and that unless she wanted a "whipping at the stake," she better do what he asked.[60]

Prior to falling under this couple's ownership, Rose and her family were owned by a man whom she described as a cruel owner who would "whip the colored folks and works them hard and feed them poorly." When her first owner auctioned off all his slaves at the start of the Civil War, her new owner made it a point to purchase Rose and her parents to keep their family intact. Rose even credited him for not separating her family, a fate so many enslaved people had endured. With this in mind, Rose concluded that she would rather share a bed and produce children with Rufus than be flogged and risk separation from her mother and father. "There it is. What am I to do? I decide to do as the master wishes, and so I yield," Rose said. Although she yielded to secure her physical safety, Rose never forgave her owner for exploiting her. "I always hold it against him," she said.[61]

Experiences like this shaped enslaved women's beliefs about marriage and relationships. Once the Civil War ended and Rose became emancipated and could legally marry any man she chose, she resolved never to marry a man or have any more children. She was unwilling to ever concede control over the most personal aspects of her life again. "After what I did for the master, I never want no truck with any man. The Lord forgive this colored woman, but he have to excuse me and look for some others to replenish the earth." This is not to say that Rose altogether abandoned the idea of having sexual intimacy in her life. She wanted nothing more to do with men, but she said nothing of engaging in sexual relations with women. The intimate choices Rose made once free are unknown, but she wanted to control her sexuality in a way that enslavement never allowed. Similarly, an enslaved woman named Lavinia refused to ever get married when her owner sold her soon-to-be husband and demanded that she marry another man instead. According to William Wells Brown, who was enslaved on a nearby plantation, Lavinia's owner was determined to flog her until she complied. He "whipped her in such a manner that it was thought she would die," he said. Brown reported that she did not die, "but it would have been the same if she had.[62]

Some enslaved women devised new ways to conceive of marriage in order to cope with the power their owners waged over their sexual and intimate lives. Pierce Butler's slave Molly concluded that although her husband had been sold away and she was forced to partner with a new man named Tony, he had not stopped being her husband. Molly and Tony received the same mandate to "bring forth" children that most enslaved "couples" received, as evidenced by the nine children they conceived together. However, Molly never divorced herself from the intimate connection she shared with her husband. Her owner could not snuff out her emotional and ceremonial attachment to him. Bethany Veney's definition of marriage was similarly influenced by the fragile nature of enslaved people's intimate relationships, which could be and too often were broken up by slave owners at any time. While Molly defined marriage as a lifelong unity that physical separation could not erode, Veney insisted that her marriage vows to a fellow bondman named Jerry reflect the uncertainty of their future together. When Veney and Jerry prepared to go before a minister, she said, "I did not want him to make us promise that we would always be true to each other, forsaking all others, as the white people do in their marriage service." Veney knew that slave marriages were not legal in the eyes of the law and therefore did not garner the same respect and protection as white people's marriages. She knew that their marriages were permitted for the economic and authoritative benefit of slave owners. She could be sold away from her husband or forced into the arms of another man at any time. She noted that although she and Jerry desired to be together, they were only able to marry because "our masters were both willing." She knew that "at any time our masters could compel us to break such a promise" as forsaking all others. She refused to enter marriage with the misconception that she and Jerry alone controlled the longevity of their union.[63]

As a young woman, Harriet Jacobs valued marriage but realized that as an enslaved person, she would never have the "right" to let her heart choose a romantic or sexual partner. Her views on sex and marriage changed when her owner, James Norcom, vehemently rejected her request to marry a man whom she loved, a free-born carpenter who also lived in Edenton. "Don't you suppose, sir, that a slave can have some preference about marrying? Do you suppose that all men are alike to her?" Norcom said that she thought too highly of herself to ask such questions. Jacobs was reminded that as a slave, her wishes did not matter, especially to Norcom, who made incessant sexual advances toward her. "Youth will be youth. I loved, and I indulged the hope that the dark clouds around me would turn out a bright lining. I forgot that in the land of my birth the shadows are too dense for light to penetrate," Jacobs wrote. She temporarily indulged the idea of controlling her sexual destiny but was quite conscious of the restrictions that enslavement placed on her.[64]

Jacobs believed that slavery robbed her of the opportunity not only to marry for love but to remain a virgin until marriage. "I wanted to keep myself pure; and under the most adverse circumstances, I tried hard to preserve my self-respect," she wrote. With marriage out of reach, "I felt as if I was forsaken by God and man; as if all my efforts must be frustrated; and I became reckless in my despair." She concluded that her prospects of remaining a "virtuous" woman were slim and thus no longer felt it necessary or possible to reserve sex for marriage. "If slavery had been abolished, I, also, could have married the man of my choice; I could have had a home shielded by the laws; and I should have been spared the painful task of confessing what I am now about to relate; but all my prospects had been blighted by slavery." She confessed that at the age of fifteen, she began a long-term sexual liaison with Samuel Tredwell Sawyer, a young white lawyer who lived near her grandmother's home and later represented North Carolina in the US House of Representatives. Over the course of several years, she gave birth to two children by Sawyer. Explaining her relationship with Sawyer, she wrote, "I was struggling alone in the powerful grasp of the demon Slavery; and the monster proved too strong for me." Jacobs did not explicitly state whether Sawyer coerced her into a sexual relationship, although it was a real possibility. She did express, however, that she gained satisfaction in being in a sexual relationship that her owner, James Norcom, had not arranged or been able to prevent.[65]

Jacobs saw her long-term sexual liaison with Sawyer as a means to feel some control over her life. She had already given up on love and marriage because of Norcom. Now she wanted something other than love and sought to achieve as much autonomy over her body and sexuality as an enslaved woman could claim. "There is something akin to freedom in having a lover who has no control over you, except that which he gains by kindness and attachment," Jacobs wrote about Sawyer. She declared him trustworthy and valued the security their association provided. Their liaison started not long after Jacobs learned of Norcom's plan to build her a private cabin several miles from the Norcom estate, where he would have been able to have uninterrupted access to her. "He talked of his intentions to give me a home of my own, and to make a lady of me," she wrote. She placed love aside and sought security and protection instead. She resolved that enslavement forced women to make difficult decisions. "There may be sophistry in all this; but the condition of a slave confuses all principles of morality, and, in fact, renders the practice of them impossible," she wrote. Jacobs was forced to choose protection over virtue and love.[66]

FOR THOSE ENSLAVED WOMEN who came face-to-face with the trauma of rape and sexual exploitation, life could not stop. They still had hard labor to perform and children—including those who were the product of rape and coerced sex—to nurture. Instead of crumbling in the wake of sexual exploitation, enslaved women found the means to navigate the various aspects of their lives, especially intimate relationships and motherhood. Sex and relationships were highly contested topics. Some felt it best to avoid relationships, and some held tight to memories of relationships destroyed long ago. Some were faced with impossible decisions—for instance, having to prioritize their safety over the sanctity of their sexuality. Because of the unfathomable nature of their circumstances, these women at times made choices that went against convention. It is hard to comprehend the kind of pain that would compel an enslaved woman to wish death on herself or her child to escape sexual assault at the hands of her owner. As enslaved women witnessed and experienced horrific instances of sexual violence and exploitation, they worked through their trauma, both individual and collective, to do the best they could regarding family, security, and sexuality.

CHAPTER TWO

She Would Rather Die a Thousand Deaths

In 1861, Pierce Bailey Jr. composed a will in which he bequeathed Adeline, a house servant, and her child Tolbert, whom he described as "good, trusty, and faithful servants," to his nephew Lawrence Battle. He requested that Battle "treat them kindly, and see that they are as comfortably provided for as their condition in life and their conduct and behavior will justify." Battle was to "treat them just as he may at all times think I would treat them if I were in life," wrote Bailey. When Bailey's will was contested before the Supreme Court of Georgia, witnesses testified to the fact that Adeline was not only Bailey's enslaved housekeeper but a sexual servant as well.[1] They also testified that Bailey openly acknowledged Adeline's son Tolbert as his biological child and expressed desires to manumit the boy and his mother and provide the child with an education. When Bailey wrote his will, he was seventy-one years old and unmarried. He openly acknowledged Tolbert as his child and determined to provide for his son's future regardless of his enslaved status.[2]

As a feature of the South's rape culture, some enslavers used enslaved women as sexual servants, which is a descriptor for enslaved women who were required to engage in sexual relations with their owners as a condition of their enslavement, often over a long period of time. Sometimes men purchased enslaved women for this express purpose. Many of these bondwomen lived and labored in plantation households as housekeepers, cooks, seamstresses, and so on. They were required to engage in sex as a form of labor to gratify their owners' sexual pleasures.[3] In Adeline's case, she might have preferred living and laboring in Bailey's home to laboring in the fields on his plantation in Warren County, Georgia. At the same time, she could have despised having sex with him, which he required as a condition of her post. She could have viewed having sexual relations with Bailey as a tolerable means for providing the best possible living conditions for her and her son. According to slave testimony, most enslaved women objected to having sexual relations with their white owners and overseers. They resented being forced into sexual relationships of any kind, including with enslaved men, preferring instead to feel a sense of control over their sexuality and choose with whom they would form romantic and sexual attachments. Some enslaved women were able to do just that—form romantic partnerships and liaisons with men, Black and white, who appealed to their emotional as well as physical wants and needs. However, their enslaved status fundamentally denied these women any real sense of autonomy over their sexuality, and none were guaranteed the opportunity to form sexual and romantic attachments of their liking.[4]

Some historians have regarded sexual servitude—historically referred to as "concubinage"—as an ambiguous state under which some enslaved women exercised more autonomy than under other conditions of servitude. Some of these long-term liaisons between white male enslavers and enslaved women have even been described as pseudo-marriages. Historical records do reveal examples of enslaved women serving as the "ladies" of their owners' households, managing other enslaved people, and living as virtually free. There is evidence of sexual servants being exempt from the hard labor of the fields and receiving finer clothes and small gifts from their owners.[5] While it is true that sexual servitude provided some enslaved women with material benefits that came along with living within the plantation household and the leverage to negotiate the terms of their servitude, there is a danger in assuming the degree to which sexual servants exercised agency, either through their entrance into sexual servitude or in their daily lives as sexual servants. Indeed, cases of sexual servants living as quasi-wives of slave owners are exceptional. Most slave owners were not eager to forgo their position of authority over any slave, even the women with whom they had sex. It was their power and money, which was derived from their slave ownership, that afforded them the opportunity to buy sexual servants and sexually exploit them at will. Ultimately, the conditions of slavery—the absolute power of slave owners over the enslaved—prevailed over even the most seemingly benevolent examples of sexual servitude.

Prior to writing his will, Bailey consulted his attorney George Bristow on how he could manumit Adeline and Tolbert. Bristow informed Bailey that due to Georgia's strict manumission laws, he could not simply emancipate them in his will. Rather, the state legislature would have to pass an act approving his request for manumission. His most promising option would be to take them to a free state like Ohio that permitted slave owners to settle enslaved people within the state.[6] Bristow encouraged Bailey to pursue this course of action because he could do it immediately and while he was still alive to guarantee their emancipation. Bailey, however, was not receptive to this option. He was an extremely wealthy man in Georgia. His father, Pierce Bailey Sr., was known as one of Georgia's most prolific financiers.[7] Bailey Jr.'s real property was estimated to be worth over $100,000, and according to the 1850 federal census, he owned at least eighty enslaved people.[8] Being a part of such a wealthy and established planting family, Bailey was reluctant to leave the slaveholding South and jeopardize his wealth and social status to emancipate two enslaved people, no matter how fondly he viewed them or how much effort Adeline might have put forth in advocating for their freedom. He would not be the first slave owner to go to his grave while his enslaved paramour and biological child remained in bondage.[9]

Dismissing his attorney's suggestion, Bailey settled for another option, which did not emancipate Adeline and Tolbert at all but merely transferred ownership of them to his nephew Lawrence Battle, who promised Bailey he would treat the two slaves as "benevolently" as he had. Bailey's will specified that after his death, Battle was to establish a $20,000 trust to be used to financially support Adeline and Tolbert. The interest earned from the trust would provide for their every need, including Tolbert's education. Although Bailey went to considerable lengths to ensure that they would live more comfortably than most enslaved people, he did not guarantee their freedom, although there were pathways for him to do so. He may have been afraid that if he took Adeline to Ohio, where she could have been emancipated or lived as virtually free, she would break her ties to him and free herself from serving him, sexually or otherwise. Keeping her in bondage, however, ensured that she would be his housekeeper and sexual servant for the remainder of his natural life. The terms of Bailey's will suggest that it was more important to him to keep her in bondage.[10]

Allowing Adeline to dictate her own path ran contrary to the foundation of Bailey and Adeline's relationship to each other. She was the mother of his child. She may have slept next to him every night and dined with him at the same table for every meal, but at the core, he was an enslaver. By law, he owned her, and he affirmed the importance of his status as a planter and an enslaver when he chose not to free her. When Bailey placed the fate of Adeline and Tolbert into his nephew's hands, to be determined long after he was dead, he willingly left their destiny up to chance. And the outcome proved to be as uncertain as Bailey's lawyer predicted. In the years following his death in September 1863, Bailey's extended family members contested his will. They hoped to acquire a portion of his bounty even though he bequeathed all his assets to his nephew. They contested on the grounds that it was unlawful for Bailey to establish a trust for the financial benefit of enslaved persons. The case went before Georgia's Supreme Court during its June 1866 term. Although the institution of slavery had been legally abolished the year prior, the high court agreed that it was unlawful at the time Bailey made his will in 1861 to establish a $20,000 trust to be used for the benefit of enslaved persons. Therefore, they declared that portion of his will null and void and ordered Bailey's nephew to distribute the $20,000 among the rest of the family. Lawrence Battle inherited the rest of his uncle's estate, minus Adeline and Tolbert, who gained their freedom at the close of the Civil War, and the $20,000 designated for their upkeep.[11]

Pierce Bailey's last will and testament and the documentation of its subsequent appeal to the Supreme Court of Georgia provide tremendous insight into Bailey's efforts to provide Adeline and Tolbert with an exceptionally higher standard of living than the rest of his many enslaved people. While he chose not to free the mother and son, he did demonstrate a commitment to their comfort and Tolbert's education at a time when educating enslaved people violated state laws. However, because Adeline's voice and actions are not captured in these documents, we do not know what role she played, if any, in helping to shape Bailey's will. Did Adeline petition Bailey for economic security for herself and her son? When she was required to share his bed at night, did she suggest that the intimate nature of her service to him warranted his special consideration for her and her son? Over time, did they develop affection for each other that blurred the boundaries of their respective positions and fostered a mutual desire for their son's freedom and long-term security?

Scholarly efforts to untangle the complexities of long-term sexual liaisons like Bailey and Adeline's have generated intense historiographical debates. At one time, prominent scholars pointed to these long-term connections as proof of loving relationships between male enslavers and enslaved women.[12] Feminist scholars responded by rejecting overly romantic and paternalistic characterizations of these relationships and contended that exploitation was and continued to be the foundation of all sexual relations between enslavers and the enslaved. It was as oppressors that white men approached Black women's bodies, said Angela Davis. And, the inherent imbalance of power made these relations exploitative by default.[13] More recent scholarship, however, has argued that in cases like that of Pierce Bailey and Adeline, it does a disservice to enslaved women not to consider their willingness or ability to pursue or at least manipulate these sexual liaisons for their own benefit, acting as power brokers within plantation households and negotiating for long-term economic security and emancipation for themselves and their children.[14] Some scholars have boldly suggested that enslaved women *knowingly* entered these long-term sexual liaisons, that the line between housekeeper and sexual servant was knowingly blurred, and that when these women assumed these positions, they understood their duties to include sex and often expected to receive material rewards in return.[15]

Indeed, these arguments are effective in expanding our understanding of enslaved women's agency within the South's rape culture because it is true that sex between enslaved women and white men did not always fit neatly into one category. As historian Cynthia Kennedy has argued, "Sex between white men and black women was coerced; it was consensual; it was a combination of both." The question becomes, How much agency is enough or too much for historians to assume that enslaved women like Adeline were realistically able to wield? How can we argue that any enslaved woman assumed or knowingly entered any labor or sexual position? The testimony of enslaved people reveals that slave owners often had well-crafted agendas for placing enslaved women into sexual servitude. That these women *entered* these relationships obscures the power that white male slave owners wielded over every aspect of enslaved people's lives, especially their sexuality.[16]

There is indeed a struggle by historians to consider every aspect of enslaved women's humanity. Historian Clarence Walker has suggested that we nuance these debates over agency and consent by shifting our efforts to exploring *how* enslaved women like Adeline perceived of themselves as agents amid sexual subjugation.[17] In my own efforts to engage with and contribute to this scholarship, I have found myself interrogating the methodological choices that we as historians, me included, make to assess agency, especially that of enslaved people. Historians have often supported claims of agency with documents produced solely by white slave-owning men. Yet slave-owning men's wills, petitions for manumission, and other attempts to grant emancipation and property to enslaved women and children shed more light on white men's power and less on enslaved women's ability to negotiate and secure physical and economic security for themselves and their families.

Historians of slavery are undoubtedly hindered by a scant archive of enslaved people's voices. We have the option to extract everything possible from sources, read the silences, and devote attention to the people whom archives wish to render invisible. I find it uncomfortable, however, to make bold claims regarding enslaved women's wants and intensions without at least drawing from their own testimony, no matter how faint. It is imperative that we never lose sight of the tenuous nature of these long-term sexual liaisons, being careful not to obscure the power that white male enslavers, as well as overseers, wielded over their enslaved women and the often violent, forceful, and coercive means by which most enslaved women first came into sexual contact with their owners. It is true that enslaved women were human beings who experienced pain and joy and desired to form familial relationships; bear and nurture children; and seek love, comfort, and pleasure through sexual expression. Yet the "chattel principle" that deemed enslaved women property reigned supreme in the slaveholding South. These women, whose bodies were legally not their own, could be bought, sold, and coerced into sexual relations and sexual reproduction at their owners' discretion.

While I am inspired by the scholars who have paved the way for new ways of thinking about enslaved women as brokers of power, I take heed to Walker's call for scholars to focus attention on the ways in which enslaved women saw *themselves* as negotiators of their own fate in a rape culture that did not relent. This chapter draws on sources produced by enslaved women, such as legal petitions to federal agencies and commissions, written correspondence, and slave narratives and interviews, to illuminate enslaved women's agency. It assesses how enslaved women perceived their ability to shape the terms and conditions of sexual servitude and long-term sexual liaisons with white men and the actions they took to improve the quality of life for themselves and their families.

In the case of Pierce Bailey and Adeline, his authority as her slave owner served as the initial and continual foundation upon which their long-term liaison rested. It is possible that Adeline sought her position within Bailey's household and campaigned for the long-term security of herself and her son, but without her voice, we cannot know for sure how much influence she was able to wield. Although Bailey attempted to secure a better life for Adeline and their child, he never lost sight of the fact that she was his property to be treated as he saw fit. According to one witness, Bailey whipped Adeline like he did his other bondpeople, just to a lesser extent. Despite coming into more intimate contact with him than anyone else, she was still his slave. Being his sexual servant may have afforded her fewer whippings than his other enslaved people and led to his consideration for her long-term economic security. Yet she remained enslaved when his natural life came to an end and beyond.[18]

UNDER THE SOUTH'S RAPE CULTURE, owners frequently had sex and sexual reproduction on their minds when they ventured to slave markets to purchase and sell enslaved people, male and female. When purchasing an enslaved woman, any practical and ambitious slave owner wanted a female who would be a productive field or household laborer and birth multiple children. Due to the unfettered power these men possessed, many also gazed upon these women's bodies with sexual thoughts in mind, considering the various ways in which they could exploit their bodies even before they returned to their plantations. During these transactions, most enslaved women were instead focused on not being separated from their children or sent away from everything and everyone they had ever known.

In cities like New Orleans and Baton Rouge, slave traders marketed enslaved women, usually of mixed raced, as sexual servants or "fancy girls," as they were called. When Jack Maddox's owner brought home a pretty mulatto girl with straight black hair who was dressed extremely neat, everyone, including the owner's wife, knew he had purchased the woman in order to have sex with her. Although his wife was not pleased, he brought the woman into their household anyway.[19] Louisa Picquet recalled a slave owner in Mobile, Alabama, who traveled to Charleston, South Carolina, to purchase a woman to be his sexual servant. According to Picquet, it was known by everyone that he "bought her for himself." Because he only intended for the woman to provide sexual labor, he did not even bring her into his home to work as a housekeeper or seamstress. Rather, he kept her boarded at a separate location. When he wanted to see her, he sent a male servant to bring her from her living quarters to his office, which was the location he designated for having sexual relations with her. The enslaved woman had no say when these meetings took place; she was expected to follow orders and travel to her owner's office when requested.[20]

Sis Shackelford's mother had the misfortune of watching her enslaver and another slave owner engage in the intense sales negotiation that would have determined whether she became a sexual servant or not. Sis Shackelford, who was a child at the time, recalled Tom Greene coming to see their owner, a man named Berry, to inquire about her mother. According to Shackelford, Greene was unmarried, and he wanted an enslaved woman for a "mistress." Greene proposed that he buy Shackelford's mother "fer his [w]'oman." Greene knew Shackelford's mother to be a nice-looking woman. He also knew that Berry would be receptive to selling her because his excessive drinking had gotten him into some financial trouble, and he needed money. According to Shackelford, Berry was more than willing to sell her mother to Greene, but only if Greene also agreed to buy her children. He considered her a valuable commodity and said he would be damned if he sold her and did not get money for her children as well. Greene balked at Berry's proposal. He said he did not want children, just a slave woman. One can only imagine what was going through the enslaved mother's mind as she watched the intense standoff between these two slave owners. An agreement in Greene's favor meant that she would not only be separated from her children but be required to have sex with her new owner as well. All she was permitted to do was watch as they decided her fate. In the end, Greene rejected Berry's terms and conditions, and Shackelford's mother narrowly escaped becoming a sexual servant. The next enslaved woman Greene pursued, however, was not so fortunate. According to Shackelford, he purchased a woman named Betsy to be his mistress. In the years to come, Betsy gave birth to three of his children.[21]

It was not uncommon for male enslavers to pursue their existing household servants for long-term sexual liaisons. Housekeepers, cooks, nursemaids, and seamstresses were ideal targets because their labor responsibilities often required them to work and live in their owners' households. It was often while they were performing their tasks in the plantation household that male slave owners would demand that they meet them in a bedroom or some other private space to have sexual relations.[22] Virginia Shepherd testified that her owner, Gaskins, was in constant pursuit of his housekeeper Diana. According to Shepherd, "He just wanted his Diana in every sense of the word." He found various ways to isolate her, including sending her to the barn to shuck corn. "He tried to cage her in the barn so she couldn't get out," said Shepherd, but she usually made every effort she could to fight back or escape.[23]

Like Diana, Louisa Picquet was determined to resist her owner's sexual advances at all costs. Picquet was familiar with the conditions of sexual servitude because her mother, Elizabeth, had been forced to be the sexual servant of their owner, David Cook. When Cook experienced a financial setback and hired out several of his enslaved people, including Picquet's mother, he turned his attention to Picquet and began requesting that she come to his bedroom at night. She had witnessed her mother give birth to three of Cook's children, so she understood why he wanted her to come to his bedroom. Picquet succeeded in avoiding Cook for a time, but he grew tired of her disobeying his orders and one day demanded that she make an appearance in his room that night. "If I didn't, he'd give me hell in the morning," said Picquet. When she did not show up again, Cook followed through on his threat and whipped her for her disobedience. In between lashes, he asked her what she was afraid of. He asked "if I could not sleep as well there as anywhere else," said Picquet. Under duress, she told him that she was not afraid and that she would obey his future commands. She had prepared, however, to "take another whippin' in the mornin'" because she had no plans of going to his bedroom that night either.[24]

To Picquet's relief, Cook never made it to his bedroom that night because he spent the evening drinking and playing cards with friends into the late hours of the night. However, the next morning, she had no choice but to knock on his bedroom door and alert him that his breakfast was ready, which was one of her many duties. She knocked with caution, afraid that he would chastise her for once again not coming to his room. To her surprise, he greeted her warmly. He summoned her to the edge of his bed, proclaiming that he had something for her. He grabbed her hand and placed a handful of half dollars in it, which was more money than she could have ever imagined seeing at one time. In his drunken giddiness, he continued to hold on to her and asked if she would come to see him later. She promised that she would, shook her hand free of his grasp, and left the room.[25]

From the moment Cook handed Picquet what she described as a fortune, she demonstrated uneasiness about the transfer that had taken place. Was Cook being unusually generous amid his drunkenness? Or had he given her the money as an incentive to end her resistance and finally obey his demand for sex. Picquet was not ashamed to admit that she was enamored by the money, even though she knew it was not a gift but an attempt to bribe her into compliance. Cook was not actually *asking* but *ordering* her to come to his room that night. Rather than hash out the implications of accepting the money, Picquet decided to go into town to buy fabric that she had been admiring for some time to make a muslin dress. She could not resist what felt like a once-in-a-lifetime opportunity to buy the fabric that was "perfectly white, with a little pink leaf all over it," she said.[26]

When Picquet returned home, she had hopes that Cook had not remembered giving her the coins that morning. But despite his inebriation, Cook remembered not only giving Picquet the handful of half dollars but also her promise to join him in his bedroom that night. Although she denied knowing anything about the money when he asked, he reiterated his expectation that she be in his bedroom that night. Picquet felt compromised. Her desire to resist Cook's sexual advances had not dissipated, but because she had accepted his money and indulged in spending it, she felt an awful and overwhelming sense of obligation to complete what felt like an exchange. "I guess I'd have to go up stairs that night," she said. Confused, she consulted an acquaintance about her predicament. She might have asked, Did his gift of half dollars make his vile commands any less vile? Why should she feel obligated to fulfill a bargain she had not willingly entered? How can someone give you a gift in exchange for your submission when they already claim ownership of your person and can whip or threaten to sell you to enforce their will?[27]

What Picquet realized was that her owner was trying to create the illusion that the two of them had engaged in an exchange, a negotiation of some sort. He had refashioned his demands for sex to look more like a request from one willing party to another—a deal that had been sealed with a generous gift. His money, however, was just another attempt to coax her into being obedient, which he already required of her as his slave. Perhaps Picquet's initial feelings of obligation were really feelings of defeat for falling into Cook's trap. After all, she had spent his money and relished in it. However, her consultation with her friend only solidified her understanding that she and Cook were not in any sort of negotiation at all. Whether she had accepted the half dollars or not, her owner held the power to rape her or beat her to death if she continued to resist. At that moment, she determined that no number of coins or fabric would ever make her stop resisting a long-term sexual liaison with Cook.[28]

These accounts of sexual servitude are important because they provide insight into how long-term sexual relationships between white men and enslaved women were imagined, initiated, resisted, or negotiated from the enslaved woman's perspective. The experiences of Diana and Louisa Picquet illustrate that being a sexual servant was not always accompanied with status within the plantation household, material benefits, or hopes for emancipation. Women like Sis Shackelford's mother were not eager to become sexual servants. Rather than being a negotiator, Shackelford's mother was forced to witness two white men negotiate over the future of her and her children. Each story reveals that enslaved women's long-term sexual relations with white men ran many different courses and were each established and sustained under unique sets of circumstances that make it hard to draw general conclusions about enslaved women's experiences as sexual servants—"concubines," "mistresses," "kept women," and "fancy girls."

It is true that some enslaved people viewed long-term sexual liaisons between white men and enslaved women as beneficial—an opportunity to potentially receive material benefits, preferential treatment, and even emancipation for the children born as a result of these relations.[29] Former bondman Willie McCullough said, "Some of the half-white and beautiful young women [who] were used by the master and his men friends or who were the sweetheart of the master only, were given special privileges." According to McCullough, some of these women worked very little and were given private quarters, and some even had great influence over the owner. Another formerly enslaved man said he and his parents received no trouble from their owner on account of his sister being their owner's "gal." Their owner was not married and decided instead to "keep Deenie up to the big house" to fulfill his needs. Although he provided no information on how his sister felt about being "kept" in the big house to serve as their owner's sexual servant, he openly acknowledged that he and his parents reaped and enjoyed the benefits. Another former bondman said his owner traveled to Baltimore, Maryland, to purchase "a light one for him," meaning an enslaved woman with a light-colored skin tone to be his sexual servant. According to this witness, although their owner had a wife, he allowed this enslaved woman to carry keys to his house, which was seen as a privilege among the rest of his enslaved people. In North Carolina, an unmarried slave owner bought an enslaved woman to live in his house to provide care for his ailing mother and be his sexual servant. The enslaved people on the plantation regarded her as their mistress, as she was treated as the lady of the household. She gave birth to eleven of her owner's children. "Yes, sir he loved that woman, and when he died he left all his property to her," said one witness.[30]

Although sexual servitude had the potential to provide amenities that other labor positions did not—such as living and eating within the plantation household—the leverage that enslaved women could acquire from these sexual liaisons was only as strong and effective as their owners permitted. An enslaved woman trusting that her sexual relations with a white man would parlay into material gains was a risky and often disappointing endeavor. For many, their efforts to broker power as sexual servants quickly unraveled. The self-emancipated William Craft argued that slave owners were eager to hand out trinkets to elicit enslaved women's affections and trust or generate feelings of ease toward what were otherwise sexually coercive relationships. Some promised enslaved women that they would live as "husband and wife" and that "if they have any children they will be free and well educated." While a few owners remained "true to their pledges," the vast majority never lost sight of the fact that their sexual servants were their legal property. "As the woman and her children are legally the property of the man who stands in the anomalous relation to them of husband and father, as well as master, they are liable to be seized and sold for his debts, should he become involved."[31]

While enslaved, William Wells Brown encountered an enslaved woman named Cynthia who was forced into sexual servitude but was promised a better life as a result. Brown's owner, Mr. Walker, was a slave trader. While on one of his slave-trading voyages, Walker purchased Cynthia and instructed Brown to put her in one of his ship's staterooms away from the other enslaved people. Brown hinted at his suspicions regarding this request. "I had seen

too much of the workings of slavery, not to know what this meant," he recalled after receiving his orders. The intention behind Walker's request became clearer once Cynthia came face-to-face with her new owner. Brown
overheard Walker make Cynthia "offers" and "vile proposals," which were
Brown's euphemisms for sex. Cynthia rejected them. Next, "he told her that
if she would accept his vile proposals, he would take her back with him to
St. Louis, and establish her as his housekeeper at his farm. But if she per-
sisted in rejecting them, he would sell her as a field hand on the worst plantation on the river."[32]

First Cynthia had to decide if she wanted to serve her new owner as a
housekeeper or labor as a field hand at a notoriously harsh plantation elsewhere. There was a general perception among members of enslaved communities that house laborers received better treatment than field laborers
and were a part of an elite class within the population.[33] Therefore, Cynthia
likely considered the advantages that working in the house might afford.
Next she had to decide if having unwanted sex with her owner was worth securing the presumably less strenuous housekeeping position. After describing Cynthia's initial meeting with Walker, Brown wrote the following about
her fate: "Without entering into any farther particulars, suffice it to say that
Walker performed his part of the contract, at that time. He took her back to
St. Louis, established her as his mistress and housekeeper at his farm."
Although Brown referred to Walker and Cynthia's arrangement as a contract, it was not a contract in the least. Cynthia's *terms* were to enter an un-
solicited sexual relationship or face harsh working conditions as a field
hand. Although it may appear that she made a choice, she had no meaningful choice at all. If she had been a free woman with full control over her
body, Cynthia would have chosen neither option.[34]

In the years to come, Cynthia labored as Walker's housekeeper and, as his
sexual servant, gave birth to four of his children. It is possible that Cynthia
settled into her position as Walker's sexual servant. She may have concluded
that it was better to have sex with Walker and bear his children than face the
unknowns of the worst plantation along the Mississippi River. This relationship, although not consensual, did provide Cynthia with security and protection. However, it is important to note that what her long-term sexual
liaison with Walker protected her from was the threat that Walker himself
had made. He was simultaneously a conduit for security and a conduit for
harm. Cynthia's "protection" from harm ended abruptly when Walker decided to get married. Now that he had a legitimate wife to serve as the lady
and domestic manager of his household, Walker chose to rid his house of

any traces of Cynthia and his four enslaved children. According to Brown, Walker sold Cynthia and her children, and they were never heard of again.[35]

Virginia Boyd faced a similar fate when she and her youngest child were placed in a slave trader's yard in Houston, Texas, in April 1853. To her dismay, she had been put up for sale at the insistence of the Honorable Samuel Boyd of Natchez, Mississippi, although she had long served as his sexual servant and he had fathered three of her children—including the child who had also been put up for sale and the unborn child that was currently in her womb. In May, while she was still being held in Houston, Virginia wrote a letter to Samuel's business partner, Rice Ballard, expressing her disappointment that he would sell her and her child considering their long-term sexual liaison.[36] Samuel was notorious for his cruelty toward the enslaved, and despite her dismay, Virginia was not exempt just because they had had a sexual relationship.[37] "Do you think after all that has transpired between me & the old man, (I don't call names) that it's treating me well to send me off among strangers in my situation to be sold without even my having an opportunity of choosing for myself," wrote Virginia. "It's hard indeed and what is still harder [is] for the father of my children to sell his own offspring, yes his own flesh & blood," she concluded.[38]

Virginia's letter to Ballard did not provide immense detail about her relationship with Samuel. Although she expressed disgust, she also suggested that Samuel had redeeming qualities that she hoped would surface in time to save her and her child from sale: "My God is it possible that any free born American would brand his character with such a stigma as that, but I hope before this he will relent & see his error for I still beleave that he is possest of more honor than that." After all, the nature of their relations required her to come into the closest proximity with Samuel, and she surely learned personal facets of his personality and character as a result. She likely made concerted efforts to gain Samuel's favor to shield her from the very predicament in which she now found herself. Each time she bore one of his children, she may have tried to facilitate a bond between father and child, reminding him that the children shared his blood even though the law declared them slaves. If this was the case, her efforts to negotiate with him for freedom and security were in vain.[39]

Virginia's hopes for herself and her children stood no chance against the domination of Samuel Boyd. In addition to being a judge, he jointly owned six cotton plantations and over five hundred enslaved people in Mississippi, Louisiana, and Arkansas with Rice Ballard. Protecting his income of approximately $100,000 per annum and his relationship with his wife, who also

Houston May 5th 1853

Dear Sir [permit?] me to address you a few lines which I hope
you will receive soon, I am at present in the city of Houston
in a Negro traders yard for sale, by your orders I was present
at the Post Office when Doctor [Burn?] took your letter out through
mistake and red it aloud not knowing I was the person the
letter alluded to, I hope that if I have ever done or said any
thing that has offended you that you will forgive me, for
I have suffered enough times in mind to repay all that
I have ever done to any one, you wrote for them to sell me
in thirty days, do you think after all that has transpired
between me & the old Man, I don't call names, that its treating
me well to send me off a mong strangers in my situation
to be sold without even my having an oppertunity of choosing
for my self, its hard in deed and what is still harder for
the father of my children to sell his own offspring yes his own
flesh & blood My god is it possible that any free born
American would hand his charter with such a stigma as
that, but I hope before this he will relent & see his error for
I still beleave that he is possest of more honer than that
I no too that you have influence and can assist me
in some measure from out of this dilema and if you
will god will be sure to reward you, you have a family
of children & no how to sympathize with others in distress all
I require or ask is for an agent to be appointed hear
to see to me and [give?] me to earn the money honestly
to bey my [children?] I have to work my finger ends off
I will earn [   ] ay every dime I do think in justice

Virginia Boyd's letter to Rice C. Ballard. This is the first page of Boyd's three-page
letter in which she protests being put up for sale due to her sexual service to Samuel
Boyd. She asks Ballard to intervene on her behalf. Rice C. Ballard Papers #4850,
Southern Historical Collection, Wilson Library, University of North Carolina at
Chapel Hill.

hailed from a prominent slave-owning family, was more important than any inkling of affection or obligation he might have developed for Virginia and their children over the years.[40] In August, three months after Virginia wrote her petition to Ballard, C. M. Rutherford, another of Samuel and Rice Ballard's associates, wrote to Ballard to confirm the sale of Virginia and her child. Her pleas for Samuel's and Ballard's consideration had fallen on deaf ears.[41]

CYNTHIA'S AND VIRGINIA BOYD'S owners never made extensive efforts to manumit them or secure their long-term financial security. Yet the last will and testament of Pierce Bailey, which attempted to establish a $20,000 trust to provide for the maintenance of his sexual servant and the child they had together, illustrates that some slave owners did, in fact, feel obligated or inspired to provide special care for their long-term sexual servants and children. However, enslavers' last will and testaments, manumission petitions, and other property transfer documents do not reveal what enslaved women anticipated in exchange for sexual servitude or how they leveraged influence within or in the aftermath of these long-term sexual liaisons. It is precarious to draw conclusions about the intentions of enslaved women like Adeline without documentation that captures their voices directly. Examining sources produced by enslaved and formerly enslaved women or sources that capture their words and actions, such as petitions to state and federal government, written correspondence, and slave narratives and interviews, provides an opportunity to understand how these women leveraged influence and perceived their ability to do so. Enslaved women did not see themselves as totally powerless or void of the capacity to negotiate, at times using and legitimizing these liaisons to secure the social and economic advancement of themselves and their families.

When writing to Rice Ballard, Virginia Boyd clearly expressed that she deserved much better than landing in a slave trader's yard, and she identified her sexual relationship with Samuel Boyd as the reason. She said that too much had happened between her and Samuel Boyd for her to be sold off, especially while pregnant. Further, she felt that it was not right that she be sold "without even my having an opportunity of choosing for myself." Her sexual relationship with Boyd should have afforded her a choice in her fate. While she expressed hope that Boyd would have a change of heart, she asked Ballard directly to cancel her sale. "I no too that you have influence and can assist me in some measure from out of this dilemma," she wrote. She said, "God will be sure to reward you." She asserted that because he had children of his own, he "no how to sympathize with others in distress." Virginia then revealed that she had written to Samuel as well with the same request. She assured Ballard that she had been discreet, using "every precaution to prevent others from knowing or suspecting any thing." Although she conveyed her willingness to protect Samuel's reputation by not putting details of their sexual liaison in writing, she wanted Ballard to know that she was willing to sling mud and air Samuel's indiscretions to save her and her child from sale. She concluded her letter with this warning: "I shall not seek ever to let any thing be exposed, unless I am forced from bad treatment."[42]

Similarly, in 1876, Susan Flowers made her appeal before the Southern Claims Commission (SCC), saying that although she was enslaved by Ignatius Flowers prior to emancipation in 1865, they then lived as man and wife. Therefore, she was entitled to the $25,155 in damages that the SCC awarded Ignatius as compensation for the property that the Union army seized from his plantation during the Civil War.[43] "I was a slave at the beginning of the war and belonged to Ignatius Flowers who afterwards became my husband," she said. Ignatius was a successful planter in Claiborne County, Mississippi, who never married. He purchased Susan, who was born in Claiborne County in 1845, six months prior to the start of the Civil War and established her as his house servant on his three-thousand-acre Spring Plain Place plantation. Spring Plain Place was not that different from the other plantations in Claiborne County that were nestled along the Big Black River, just a few miles outside the township of Rocky Springs.[44]

Ignatius's ownership of Susan was the foundation on which their relationship was built, although they produced five children and lived together for thirteen years, both before and after the Civil War. When defining their relationship for the SCC, Susan appropriated the language of marriage, suggesting that their transition from enslaver and slave to husband and wife had been a natural and conscious one. Susan needed to validate her relationship with Ignatius if she was going to successfully persuade the SCC to designate her next of kin and give her Ignatius's sizable settlement. The $25,155 sum would have created economic independence and generational wealth for her and their three surviving children, fifteen-year-old Washington, twelve-year-old Parilea, and eleven-year-old Rosa Ann. The legality of Susan and Ignatius's ties were much more complex. When Susan was Ignatius's bondwoman, she did not have the right to enter into a marriage or any legal contract. There were no courts or legislative bodies to which she could have appealed if she no longer wanted to be Ignatius's "kept woman." While she claimed that Ignatius had become her husband after the Civil War, the laws of Mississippi said otherwise. The Mississippi Black Code of 1865 stated that "freedmen," "free negroes," and "mulattos" could intermarry one another, but that it "shall not be lawful for them to intermarry any white person."[45]

When Susan testified before the SCC in 1876, she knew to anticipate challenges. For one, she was appealing to a government agency for financial support during a time when the federal government's efforts to help former bondpeople transition into freedom were waning. By the early 1870s, radical Republicans, Black and white, were beginning to lose control of state and local governments. As ex-Confederates became enfranchised, they were able to reorganize the Democratic Party. By 1875, states such as Mississippi, where Susan lived, had been "redeemed" by Southern Democrats, and they began re-creating a racial order characterized by Black deference in economic, political, and social arenas.[46] As for the SCC, it was created by Congress in 1871 and provided Southern loyalists with the opportunity to seek compensation for property that was commandeered or destroyed by the Union army during the Civil War. Ignatius petitioned the SCC for damages for the corn, livestock, fodder, and cured meat he claimed the Union army seized from his Spring Plain Place plantation. Ignatius died during a cold spell in 1873, shortly after submitting his petition and before a judgment could be made on his claim. At that time, Susan assumed the role of administrator of the petition. All she had to do was convince a committee of white male commissioners that as the formerly enslaved "wife" of Ignatius, a prominent plantation owner, she was entitled to over $25,000 of government money.[47]

When Susan offered her deposition to an SCC commissioner, she took the initiative to define her relations with Ignatius in her own terms, even if they defied legal and social conventions. She said, "I claim to be the widow of Ignatius Flowers." She was careful to acknowledge her formerly enslaved status alongside her declaration of marriage. This was possibly an effort on her part to present their liaison in a way that was less threatening to the South's ante- and postbellum social sensibilities, which did not approve of white men and Black women living openly as man and wife. Yet she reiterated the strength of their connection, emphasizing that although she was emancipated, she continued to live with and conceive children by him for eight years. This was her way of claiming that despite her formerly enslaved status, her sustained ties to Ignatius had meaning. When she declared herself his widow, she was building her case that she was the lawful recipient of his federal compensation. Susan was actively shaping the narrative of her relationship with Ignatius, which was founded on slave ownership, into an opportunity to seek economic and social advancement for herself and her children.[48]

The SCC provided Susan with a grand stage on which to assert her agency. "There was no legal ceremony ever performed," said Susan. "But under the Constitution adopted by the State of Miss., in 1869, we became man and wife." The Mississippi Constitution of 1869 was drafted to satisfy the Republican-controlled US Congress's terms of reinstatement into the Union. Of marriage, it said, "All persons who have not been married, but are now living together, cohabiting as husband and wife, shall be taken and held for all purposes in law as married, and their children, whether born before or after the ratification of this Constitution, shall be legitimate; and the Legislature may, by law, punish adultery and concubinage." Unlike the state's 1865 Black Code, the new Mississippi state constitution did not specifically prohibit interracial marriage. However, the constitution's crafters did not necessarily abandon the anti-miscegenation sentiments that were reflected in the 1865 Black Code. Rather, they had to appease state Republicans and Congress by producing a document that respected the Fourteenth Amendment's provisions for guaranteed citizenship and due process for all Americans, Black and white. Social customs still dictated that interracial relationships were not legitimate in the eyes of most Southern communities.[49]

Regardless of social customs, Susan pled her case. She said, "Before his death he made a will, although not a legal one, in a letter to Bryant Willie in which he acknowledged me as his lawful wife and the children as his and wanted us to have his property." Knowing that Ignatius had never legally married or produced white heirs who could challenge her petition, she said, "No one beside myself and my children have any interest in this claim." It was later revealed in testimony by W. D. Spratt, an acquaintance of Ignatius, that while he left no white heirs, he did "raise two colored families." In her testimony, Susan carefully and explicitly represented herself and her surviving children as the sole claimants to Ignatius's hefty estate.[50]

Despite Susan's efforts to legitimize her "marriage," the SCC determined that Susan and Ignatius were not legally married. Because she was not legally his next of kin, she was not entitled to the compensation that would have been due to him had he not died. Although Mississippi's 1869 constitution decreed all cohabiting couples, even those that did not have prior documentation of marriage, legally married from that moment onward and did not explicitly outlaw interracial marriage, the SCC did not recognize Susan's testimony as proof that she, a former slave, was the lawful wife of her wealthy former enslaver. In a fact-finding brief, the commission reported, "No letters of Administration appear to be on file, and it is submitted that claimant's testimony is not sufficient to prove that she has the legal right to prosecute this claim." Despite her efforts, Susan was denied her claim to Ignatius's $25,155 settlement.[51]

In contrast to Susan Flowers, the formerly enslaved Susan Bryant did not speak at all to her long-term sexual liaison with her former owner, Thomas Brown, or to the ten children she had by him when she was asked to provide detailed information on her marital history and parental status to secure a widow's pension from the federal Bureau of Pensions. In 1875, she had married the formerly enslaved William Bryant, who received a monthly pension of twenty dollars due to his service as a private in Company B of the Sixty-Sixth Regiment of the United States Colored Infantry during the Civil War.[52] When William died in January 1917, Susan filed a Declaration for Widow's Pension form to continue receiving William's monthly benefits. When Susan filed on February 17, 1917, she completed a deposition, answering the questions asked and providing information that she felt was most pertinent to her case. She testified that "she is the widow and heir of William Bryant—deceased, who was a pensioner, his certificate being 1039.101; that he died January 18, 1917; that said Bryant had no children or heirs except herself. And that she now makes claim for the pension money due said Bryant at the time of his death so that she may pay for funeral expenses and medical bills." Although her request for a widow's pension was not out of the ordinary during this time for either white or Black women, her petition set off alarms when bureau commissioners later discovered that Susan had given birth to ten children and none of them belonged to William.[53]

In 1915, two years before he died, William Bryant was asked by the Bureau of Pensions to complete a form for the purposes of identifying his next of kin. A notice in type print at the top of the form read: "The information is requested for future use, and it may be of great value to your widow or children." When asked his date and place of birth, William wrote, "Claiborne County, Mississippi." Where he was asked to provide the full name of his wife and when and by whom they were married, he wrote, "Susan White" and "8 April 1875, by Rev. John Bertram." William also indicated that he had never been married to any other woman, Susan had never been married to any other man, and they "have lived continuously together since marriage." In Susan's deposition, she also testified that William had no biological children, that they had no children together, and that she had never been married to any other man. Susan did not offer that she had ten biological children of her own. It is possible that Susan did not mention her children because the bureau did not specifically ask if she had children independently of William, the pensioner. If she had voluntarily mentioned her children, she would have had to confirm that William was not the father and possibly name who the father was. By not identifying herself as a mother, Susan avoided having to speak about any sexual relationships she may have had prior to marrying William. She may have suspected that mentioning children would have prompted questions about previous marriages and wanted there to be no doubt about the legitimacy of her marriage to William. Yet to bureau special examiner J. B. Steed, it was the fact that Susan did not mention her children that made him wonder if she had been married before or was still married to her children's father, which would have made both her marriage to William and her request for his pension null and void.[54]

By the time Steed was able to convene witnesses to testify to the legitimacy of Susan and William Bryant's marriage and the paternity of Susan's children, Susan had suffered a massive stroke that "rendered her wholly incompetent to give testimony in her case," reported Steed. Therefore, he had to rely on the testimony of people who knew Susan best, including her children and the white children of her former owner, Thomas Brown. Susan's son Jack Brown testified that his mother had never been married until she married William Bryant. "They were married when I was a baby so my mother always said," said Jack. He told Steed that yes, his mother had birthed all ten of her children before she married Bryant, whom he referred to as his stepfather. "Thomas Brown, a white man, now dead, was the father of mother's ten children," declared Jack. He then testified, "She was the slave of Thomas Brown and he kept my mother as servant there in the home and she had the ten children by him. I am the youngest of the children."[55]

While she was enslaved, Susan had served as Thomas's sexual servant. L. C. Fischer, a neighbor and acquaintance of Thomas, testified that he used to visit Thomas often and knew that he owned Susan and "kept her in his yard there on the place." He then said, "Susan had ten children in all by her old slave owner. The children were known as the Brown children and I don't think Thomas Brown made it any secret about his being the father of Susan's children." Fischer even added that Thomas "kept Susan there on the place till she married William Bryant." While Fischer's testimony confirmed that Thomas was Susan's slave owner, it also provided details on the longevity and complex nature of Thomas and Susan's long-term sexual liaison. For one thing, Thomas openly acknowledged fathering children by Susan; for another, she and her children remained on Thomas's land for almost ten years after the Civil War ended.[56]

In their depositions before Steed, Susan's sons, Jack and Lee, both testified that they were born after 1865, which means that Susan continued to have sex with and bear children by Thomas although she was no longer enslaved. Like Susan Flowers, her intimate connection with Thomas lasted beyond their legal connection as enslaver and enslaved. Unlike Susan Flowers, Susan Bryant did not represent her relationship with Thomas as a marriage. In fact, when questioned about marital and parental status, she did not speak of him or the children who carried his name. It did not benefit her to do so. For one, Thomas Brown had a lawful wife, Ann, whom he was married to during the entire time he was fathering children by Susan. And despite having ten children with Thomas, William Bryant was the only lawful husband she ever had. When asked to testify about the paternity of Susan's children, Thomas and Ann Brown's children were also invested in diverting attention away from Thomas and Susan's sexual ties. Thomas Brown, named for his father, said, "Yes, Susan had children before she married Bryant. . . . They were all known as the Brown children." He went on to say that while Susan's children were fathered by a white man, he had no idea who that man was. He professed, "I rather not discuss that feature of the case. I am sure though that all her children were begotten by some white man."[57]

In Susan Bryant's case, it was not her long-term sexual liaison with Thomas Brown but her marriage to the formerly enslaved William Bryant that was going to sustain her financially in her old age. When asked, she and her sons shaped the narrative of her relationship to Thomas to fit their economic needs. When Susan's silence about her sexual liaison with Thomas threatened her pension, her sons confirmed that she had been Thomas's sexual servant but never his wife. They were able to convince the Bureau of Pensions that William and Susan had been truthful in their claims and had never been married before they married each other. On December 6, 1918, the Bureau of Pensions granted Susan's request for back pay and future widow's pension payments, stating that she was "entitled a pension at the rate of twenty dollars per month, to commence February 21, 1917, and twenty-five dollars per month from October 6, 1917, and to continue during her widowhood." Susan died two months before their ruling due to complications from her massive stroke. However, her efforts to obtain this money did not go unrewarded. Susan's son Lee, who had taken care of her during her illness, filed a petition to be reimbursed for all the payments his mother would have received until her death in October 1918. His request was granted, and Susan's pension claim was officially closed on January 7, 1919.[58]

HOW AND WHEN ENSLAVED WOMEN demonstrated their agency as sexual servants is critical to our understanding of slavery and sexual exploitation, agency, and consent. Yet even with an examination of enslaved women's voices, it is hard to look back into the past and fully understand the complexities of sexual servitude, specifically the roles that enslaved women were able to play in shaping the nature of these relationships. Based on Susan Flowers's testimony before the SCC, in which she stated that she and Ignatius Flowers had lived as husband and wife, it appears that the former bondwoman and slave owner engaged in a relationship based on mutual affection. It is possible that Susan did not view her relationship with Ignatius as coercive. Or maybe she found it to be coercive in the beginning, but after years of living with him and serving as his housekeeper and pseudo-wife, as well as the mother of his children, she found the relationship to be beneficial, providing a sense of security for herself and their children. However, we are unable to decipher most of the details of their life together based on her petition alone.

When Susan assumed the role of executor of Ignatius's original petition and went before the SCC for her own benefit, she stood to gain a considerable amount of money. Considering the limitations placed on formerly enslaved people's labor and mobility after the Civil War, she was willing to go to the furthest extent, even claiming to be in a legal marriage with her former slave owner, to secure access to the money he left behind. Although Susan's testimony does not provide concrete evidence of the dynamics of their life as slave owner and sexual servant, it does illuminate how she was able to define for herself the meaning and terms of their relationship in its aftermath and use their connection to seek a substantial financial reward.

There is no ideal source that could answer every question about agency or provide a comprehensive understanding of how each enslaved woman experienced long-term sexual relationships with slave-owning men. Susan's testimony does, however, illustrate her agency—not when she was first made to live in Ignatius's house on the eve of the Civil War or the first time Ignatius required her to have sexual relations with him but as a free woman who was presented with an opportunity to capitalize on her connection to her former slave owner to claim monies that he was unable to collect. Sources like Susan's require that we not only reconsider what agency for enslaved women looked like but consider when and where that agency took place. Most sexual servants were not afforded much latitude to negotiate if, and for how long, they would be a sexual servant. And most were not given free rein over their owner's households. Perhaps many sexual servants were like Susan in that their ability to shape and define the nature of their sexual servitude for their own benefit came once they were no longer bound to their slave owners. Maybe their negotiations did not take place while they were within the plantation household but outside it. Slave narratives and interviews support the fact that slave owners overwhelmingly dictated the terms of sexual servitude, deciding who would be their sexual servants and for how long. For Susan, her most significant negotiations over what her sexual servitude meant occurred after her owner was dead. While we will never know the true dynamics of Susan and Ignatius's relationship, we can conclude that during the moments she was before SCC commissioners, she felt empowered to claim herself as his legal wife. To her thinking, as the mother of his five children, she was the only true claimant to the assets he had accumulated over the course of his life—a conclusion she reached on her own.

CHAPTER THREE

The Men Had No Comfort with Their Wives

While Josiah Henson's father was going about his daily work, he was disturbed by a woman's screams. He ran toward the commotion and soon found his wife in a physical struggle with their overseer. The overseer's plan to sexually assault Henson's mother had been put into motion much earlier that day when he intentionally sent her to a remote location away from the other field laborers. He then approached her and tried to coerce her into having sex with him. When this failed, he "resorted to force to accomplish a brutal purpose." It was at this moment that Henson's father ran onto the scene, and "furious at the sight, he sprung upon him like a tiger." Filled with rage, he was determined to kill the man, and he would have had his wife not encouraged him to restrain himself. She knew the consequences her husband could face for killing a white man. His valor would have been praised among Southern society had he been a white man. Yet because he was enslaved, neither he nor his wife possessed rights or privileges that Southern whites had to respect.[1]

When Henson's father attacked the overseer, he was responding to his desire to protect his wife and avenge harms committed against her. Although his wife had suffered the greatest atrocity, he also felt "beside himself with mingled rage and suffering." He was her husband and she was his wife. Yet the threads that held enslaved marriages together were delicate. Their condition of enslavement limited the extent to which enslaved men and women could hold claims to one another. Unlike Southern patriarchs, enslaved men were not entitled to patriarchal authority to guard over women and children. This was made most evident by the forcible separation of enslaved families and enslavers' sexual and reproductive exploitation of the enslaved, both male and female.[2] Nonetheless, some enslaved men correlated manhood with the responsibility to provide for and protect their families. They exhibited manliness through strength and power and sought authority within their families and communities at large. Henson's father fought back with the understanding that as a man, he had an obligation to protect his wife from harm. In his eyes, he was justified in beating the overseer.[3]

Word immediately spread through their community in Charles County, Maryland, that an enslaved man "has struck a white man." Henson explained that when an enslaved person showed aggression toward a white person, it "was enough to set a whole county on fire." According to Henson, no one cared to ask what had provoked his father to attack the overseer. Without question, "the authorities were soon in pursuit of my father." The architects of American slavery considered enslaved people's use of violence against their enslavers or any form of rebellion as a threat to the South's slave economy on which their status and wealth rested. To safeguard slave owners and their agents from physical violence, they inscribed enslaved people's subjugation into law and social custom.[4] As early as the colonial period, statutes stipulated severe penalties for the enslaved who inflicted violence against white people or conspired to revolt. The 1690 slave act of South Carolina mandated that a slave be "severely whipped, his or her nose slit, and face burnt in some place," even put to death for repeated offenses. The message slave owners wished to communicate was that preserving the system of slavery and its economic and social benefits was far more important than preserving the lives of enslaved individuals who wished to challenge the system.[5]

As Henson's mother suspected, the county authorities were not moved by the cause of her husband's violent actions and sentenced him to one hundred lashes on his bare back, and his ear was to be nailed to a whipping post and subsequently severed from his body. This harsh penalty served not only to reprimand Henson's father but to discourage other enslaved men from challenging white men's authority. At least one of these missions was accomplished. According to Henson, his father was never the same. Previously, he had been good humored and lighthearted. "But from this hour he became utterly changed. Sullen, morose, and dogged, nothing could be done with him."[6]

Henson's story reveals that enslaved women did not carry the burden of sexual exploitation alone. A part of living in the South's rape culture meant that enslaved men knew how vulnerable their wives, daughters, sisters, and mothers were to sexualized violence and exploitation and that their sense of obligation to shield them from these offenses was not recognized by those who enslaved them. In the sources they left behind, enslaved men frequently described white men's sexual abuse of enslaved women and the physical and emotional trauma that resulted. Their stories, however, did not end there. These men articulated their own feelings of anger and regret over being unable to protect enslaved women, a responsibility they assumed as men.[7]

White men put forth much effort to deny Black men the right to fully exercise their markers of masculinity in order to fortify their self-proclaimed rights as white men to be masters over the white and Black dependents in their households and society at large. This included enslavers committing or threatening acts of violence against enslaved men who attempted to stop or avenge sexual assaults on enslaved women. Despite their status within the South's patriarchal paradigm, many enslaved men held tight to their claims of masculinity, especially the responsibility to protect their families and communities from the violence of enslavement.[8]

The South's rape culture ensured that enslaved men and boys would repeatedly witness or even have to participate in the rape and sexual exploitation of enslaved women. This chapter illustrates that despite the consequences, some enslaved men responded to rape and sexual exploitation by acting in defiance of the legal and cultural parameters set forth by their enslavers. These men used violence, at times lethal, to prevent and avenge sexual abuses against enslaved women. These efforts, however, rarely went unpunished. The slave-owning class and their governing bodies inflicted acts of ritualized violence and issued death sentences to reinforce their mastery. By striking fear and feelings of powerlessness in the hearts of all enslaved people who witnessed these acts, they hoped to ensure enslaved people's subjugation and obedience. Enslaved men's confessions of powerlessness and regret in regard to the rape and sexual exploitation of enslaved women prove just how effective these threats of corporal punishment were. Although enslaved men were unable to dismantle this rape culture, which troubled many even after slavery's end, some never abandoned the notion that as men they had the right and responsibility to protect, provide for, and exercise authority over their families.[9]

WHEN ENGLISH-BORN FRANCES KEMBLE made her first visit to her husband Pierce Butler's Georgia slave plantations in 1838, she encountered an enslaved family consisting of a husband, Frank; a wife, Betty; and a son, Renty. She learned that Renty was not Frank's son but the son of the Butlers' overseer, Roswell King Jr., who was notorious for sexually assaulting the enslaved women under his charge. King had been a trusted employee of the Butlers since 1819, working alongside his father, Roswell King Sr. The elder King first began overseeing daily operations in 1802.[10] Kemble did not know how long "Mr. King's occupation of Frank's wife continued," but she became particularly concerned with how Frank "endured the wrong done to him." Without doubt she felt concern for Betty's well-being, but her concern for Frank illustrates her awareness that the sexual exploitation of enslaved women had consequences for enslaved men as well. Kemble believed King's abuse of Betty to be an "outrage upon this man's [Frank] rights." Kemble believed that although Frank was enslaved, he had a right as a man to protect his wife from abuses, such as sexual assault. According to Kemble, the denial of this authority left Frank a "grave, sad, and thoughtful-looking man."[11]

In the years following American independence, enslaved men like Frank were forced to watch white men like Pierce Butler and Roswell King Jr. indulge in patriarchy's privileges. White men's definitions of masculinity were deeply rooted in the concept of mastery, especially the right to master over the bodies and labor of their white and Black dependents. According to historians Craig Friend and Lorri Glover, freedom, landownership, an independent household, "a submissive wife and children, and ideally, slaves" were all marks of a Southern man—a patriarch.[12] White men discovered that the best way to display their masculinity and bolster their authority was to deem their dependents incapable of managing these responsibilities and inscribe it into law. They believed that only white men possessed the capacity for reason and self-control, qualities needed to manage a household. By claiming that women and Black people lacked these qualities, they could perpetuate the belief that dependency was a natural component of their character.[13]

The South's patriarchal structure also ensured that propertied white men held dominion over local and state government and other public entities. While free men of color were often permitted to acquire land, participate in local economies, and even purchase and own slaves, their skin color placed limits on their mobility, claims of citizenship, and participation in the legislative and judicial process. By law, free Black men were not permitted to hold public office or vote. North Carolina, Maryland, and Tennessee were the exceptions to the rule in regard to voting; however, by the 1830s, these states instituted statutes that prohibited free Black men from voting as well. Cities like Charleston, South Carolina, required free people of color to pay an annual capitalization tax of two dollars and register their names with local courts, which served as a means to monitor the growth and movement of its free Black population. South Carolina also forbade free Black people from leaving the state unless they planned to relocate permanently.[14] While free Black people's status as citizens of the United States was always tenuous due to these restrictions, they were formally denied the claims of citizenship in 1857, when the Supreme Court ruled in the *Dred Scott v. Sandford* case that Black people, free or enslaved, were not citizens of the United States and therefore had no legal standing before the court. For free Black men, being free and male was not enough to entitle them to all that Southern patriarchy afforded.[15] And although white women, especially those from landed and slave-owning families, enjoyed privileges of whiteness and social status, their gender subordinated them to white men. Adolescent and unmarried women were dependents of their fathers, and when they married, they became dependents of their husbands. Laws of coverture limited white women's property rights and forbade them from keeping their own wages, making contracts, and even claiming parental rights over the children they bore.[16]

While white women and free people of color had limited rights, the enslaved had neither the benefit of freedom nor white skin to save them from absolute subordination under the law. Enslaved men and women could not own property, make contracts—including the contract of marriage—or bring charges against white people in court. Legally categorized as property, they were noncitizens who had no civil rights in the eyes of the law, and their fate was largely determined by their owners.[17] According to historian Edward Baptist, the emasculation of enslaved men was an essential element in establishing white men's patriarchal authority and enslaved people's subordination. Baptist argues that "concepts of white manliness that structured households, animated political conflict and consensus, and authorized violence [in America] depended on the disempowerment of blackness." White men justified their superiority to Black men by arguing that because of their Blackness, these men lacked the material substance of masculinity and therefore were not entitled to independence. They were unfit to own property, control households and dependents, and hold political rights, all qualities that "marked men as men."[18]

White men's devaluation of Black masculinity—the effort to discredit Black men's capacity to possess and exhibit qualities of reason, civility, and independence, which white men deemed essential to their own masculinity— did not begin with Roswell King Jr. and Frank but began centuries before, even before the first Africans were brought to the colony of Virginia in 1619.[19] As early as the fifteenth century, western Europeans traveled to the coasts of Africa to establish trade relations. These newly formed networks afforded them the opportunity to observe the familial structures, strategies of warfare, hunting practices, and physical characteristics of the various groups of African people they encountered. These travelers acknowledged African men as strong, aggressive, and capable of establishing kingdoms and engaging in precise warfare, which were all masculine qualities in their view. However, they refused to acknowledge them as civilized, which was an essential quality to possess in order to be placed on par with white masculinity. Instead, they viewed African men's behavior as "savage," "bestial," and "brutish." They considered their semi-naked bodies and physical prowess to be animalistic and hypersexual. They described African men's genitals as "large propagators," claiming that they were so large as to be "burthensome unto them." Similarly, they described African women's breasts and bodies as beastly, and noted their supposed ability to suckle their young over their shoulders and labor like men, which reinforced their beliefs about Africans' animalistic nature.[20] To these traders and travelers, African people's Blackness was the only logical source for what they perceived to be their beastliness and lack of civility.

Over the next two centuries, as it became critical to secure a reliable labor force in British North America and the Caribbean, Europeans pointed to the color of African people's skin and their cultural differences to make claims of their inherent inferiority to white people, thus making them ideally suited for perpetual slavery. In 1662, officials in colonial Virginia passed a statute stating that a child's status as free or enslaved was determined by the status of its mother, which was a departure from traditional English common law that said that a child gained their status from their father. Therefore, the children born to enslaved African women would also be enslaved, even if their fathers were of British descent, a frequent occurrence. This was the first step in inextricably linking enslavement to Blackness in Virginia. The law made slavery an inheritable trait, and now men and women of African descent were bound to this system that would serve as the economic and social foundation upon which American freedom for whites was won.[21]

Enslaved men were very much aware of the limits placed on their ability to fully exhibit their masculinity and exercise authority within enslaved communities, as historian John Blassingame noted, "The master and not the male slave furnished the cabin, clothes, and the minimal food for his wife and children."[22] Although enslaved men most likely built these cabins and were often tasked with planting, hunting, and fishing in order to significantly supplement the food their owners provided, slave owners took credit for supplying the enslaved with these basic necessities. It was essential for slave owners to reinforce the notion that enslaved men were just as much dependents as enslaved women and children. Former bondman James Pennington called this state of being the "chattel relation" and argued that it indeed challenged enslaved men's notions of manhood. Pennington argued that enslavement transferred an enslaved man's "proprietorship of his wife and children to another." Pennington's thoughts reveal that enslaved men desired and felt entitled to proprietorship over their wives and children, but as much as they were invested in gaining this proprietorship, slave owners were invested in denying them of it.[23]

At the same time, enslaved men constantly received contradictory messages from slave owners concerning their roles as husbands and fathers within their communities, which created more uncertainty and pain. When crafting codes of conduct for the enslaved, many owners instructed enslaved men and women to assume the same traditional gendered responsibilities that took place in white households during the antebellum period. From the late 1830s to early 1850s, William Ethelbert Ervin, a cotton planter from Lowndes County, Mississippi, kept very meticulous journal records concerning the buying and selling of enslaved people, crop cultivation, and other farming activities. He was especially diligent in recording his rules for slave conduct, including the duties of husbands and wives, and guidelines for punishing those who stepped out of line. In the entry titled "Rules to be observed on my place & after the First of January 1847," Ervin revealed his expectations that within the slave quarters, enslaved men would function as heads of household, responsible for providing for the basic needs of their family. His second rule dictated "each family to live in their own house. The husband to provide firewood and see that they are all provided for, wait on his wife." In turn, the wife was to "cook & wash for the husband and her children and attend to the mending of clothes." But to what extent could an enslaved man really serve as the head of his household under slavery? Although slave dwellings were typically built by the enslaved themselves, they were made from materials purchased and provided by their owners and built on land owned by their owners. Although an enslaved man might establish a family with a wife and children, he did so only with his owner's permission.[24]

Although Ervin instructed enslaved men to secure firewood and make sure their families were provided for, the reality is that these men could not shield their wives and children from any task he might assign, any punishment he might inflict, or any assault he might commit. Despite Ervin's charge that enslaved men serve as the heads of their families, his position as the ultimate authority over the enslaved was made evident in his next rule: "Failure on either part [of the husband or wife] when proven shall and must be corrected by words first but if not reformed to be corrected by the whip." In other words, Ervin's bondmen could act patriarchal only at his invitation and under his supervision. For Ervin's household to be deemed respectable and economically sound, he needed the power to dictate their every action. His fourth rule was that a horn would be blown every night at 9:00 P.M., "which is to be a signal for each to retire to his or her house and there to remain until the morning." For those who failed to obey, "they shall be delt with as having broken the third rule and shall be delt with accordingly." If any of Ervin's enslaved men doubted that he held the ultimate authority on his plantation, his use of the power of the lash resolved any confusion.[25]

Like Ervin, Virginia planter Richard Eppes conveyed mixed messages to the enslaved with his rules of conduct. His rules on sexual conduct serve as an excellent example. For one, he defined adultery among the enslaved in gendered terms, only establishing guidelines for how to proceed when an enslaved woman committed adultery against her husband. Only acknowledging a woman's extramarital relations as a punishable offense suggests that he applied traditional beliefs of women's dependence and subordination to men to his enslaved population. The penalties he outlined reflect similar sentiments. For a first offense, "the man shall receive from the husband of the woman on his bare back twenty stripes," he said, permitting the husband to impose consequences on the intruding man for disrupting his household, a right that white male heads of household would have possessed by default. By permitting these enslaved men to exercise patriarchal rights under well-defined circumstances, he was conveying that these limited rights could only be given and supervised by him. For the woman's part, Eppes instructed that she "shall receive fifteen stripes from her seducer." Although both the male "seducer" and the enslaved woman were guilty of adultery, Eppes placed the male "seducer" in a position of privilege and authority over his female accomplice.

These penalties reveal that in some instances, Eppes fostered a culture of male dominance among his enslaved population. But these moments of empowerment were not intended to suggest that his enslaved men could impede on his patriarchal authority. In fact, Eppes was a meticulous owner who gave periodic lectures on proper moral conduct to the people he owned, and he monitored their behavior closely. His plantation journals provide detailed descriptions of slave misconduct and the actions he took to correct their behavior. The ritual he designed for punishing adultery was intended to humiliate the guilty parties and repudiate their immoral behavior, not to empower enslaved men. The enslaved men and women likely understood these brief moments of male empowerment for what they were—a part of Eppes's compulsion to maintain strict control over all of the enslaved.[26]

Through the systematic use of violence against the enslaved, slave owners were able to terrorize enslaved men into submission and neutralize their defenses against sexual assaults on enslaved females. According to former bondman Austin Stewart, this process of brutalization and emasculation began at birth and continued throughout an enslaved man's life, despite his becoming a husband or father. The enslaved man has "from his infancy been taught to cower beneath the white man's frown, and bow at his bidding, or suffer all the rigor of the slave laws."[27] According to Harriet Jacobs, white men were able to "lash" the fight out of enslaved men. "Some poor creatures have been so brutalized by the lash," said Jacobs, "that they will sneak out of the way to give their masters free access to their wives and daughters."[28]

This violence against enslaved men was crucial to clearing the pathway for white men to rape and sexually exploit enslaved women and allowing the South's rape culture to flourish. William Ward's owner threatened him with murder if he tried to block him from having sex with Ward's wife. "One day he tol' me dat if my wife had been good lookin', I never would sleep wid her again 'cause he'd kill me an' take her an' raise chilluns off'n her," said Ward. His owner found pleasure in telling him that there was nothing he could do to stop him. Owners like Ward's knew it was important to establish this precedent not only among enslaved women but among enslaved men as well. Although Ward's owner never made good on his threat, he succeeded in communicating the consequences his enslaved men would face if they challenged him. If he wanted to have sex with an enslaved woman, he would, even if it meant killing enslaved men in the process.[29]

Former bondman Lewis Clarke recalled how slave patrollers who were granted authority by slave owners to police the behavior and whereabouts of enslaved people would enter slave cabins at night during their patrols with the intentions of sexually assaulting women. Even if husbands and fathers were present, they "act just as they please with his wives and daughters." They knew they could participate in this rape culture and enter these cabins with ease because the enslaved husbands had been conditioned through the use of violence to show no objection. According to Clarke, if a husband did try to fight off a patroller, his hands were tied behind his back and he was given "thirty-nine lashes." He suggested that these patrollers' actions were motivated not only by the possibilities of having sexual relations with the women but by the prospects of provoking the men. Therefore, their sexual exploitation of the enslaved women was just as much about torturing the men as the women. According to Clarke, when they attacked a woman, they looked to see if the man would get "cross" so they would have an excuse to "give him a flogging."[30]

Slave owners and overseers often used their authority to dictate enslaved men's whereabouts to place physical distance between them and their female family members when needed. All an owner or overseer needed to do was occupy an enslaved man's time and attention with an arduous task like plowing a field or constructing a barn to separate him from his wife for an extended amount of time. This would give a would-be perpetrator all the time he needed to secure a moment of privacy with the chosen woman. While the enslaved man possessed the faculties to disobey the command in order to be near his wife or daughter if he suspected she was in danger, he knew this course of action would come with consequences. Ishrael Massie said that while he was enslaved in Virginia, masters and overseers were notorious for coming into the slave quarters and directing enslaved husbands to get out of bed and go to work "milkin' cows or cuttin' wood." Then they would get in bed with the women and force themselves on them, causing some women to "fight and tussle," while others offered no resistance for fear of being beaten. "My blood is boiling now at the thought of them times," said Massie, when he was interviewed seventy-two years after slavery had ended. When he and other husbands learned of these attacks, they felt unable to do anything to stop them. According to Massie, it made no difference if a wife told her husband or not because "he was powerless."[31]

Enslaved men also could be forced to participate or aid in the sexual assault of enslaved women. In New Kent County, Virginia, a planter named John Francis developed a reputation among his enslaved people and his neighbors for being licentious with enslaved women. He paid particular attention to a young woman named Peggy and stated his intentions "to cohabit with Peggy, to which she objected." Francis was known to chain Peggy to a block and threaten her with violence because she resisted his sexual advances. On one occasion, he warned her that he would have two enslaved men, Patrick and Jesse, hold her down while he raped her if she continued to resist him. If forced to hold Peggy down, Patrick and Jesse would have found themselves in a devastating position. If they refused Francis's order, they would have been punished. If they obeyed, they would have suffered a different kind of consequence: knowing that they had aided their owner in causing Peggy great physical and psychological trauma. The fact that Patrick later conspired with Peggy to kill Francis reveals that he was inclined to protect Peggy from such vile and vicious attacks. In another instance, Henry Bibb's owner, Francis Whitfield—a cotton planter who claimed to be a pious man—instructed an enslaved male to flog a young female for resisting an unwanted sexual relationship.[32] According to Bibb, Whitfield told the young woman that "he had bought her for a wife for his boy." She rejected the partnership, however, claiming to have felt no affection for the young man. It was in his fit of rage that Whitfield, displeased with her resistance, ordered the enslaved man to flog her until she agreed to comply. The same enslaved man was later ordered to strip his own wife naked and whip her on her bare back for not following Whitfield's orders. Surely it must have been extremely difficult for the man to be forced to inflict these women with pain.[33]

According to Thomas Goodwater, his parents' owner, Lias Winning, was a mean man who "liked his women slave[s]." Therefore, it was no surprise to Goodwater's mother when Winning tried to attack her while she was working alone in the field. When Winning attempted to grab her, she "pulled his ears almost off" and ran. Winning then went in search of the woman's husband, and when he found him, he instructed him to talk to his wife and reprimand her for her disobedience and for injuring his ears. Although Winning made it this enslaved man's responsibility to chastise his wife and exercise authority over her, his authority in that moment was nothing more than an extension of Winning's dominance. Although Goodwater said that his father laughed when he heard what his wife had done to Winning's ears, it is easy to imagine that most men would have become angered or, at the very least, perplexed if asked to rebuke their wife for refusing to have sex with another man. It must have felt otherworldly to be ordered to make your wife submit to someone else's unwanted touch. Demands like this further complicated enslaved men's perceptions of themselves as protectors and providers for their families and communities.[34]

Because slave owners relied greatly on the natural increase of their enslaved labor force, some enslaved men found themselves forced to have sex with enslaved women to produce new generations of enslaved laborers.[35] Forced coupling was merely one of the ways that enslaved men and women were sexually exploited. In an interview, formerly enslaved Sam and Louisa Everett recalled that on their Florida plantation, if their owner, Big Jim, thought a certain man and woman might produce healthy offspring, he would force them to have sexual intercourse, even if they were married or coupled with other people. They noted that if either party showed the slightest reluctance, Big Jim would force them to have sexual intercourse in his presence. These men and women were essentially used to sexually violate each other and forced to disrupt the marital bonds that they had established with their respective spouses, which many men and women deeply valued despite the fragile nature of these unions. Although unmarried at the time, Sam and Louisa were "brought together" under these coercive circumstances. According to Louisa, Big Jim called her and Sam to him, and he "ordered Sam to pull off his shirt." With this being his only article of clothing, Sam stood naked before Jim and Louisa. It stands to reason that Sam was just as embarrassed and ashamed as Louisa, who said that she covered her face to shield herself from Sam's nakedness. Next, Big Jim asked, "Do you think you can stand this big nigger?" meaning could she physically sustain sexual intercourse with him. Although Jim offered his words in the form of a question, Louisa, observing his "old bull whip flung across his shoulder," knew it was not a question at all but a command. She knew she had no choice but to "stand" Sam and take him as her husband and have as many children as possible. "So, I just said, yes sir," said Louisa. "He told us what we must get busy and do in his presence," she said. Like Jim's other enslaved people, Sam and Louisa were forced to have sex in front of him, undoubtedly for his own personal pleasure. According to Louisa, he enjoyed watching enslaved people have sex and "often entertained his friends in this manner."[36]

Enslaved men occupied a unique position within the South's rape culture. While being sexually exploited for their own reproductive capabilities and presumed sexual virility—the subject of both white men's and white women's erotic fantasies—and even made to participate in assaults against enslaved women, some enslaved men also used this sexually exploitative landscape and "validated their manhood through expressions of sexual dominance." In seeking to perform their masculine identity, they assumed power and privilege over the courtship process and within intimate relationships. Their sexual dominance could take the form of coercion, threats of violence, and even force. In his testimony, John Cole conveyed that if an enslaved woman showed no interest in having a relationship, "a good, hard-working hand could always get the master to make the girl marry him—whether or no, willy-nilly." Historian David Doddington notes that while enslaved men were undoubtedly "constrained within a racist and oppressive system," sexual dominance over enslaved women was an accessible tool for constructing an identity based on power and virility. Nevertheless, slave owners' desire to reinforce the "chattel relation" and maintain unfettered access to enslaved women was strong. Denying or limiting enslaved men's claims to the responsibilities and privileges of manhood, including the right to combat the sexual exploitation of enslaved woman, was one way of securing their power.[37]

ENSLAVED MEN'S LONGING to be heads of household, responsible for providing economic security and physical protection for their wives and children, is made evident in the sources they left behind. Scholar bell hooks described the image of Black masculinity that emerged from slave narratives and interviews as "one of hard working men who longed to assume full patriarchal responsibility for families and kin." Many sought a masculinity defined by their ability to provide protection and leadership rather than mastery, which is what spurred white men's definitions of masculinity and patriarchal authority.[38] In his narrative, Henry Bibb expressed his belief that all men are "free, moral, intelligent, and accountable human beings." Bibb argued that a man had a right to wages for his labor, the right to pursue liberty and happiness, and "a right to his own wife and children." Although Bibb was firm in his belief that he was endowed with these rights by "the All-wise Creator," he was aware of the restraints placed on him by man-made laws that bound him in slavery: "I was a slave, a prisoner for life; I could possess nothing, nor acquire anything but what must belong to my keeper."[39]

Although Bibb might have been inspired by the patriarchal rhetoric of the American Revolution, men of African descent shared a longer tradition that embraced masculinity and patriarchal authority. Historian Daniel Black argues that "the ideas of male dominance, power, and control were well-established aspects of the West African concept of manhood centuries before the European ever arrived in Africa."[40] For example, the Mende, who lived in what is today Sierra Leone, organized themselves into patrilineal societies. A family's identity was defined by its male line, and it was through the male line that status and property were passed down. Mende men were expected to be rulers of their wives, children, and slaves. Also, these men were permitted to have more than one wife, and the number of wives, children, slaves, and cattle a man had was a symbol of his wealth and status.[41] A multitude of cultural understandings and practices survived the Middle Passage from the west coast of Africa to British North America. Although these newly settled Africans merged their various cultural understandings with influences from European cultural practices, many managed to hold on to some semblance of their African identity.[42] It is no wonder that many enslaved men considered their owners' claims of benevolence and paternalism—providing shelter, food, and clothes to their families—a direct challenge to their masculinity. The South's rape culture, which fostered white men's cavalier sense of entitlement to Black women's sexuality, added insult to injury.[43]

Enslaved men often had to grapple with their deep-seated want for authority within their communities alongside their feelings of powerlessness and pain. Women's sufferings due to rape and sexual exploitation elicited some of the most heart-wrenching declarations of powerlessness from these men. To avoid the pain of being unable to protect his wife, Malinda, from sexual abuse, Henry Bibb concluded that it was best for him to live apart from her.

If he was powerless to prevent these assaults, he felt it was best not to witness them either. He lived on the same plantation as his wife for the first time when he was sold to William Gatewood, Malinda's owner. Previously, he had been owned by a man who lived seven miles away from Gatewood's plantation, and because he was only permitted to visit with Malinda on Saturdays and Sundays, he was shielded from any abuse she might suffer during the rest of the week. Living on Gatewood's plantation meant he would be exposed to every whip of the lash or unwanted sexual advance from Gatewood or his overseer. This proved to be too much for Bibb to handle. "To live where I must be eye witness to her insults, scourgings and abuses, such as are common to be inflicted upon slaves, was more than I could bear," he said. "If my wife must be exposed to the insults and licentious passions of wicked slave-drivers and overseers; if she must bear the stripes of the lash laid on by an unmerciful tyrant . . . heaven forbid that I should be compelled to witness the sight."[44]

After several attempts to escape, Henry and Malinda and their young daughter, Frances, were sold by William Gatewood to a slave trader named Madison Garrison. It was while under the ownership of Garrison that Bibb came face-to-face with his biggest fear. Garrison was known for raping the women he bought and sold in the interstate slave trade. He had already attempted to rape Malinda once, but she was able to fight off his attack despite his efforts to subdue her with lashes from his whip and a threat to separate her from her child forever. According to Bibb, Garrison never succeeded in having sexual intercourse with Malinda, but he settled for whipping her, which he considered the next best thing. "I have often heard Garrison say that he had rather paddle a female, than eat when he was hungry—that it was music for him to hear them scream," said Bibb. He recalled a day when Garrison got angry with Malinda and dragged her off to a separate room with a paddle in hand. Left behind to imagine the horrible things that Garrison intended to do to Malinda, Bibb suffered with this thought: "I could afford her no protection at all, while the strong arm of the law, public opinion and custom, were all against me." His fear became a reality; he felt powerless to protect his wife from her lecherous owner, and all he could do was be a witness.[45]

William Craft said that the thought of enslaved women being forced to endure rape and sexual coercion, what he called "the greatest indignity," was enough to shake a man to his core. His own wife being the product of a sexual relationship between a slave owner and an enslaved woman, he knew firsthand not only how vulnerable these women were but how pained enslaved men felt as a result. "If there is any one thing under the wide canopy of heaven, horrible enough to stir a man's soul, and to make his very blood boil, it is the thought of his dear wife, his unprotected sister, or his young and virtuous daughters, struggling to save themselves from falling a prey to such demons!"[46] Another enslaved man described this sense of powerlessness as a wild throbbing in an enslaved man's chest. He explained that an enslaved husband was forced to watch his wife "exposed to the rude gaze of a beastly tyrant," yet his throbbing heart had to be suppressed and "his righteous indignation find no voice."[47] Although these men articulated the pain and powerlessness they felt in these situations, they never lost sight of the fact that enslaved women carried the heavier burden. Josiah Henson said that the condition of the enslaved female, "compelled to perform unfit labor, sick, suffering, and bearing the burdens of her own sex unpitied and unaided, as well as the toils which belong to the other, has often oppressed me with a load of sympathy."[48]

Sources show that many men were deeply concerned about enslaved women's vulnerability to sexual exploitation and carried deep regrets about their limited ability to prevent these incidents. However, in a few instances, enslaved men chose instead to emphasize what they perceived to be enslaved women's complicity in sexual relations with white men. They argued that some women were calculated in their efforts to establish sexual connections with wealthy white men who could improve their condition or that of their children, even providing emancipation from slavery altogether. When Robert Smalls was interviewed by a member of the American Freedmen's Inquiry Commission, an agency tasked with integrating the formerly enslaved into the Union at the conclusion of the Civil War, he was asked very specific questions about enslaved women's sexuality. In response, he said that bondwomen would rather have sex with white men than their male counterparts, and he knew them to start "as young as twelve years." When asked if these young women do this for money, he said, "The majority of the young girls will for money." According to Smalls, enslaved women were preoccupied with material gains, creating this interest in having sex with white men instead of Black men. Smalls, himself, was born to an enslaved woman and fathered by a white man. Yet despite his claims, his mother's own sexual relationship with this white man did not provide her or her child with any substantial benefit. It was only by his own efforts that Smalls acquired his freedom in 1862 while working aboard the *Planter*, a Confederate transport steamer. He had worked his way up from deckhand to captain, and in May of that year, with his wife and children in tow, he commandeered the steamer, leaving its white crew onshore, and sailed toward the nearest Union blockading ship.[49]

Lewis Clarke offered similar claims that enslaved women benefited from having sexual relations with white men. He said a master might provide them with fancy clothes, give them small presents, or extend more privileges, all "while the whim lasts." However, he did not totally lose sight of the fact that enslaved women had little choice in whether to have sex with white men. If ordered by their owner to have sexual relations, "they know they must submit to their masters," said Clarke. However, he suggested that they saw these small trinkets as consolation, feeling that it was better to receive something for their suffering than nothing at all. Regardless of what Clarke believed, small presents and fancier clothes could hardly diminish the trauma of rape and sexual harassment.[50]

The trauma enslaved men suffered due to the South's rape culture made a notable impact, leading some to regret their decisions to become husbands and fathers. In his narrative, Henry Box Brown declared, "And here let me state, what is well known by many people, that no such thing as real marriage is allowed to exist among the slaves. Talk of marriage under such a system!" His conclusion that enslaved people could never maintain a virtuous and untainted marriage was inspired by a conversation he and his brother had with a group of enslaved men who all lived on the same plantation. They conveyed their owner's refusal to let them marry women from neighboring plantations, choosing instead to make his enslaved people marry each other, "whether related or not." For this reason, along with Brown's belief that "the greater part of slaveholders are licentious men," he saw no need for an enslaved man to pursue marriage. According to Brown, "The slave's wife is his, only at the will of her master, who may violate her chastity with impunity." Therefore, "the slave is placed under strong inducements not to form a union of love, for he knows not how soon the chords wound around his heart would be snapped asunder, by the hand of the brutal slave-dealer."[51]

Despite his reservations, Brown eventually considered getting married and formed a strong attachment to a woman named Nancy who belonged to a man named Lee. He said he felt his chances for having a secure marriage were increased because Lee was a member of the Presbyterian Church and was known as a very pious man. Although Lee promised he would never sell Nancy, he confirmed Brown's beliefs that an enslaved man's wife was only his as long as the union satisfied the needs of the owner. Lee's "conscientious scruples" quickly vanished, and he sold Nancy without mention or explanation.

Lewis Clarke met a fellow bondman named Nathan who shared a similar experience and vowed to never marry another enslaved woman. While Brown's wife was sold, Nathan's wife was actually killed due to "hard usage." Although devastated by her death, Nathan did not give up entirely on marriage, just the idea of marrying another enslaved person. According to Clarke, Nathan vowed never to take a slave for a wife, and he selected a free woman as a companion instead. Although his owner was vehemently opposed to the match, Nathan stayed true to his vow and was eventually sold "down south" as a consequence. Although he was ultimately separated from his new wife, his wife's free status spared him from the burden of worrying about any ill treatment she might receive from a violent or lewd owner.[52]

Henry Bibb expressed similar regrets about fatherhood. "If ever there was any one act of my life while a slave, that I have to lament over, it is that of being a father and a husband of slaves," said Bibb. The love he had for his daughter, Frances, could not be questioned. He described her as a pretty, playful, bright, and interesting child with "the very image of her mother . . . stamped upon her cheek." But "I could never look upon the dear child without being filled with sorrow and fearful apprehensions," said Bibb. Like his wife, his daughter was enslaved, and in Bibb's words, her female virtue could be trampled underfoot with impunity. His wife had been previously sexually assaulted and beaten severely for her resistance, and this made his concerns for his daughter that much more intense. In fact, Bibb became determined to never bring another child into slavery. "She was the first and shall be the last slave that ever I will father, for chains and slavery on this earth," said Bibb. "I have the satisfaction of knowing that I am only the father of one slave."[53]

DESPITE THE CONSEQUENCES, the enslaved acted in ways that challenged the parameters set forth by slave owners.[54] When placed in the precarious position of witnessing or even having to participate in the sexual exploitation of enslaved women, enslaved men sometimes responded in ways that slave owners did not anticipate or tolerate. Motivated by their desires to lead and protect their families, these enslaved men fought back to prevent and avenge sexual offenses against enslaved women. William Hayden, a bondman from Virginia, declared that despite white men's expectations, he was a man, and although the rights that came along with manhood were not freely granted to him, he intended to exercise them anyway. Hayden was often challenged by his owner's business partner, Mr. Stone, and Stone's instigation generated anger within him. He already resented having to obey any man, much less one who did not lawfully own him. He was particularly angered by Stone's abuse of "the poor oppressed slave, especially the female portion," and challenged Stone's authority over him at every turn. However, he did not characterize his behavior as mere disobedience. He determined, he said, to "stand firmly upon the rights of my manhood." According to Hayden, Stone was surprised by his audacity and began foaming at the mouth and sweating and threatened "his deep revenge."[55]

When Alfred, an enslaved resident of Hinds County, Mississippi, confessed to murdering John D. Fondren's overseer, Coleman, he sent waves of fear and confusion through the four white men who heard his confession. According to court records, minutes earlier, Dr. James, a neighbor who was visiting the Fondren plantation, along with two of Fondren's employees, heard a loud commotion. The three men rushed toward the noise, running the two hundred yards from the Fondren house to the stable lot. When they arrived, James asked Alfred, who was standing outside the stable, "what was the matter?" Without hesitation, Alfred replied, "I have killed the overseer." When Fondren arrived on the scene a few minutes later, Alfred repeated his confession. His wife, Charlotte, was also owned by John Fondren and therefore placed under Coleman's control. Earlier that morning, Coleman had ordered Charlotte to a remote area of the plantation, where he raped her. When Alfred heard what Coleman had done, he determined to confront and eliminate him as a future threat to his wife.[56]

Alfred was formally charged with murder and tried before one of Hinds County's two district courts. Charlotte wished to testify before the jury to explain why Alfred had taken such extreme measures to protect her, but her testimony was rejected on two grounds. First, the prosecution argued that Charlotte's testimony would have no profound impact on Alfred's fate. Even if she presented circumstances that could reduce Alfred's charges from murder to manslaughter, the outcome would be the same: death. Second, the prosecution argued that because Charlotte and Alfred were not legally married, she could not provide testimony in his defense.[57] They knew she'd say that Alfred was provoked to murder Coleman because he had raped her. If Charlotte's testimony was deemed admissible, it had the potential to tug at the heart strings of at least one member of the all-male, all-white jury, who, as a husband or father, might feel sympathy for Alfred's predicament and be willing to disregard his enslaved status when casting his vote regarding guilt or innocence. With their position, the prosecution contended that an enslaved man was not entitled to the unbridled passions that could drive a husband to commit murder in defense of his wife. If a white couple in Hinds

County had provided similar evidence of a rape, a judge or jury would have likely considered the man's actions justified and applied the lesser offense of manslaughter. Alfred was eventually found guilty and sentenced to hang for his crime.[58]

In 1836, Thomas Ruffin, chief justice of the North Carolina Supreme Court, issued a ruling in *State v. Samuel* that marriage among the enslaved was inconsistent with the institution of slavery.[59] Marriage was a contract entered into by individuals with consent. Ruffin argued that because the law did not recognize the enslaved as such, enslaved men and women could not enjoy either the burdens or the benefits of marriage. Samuel, the appellant in the case, claimed that his conviction for murder should be overturned because the prosecution's evidence hinged on his wife's testimony. Because they were married, she should not have been compelled to testify against him due to spousal privilege. Ruffin argued, "It has never been decided by our predecessors, that the marriage of slaves, such as existed in this case, and such as usually exist in this State, consisting of cohabitation merely, by the permission of the owners, constitutes the relation of husband and wife, so as to attach to them the privileges and disabilities incident to that relation by the common law." At best, he said, the relationships among the enslaved could be considered concubinage, "which is voluntary on the part of the slaves, and permissive on that of the master." It is the only union "with which alone, perhaps, their condition is compatible."[60]

Although such a restrictive precedent regarding the legality of enslaved marriage had been set in North Carolina, Alfred's attorney, B. F. Trimble, appealed to Mississippi's High Court of Errors and Appeals to have Alfred's conviction of murder overturned by asserting his right as a man and a husband, in particular, to become impassioned and provoked to violence at the knowledge that his wife had been sexually assaulted.[61] Trimble was careful, however, not to lose sight of his audience, a panel of white male jurists who were beneficiaries of the white supremacy and patriarchal authority that slavery ensured. One justice, William L. Harris, owned fourteen enslaved people and became a staunch supporter of state sovereignty and Southern secession.[62] These jurists' power rested in the subordination of the enslaved, and it was evident to Trimble that Alfred's murder of a white man chipped away at white men's feelings of security. To reassure them, Trimble acknowledged that "it is inconsistent with the master's right of removing his slave any distance from his wife, or her husband, that he or she, should claim the privileges of the marital relation." It is also inconsistent with slavery "that the slave should be compelled to maintain his wife and children." Trimble realized that legally recognized marriage among the enslaved would change the way slave owners operated day to day. It would hinder their ability to separate and sell enslaved spouses to pay off debts, or break up marriages in order to create new ones in hopes of producing strong and healthy offspring—actions that were quite routine.[63] By legally permitting bondmen like Alfred to "maintain his wife and children," they would be extending to them some of the rights of patriarchy that white men enjoyed, such as dominion over their wives and children. Trimble understood that these changes went against slave owners' social and economic interests.[64]

Still, Trimble's challenge was to get the jurists to see Alfred as he saw himself—a man, a human being, a husband. Alfred's defense rested on the notion that as a husband, he had the right and obligation to avenge this most vicious crime committed against his wife, Charlotte. He could not point to any legal statutes to support his claims, but his attorney, speaking on his behalf, pointed to a higher law—the law of humanity that affirmed that even enslaved men like Alfred had a calling to be protective husbands to their wives. Trimble argued that Alfred was answering this call when he attacked and killed Coleman. "The humanity of our law regards them as human beings," he said, "with lively emotions and social instincts." Therefore, the law should regard "with as much tenderness the excesses of outraged conjugal affections in the negro as in the white man." After all, "the servile condition of the negro has not deprived him of his social or moral instincts." Despite Trimble's pleas for recognition of enslaved men's patriarchal instincts, the high court upheld the lower court's decision that Alfred could not claim the rape of his wife as provocation for murder. Like Thomas Ruffin in North Carolina, Mississippi's chief justice, Cotesworth P. Smith, argued that as a slave, Alfred was not entitled to the benefits or burdens of marriage, which in this case was the right to protect his wife and seek justice for her rape. Despite the court's ruling, Albert had claimed for himself the right to defend his wife and even redress the harm done to her when he killed Coleman and stood over his body. He knew the consequences would be deadly. Yet per witness testimony, he confessed boldly and without hesitation to the murder.[65]

Another enslaved man, Ben, not completely on his own accord but at a slave owner's insistence, killed the man who had been having sexual relations with his wife. Ben was owned by William Ware of Chesterfield County, Virginia, and was married to an enslaved woman owned by John Bass. With Bass's permission, Ben visited his wife weekly on the Bass plantation. After several years of being husband and wife, their relationship was brought to an abrupt end when Bass banned Ben from visiting his wife. Bass no longer approved of the couple's relationship after Joe Gooding, a free man of color who had recently fallen into Bass's good graces, expressed interest in having a relationship with Ben's wife. Bass granted Gooding permission to pursue the enslaved woman; however, his favor was short lived. For unknown reasons, Bass suddenly withdrew his permission for Gooding to see her.[66]

Ben heard of the conflict between Bass and Gooding and, careful to follow protocol, asked Bass once more for permission to commence his relationship with his wife. Seeing an opportunity to eliminate his newfound enemy, Bass approved Ben's request on the condition that he first "put Joe [Gooding] out of the way." Bass worked to incite feelings of jealousy within Ben, telling him that Gooding had "taken his wife from him," although in actuality it was Bass who had taken his wife from him, with no regard for the bonds they had formed. Bass was the one who controlled their fate, as he alone possessed the authority to approve of enslaved marriages, which made Ben's ties to his wife so fragile. This realization would not have been lost on Ben, but in that moment he was being granted permission by his wife's owner to seek vengeance against Gooding, which he may have wanted to do with or without Bass's permission.[67] Ben agreed to murder Gooding and do Bass's dirty work, since it meant restoring his relationship with his wife and ridding the world of the man who had been permitted to come between them in the first place. Things went awry, however, when Ben set his plan to murder Gooding into motion. Ben intended to poison Gooding's food, but Ben's wife ingested the poisoned food instead and died immediately. Stricken with grief over the death of his wife, Ben determined to rectify his mistake. He stole his owner's shotgun and went to Gooding's house, where he shot him dead. For his crime, Ben was tried and found guilty of murder.[68]

Sometimes enslaved women worked alongside enslaved men to commit these violent acts against the men who raped and sexually exploited them. Peggy, who was owned by John Francis, had more than enough motivation to put a permanent end to Francis's incessant sexual harassment. According to witnesses, Francis had plans to "cohabit" with Peggy, and when she resisted, he used a range of strategies—tying her to a block, locking her inside his meat house, and threatening to sell her—to make her submit to his plans. Peggy was determined not to have sex with Francis because in addition to being her owner he was also her father, and she "could not do a thing of that sort with her father." Things reached a critical point when Francis declared that he would have his enslaved men, Patrick and Jesse, hold her down so that he could rape her. He also threatened to "beat her almost to death . . . if she did not yield to his wishes." Threatened with rape and death, Peggy conspired with Patrick to kill Francis. On the night of August 22, 1830, Patrick and Peggy, armed with a stick and an axe, entered Francis's home and attacked him, beating and slicing him all over his body. Once finished with the physical assault, they left the house and set it on fire. The house burned to the ground with John Francis inside.[69]

Soon after, Peggy, Patrick, and two other enslaved women, Franky and Caroline, found themselves before the New Kent County Court in Virginia in September 1830. The court's main objective was to determine whose idea it was, Peggy's or Patrick's, to fatally beat and burn John Francis. In her testimony, Peggy admitted to beating her owner with a stick but adamantly denied murdering him. She claimed to have been provoked by a severe beating Francis had given her and his threat to sell her away from her family some time before. She then pointed the finger at Patrick, testifying that it was he who attacked Francis with the axe and likely brought about his death. Likewise, Patrick told the court that he was the one who carried the stick and that it was Peggy who used the axe to slash her owner's body. Neither took responsibility for the fire but claimed that it had been set before they entered the house. Francis's other enslaved people offered testimony that made assigning fault even more difficult. One testified that Peggy had verbalized her intentions to beat Francis the day before the murder, but it was Patrick who they saw set the house on fire. Another witness said they saw them both enter the house with weapons and both placed quilts filled with straw inside the house and set it on fire. While witnesses conceded that Patrick had the physical ability to kill Frances, they doubted that he had the mental capacity to plan the murder, citing his severe mental disability. The court found Peggy, Patrick, and Franky guilty of murder, having dismissed the charges against Caroline. The reality was that Peggy and Patrick had motive to kill Francis. They were both his victims, and together they decided to take his life to put an end to his sexualized violence.[70]

In his narrative, Charles Ball recalled a similar incident in which an enslaved couple, Frank and Lucy, conspired to kill the woman's owner. Lucy had been laboring as her owner's housekeeper and sexual servant when she developed an interest in Frank, who lived on an adjoining plantation. Threatened by the presence of this young enslaved man, Lucy's owner forbade Frank from visiting his home. He wanted to create distance between the enslaved lovers and protect his own interests in Lucy. His command, however, did not thwart the enslaved couple's determination to be together. Instead, they designed a plot to "destroy the master." With Lucy providing the means and opportunity and Frank providing the gumption to execute the murder, together they killed him. Familiar with her owner's daily routine and the terrain of his house, Lucy knew exactly where he stored his shotgun and when it would be safe to place the weapon in Frank's hands. Next, she created a gap between the logs of the house's exterior through which Frank could nestle the barrel of the shotgun and shoot her unsuspecting owner in the back while he ate his supper. That evening, she served him his meal as she did every day, but what came next was a departure from the usual. At Lucy's signal, Frank aimed the shotgun at his target and unloaded a round of buckshot squarely into her owner's back. After jumping up from his seat, the maimed slave owner fell to the floor and died right next to the dining room table. Lucy could finally enjoy a sense of freedom from her owner's grasp, if only for a night. The next day she traveled to a neighboring plantation and gave word of his death.[71]

In the beginning, Lucy and Frank felt no need to reveal their guilt. But Lucy's resolve proved to be greater than Frank's. When the justice of the peace and coalition of neighboring planters forced Frank to come face-to-face with and touch the body of the deceased, he became overwhelmed with fear and cried out that "Lucy had made him do it." Lucy remained steadfast and declared her innocence, insisting that if Frank did kill her owner, he did so without her "knowledge or advice." The court officials and neighbors remained unconvinced. Living in close proximity to the deceased, they would not have been naive about his sexual relationship with Lucy, nor did they underestimate her capacity to conspire against the man who held her as a sexual servant. And in light of her and Frank's budding romance, he was the logical co-conspirator. In the end, Frank's confession to their collaborative effort to kill her owner was sufficient evidence for a jury to convict and sentence them both to die for committing murder.[72]

The execution of Frank and Lucy drew a large crowd. Charles Ball, living on a nearby plantation, was forced to attend by his owner, who, along with the other slave owners, hoped that the enslaved would remember the spectacle the next time they contemplated breaking the rules established for them. A preacher was commissioned to deliver a sermon. He likely beseeched the enslaved people assembled to avoid Frank and Lucy's fate by being obedient to their earthly masters as they were to their heavenly master.

Frank and Lucy were left to hang for half an hour before the ropes were cut. As if to communicate their excitement over ending these two lives, members of the slave-owning community commenced in "music, dancing, trading in horses, gambling, drinking, fighting, and every other species of amusement and excess to which the southern people are addicted," said Ball.

White slave owners sustained the South's rape culture as well as enslavement as a whole through these spectacles of violence and subsequent displays of entertainment. They conveyed enslavers' reach and willingness to destroy the lives of those enslaved people who dared to challenge their authority. For Charles Ball, the message was received loud and clear.[73]

ENSLAVED MEN LIKE ALFRED, PATRICK, AND FRANK demonstrated incredible boldness for confronting the men who they believed had raped and sexually exploited the enslaved women in their lives because acts of rebellion, disobedience, and vengeance were almost always met with grave consequences. When Josiah Henson recounted his memories of his mother's rape and his father's subsequent beating, he paid much attention to the injurious and lasting impact the experience had on his father's spirit. His once jovial nature was forever changed and replaced by a sad and gloomy disposition. Henson claimed he no longer had the capacity to care about himself or anyone else. According to Henson, "The milk of human kindness in his heart was turned to gall." Certainly, the physical trauma he experienced, having his ear severed from his head and being beaten severely, played a significant part in creating his sullen attitude. But what may have been even more traumatic for this enslaved husband and father was being forced to accept the limitations that enslavement placed on his masculinity.

Although he desired the right and responsibility to rescue his wife from an impending sexual assault, the system under which he lived dictated that his inclination to protect his family did not matter. Both his owner and the county authorities considered him incapable of being a patriarch and punished him severely when he attempted to protect his wife. They felt it was crucial to remind him of his dependent status and that his actions needed to fall within the boundaries set by his owner. Enslaved men were expected to abide by these terms and conditions or face consequences that ranged from violent beatings to death. Deciding whether to preserve one's own life or protect one's wife from sexual exploitation could not have been an easy decision for any enslaved man to make.[74]

When Henson's father prioritized his need to protect his wife from harm over his overseer's prerogative to abuse her, the local authorities determined that he needed to be reminded of his subordinate station. Yet his penalty, a flogging on his back and the severing of his ear, served a much larger purpose. The floggings and death sentences issued to men like Henson's father, Alfred, Patrick, and Frank were designed to implant feelings of fear and powerlessness in the hearts of all enslaved men who witnessed them.

Of course, this intense violence was also intended to strike fear in the hearts of enslaved women and likely discouraged some women from sharing their experiences with sexual exploitation with others. It also served to teach enslaved children the importance of deference and obedience. Enslaved men's frequent confessions of powerlessness and regret in regard to the sexual exploitation of enslaved women prove just how effective these threats of corporal punishment were.

For Henson's father and others who attempted to offer enslaved women protection from sexual abuse and challenged slave owners' authority in the process, the emotional consequences sometimes proved to be too great. Although Henson's father managed to escape a death sentence, the sullen and disagreeable attitude he developed as a result of his ordeal was not well received by his owner, who made numerous threats to sell him to "the far south" if his attitude did not improve. His father's disposition, however, did not change. He probably did not feel that his physical location would make much difference to his broken spirit. Regardless of where he lived, he would still be enslaved and would still be denied the fundamental rights he believed he deserved. To Henson's and his mother's dismay, his father was eventually sent off to Alabama, and neither one of them ever heard from him again.[75]

CHAPTER FOUR

The Greater Part of Slaveholders
Are Licentious Men

On January 15, 1843, five months prior to his marriage to Helen Brooke, Robert Hamilton of Virginia wrote his fiancée a detailed letter in which he expressed his anxiety about their upcoming nuptials: "You will find this letter more serious in its tone than those which have preceded it." Robert believed he needed to share his feelings before they entered into marriage, a compact that could be "dissolved only by death or by circumstances more painful than death." Prior, Helen had expressed concern about not being able to please him sexually. Robert also questioned whether he and Helen would be sexually compatible and if she could accept his unique sexual needs, which he described as his "peculiar feelings—my most unfortunate eccentricities." He said he would be surer "if I were like yourself in my temper & disposition—if I were like other honest & honorable men." Helen satisfied all of Robert's qualifications for an honorable wife: "You are all that can be reasonably asked or that a reasonable man could need in a wife." He noted that she was amicable, gentle, generous, and—most importantly—yielding. Yet Robert had no misconceptions about the kind of man he was. He believed his sexual needs and wants could raise eyebrows and place him outside the definition of an honorable Southern gentleman. He felt his future wife should be warned that his "peculiar disposition" was like nothing that had ever been seen before, and that he was "the most unfortunately constituted being that was ever made in the human form."[1]

Southern white men like Robert, whether married or single, were afforded a lot of sexual latitude. Although same-sex relationships and incest were proclaimed outright intolerable by antebellum Southern society, soliciting prostitutes, fathering children out of wedlock, and having sex with Black women—free or enslaved—were declared illicit but were tolerable behaviors as long as they did not lead to public scandal.[2] Although Robert did not identify the sexual desires that made him so "unfortunately constituted," his sexual intercourse with enslaved women would ultimately be the major point of contention in his marriage with Helen. He knew Helen might reject him as a respectable suitor if he professed a need or desire to have interracial sex. He did not wish to dissuade her from marrying him, but he did want her to know what she would be conceding to if she became his wife, which was his purported inability to curb his "peculiar disposition" for the sake of her happiness. "You cannot be happy with me. I am too exacting, too unreasonable, too monstrous in my requirements," he wrote. Then he said, "Some of them [his sexual needs], it is true, might be fulfilled & that very easily." He wanted his future wife to know that she *could*—if she were willing—fulfill some of his "monstrous" sexual urges. "But you will not fulfill them. Altho I tell you that your happiness for life depends upon it, you will not," he wrote. Robert was telling his future wife that if she failed or refused to accept his needs, she would be to blame for their unhappiness and not him. He gave Helen two choices. Once they were married, she could either broaden her conception of tolerable sexual practices to align with his or agree to turn a blind eye and resist any feelings of jealousy or discontent.[3]

For elite slave-owning men, engaging in interracial sex with enslaved women was considered a privilege of mastery. If they were discreet and avoided bringing shame on themselves and their families, they expected to receive little to no scrutiny from family and community. When faced with pushback, men were often quick to absolve themselves of wrongdoing and expected their families to respond in kind. Individual men, as well as political and moral leaders, offered a variety of well-calculated excuses that were rooted in their assertions of white supremacy and patriarchal authority to dismiss or minimize the shame or discontent that their sexual relations with enslaved women could generate among their families and communities. In public addresses, private correspondence, and court documents, these men argued that there was a clear distinction between an honorable white man's true character and his flawed and sinful nature, which occasionally led him to succumb to temptations, such as enslaved women's purportedly inherent sexual nature. These dispositions, therefore, were not mutually exclusive. Robert's strategy was to forewarn his wife about his "objectionable" sexual wants so that he would not have to answer to any complaints down the road. If he had sex with enslaved women, it would be her burden to bear or mitigate her feelings and any foreseen or unforeseen consequences. "If you cannot unravel the secret mysteries of my character with the insight I have now given you, it must remain always a sealed book to you," he wrote. "I have now presented to you the worst side of this picture of myself," he declared. His final message to Helen was this: if you still want to marry me, you "need not expect to be happy with me unless you marry me with the determination to make up for the deficiencies in my conduct by your own."[4]

ROBERT AND HELEN were married on June 1, 1843. Less than a year into their marriage, Helen was confronted at last with her husband's forewarned sexual behavior. She was recuperating at her parents' home—a sizable plantation named St. Julien in Spotsylvania County, Virginia—from what had been a difficult pregnancy and a delivery riddled with complications when she learned that her enslaved nurse, Louisa, was pregnant by none other than her husband, Robert.[5] Prior to Helen's pregnancy, Louisa's daily responsibilities were to take care of Helen's personal needs, which likely included helping her bathe, pick out clothes, and dress, as well as coiffing her hair and making sure she received all her meals. Once Helen gave birth to her and Robert's first and only child, Mary—a daughter named for Helen's mother—Louisa's duties probably became even more intimate in nature. She had to ensure that Helen was healing properly and remained free of infection. She likely aided her with breastfeeding and diapered her infant daughter when needed. This intimate contact is what led Helen to discover Louisa's pregnancy. It is unclear whether Louisa told her that Robert had impregnated her or Helen questioned her about the pregnancy after noticing her expanding midsection. Either way, according to Helen's mother, the news that Robert had impregnated Louisa "threw my daughter into a paroxysm of grief."[6]

Helen's parents—the Honorable Francis T. Brooke, a jurist on the Virginia Court of Appeals, and Mary Champe Brooke—were Louisa's actual owners. The Brookes had loaned Louisa to Robert and Helen after the newly married couple moved to Richmond. Helen had originally brought a different enslaved woman to Richmond to serve as her personal servant. Priscilla, who was around forty years old, was an experienced servant of the Brooke family and a logical choice to help the newly married Helen establish a home. Robert, however, was not pleased with Priscilla. He complained about her age, calling her an "old settled servant." He requested that she be sent back to St. Julien and replaced by the much younger Louisa. At the time, Helen's mother was not suspicious of her son-in-law's request and did not make any objections. But why did Robert object to having Priscilla in their home, especially since her responsibility was to serve Helen and not him? Did he believe a younger servant would better meet his wife's needs? Priscilla's experience belies any claims Robert could have made about her effectiveness. Robert's request appears to have been much more nefarious. He likely wanted access to Louisa's more youthful body, and he may have assumed that he'd have an easier time coercing the younger woman to have sex with him.[7]

White men and women alike exploited the myth that Black women, unlike white women, were more interested in matters of the flesh than piety and domesticity. According to historian Deborah Gray White, colonial and antebellum white society accepted and maintained the belief that Black women were governed almost entirely by their sexuality, making them "the counterimage of the mid-nineteenth-century ideal of the Victorian lady." White men relied on this myth of Black women's hypersexuality to excuse their choice to engage in sex across the color line. Although empowered by law and custom to rape and sexually coerce enslaved women, many spoke of "succumbing" to Black women's seductive nature instead.[8] While on a visit to Charleston, South Carolina, Ebenezer Appleton, a native of New Hampshire, wrote to his childhood friend about the bustling sex trade in Charleston and stated that "there is more illicit commerce on here with blacks & mulattoes than white girls." Appleton assured his friend that he was too much of a "yankee" gentleman to solicit sex from any of the Black women, many of whom were enslaved. However, he listened intently as "connoisseurs" told him about the ways in which Black women were "better in all respects" than white women when it came to sexual relations.[9]

In many ways, white Southerners actively encouraged young boys and men to explore their sexuality with enslaved women and mostly withheld any judgment. Enslaved men and women reported that white adolescent boys were taught to regard the young girls in the slave quarters as their training ground for gaining sexual experience.[10] A formerly enslaved man, Walton, reported that his owner took his son down to the slave cabins to teach him how to have sex. After the father selected one of the enslaved women, "they both took her—the father showing the son what it was all about."[11] Pro-slavery advocates claimed that interracial sex between white men and enslaved women would allow men and boys to gain sexual experience as well as indulge any lustful or illicit desires on the allegedly well-suited enslaved woman, thus preserving the sexual purity and respectability of white womanhood.[12] Chancellor Harper of South Carolina argued that the "warm passions" of young white men "give rise to licentious intercourse." Although he condemned interracial sex in principle, he excused these young men's behavior, claiming that "the intercourse which takes place with enslaved females, is less depraving in its effects, than when it is carried on with females of their own caste." Chancellor proclaimed that as long as the sexual intercourse was casual and the male did not become "tainted" by the enslaved woman's habits and manners, he was excused. Chancellor professed that when a Southern boy was eventually ready to become an honorable man, he would leave enslaved females alone because, after all, "the female of his own race offers greater allurements."[13]

Robert Hamilton could have been motivated by the obligation to preserve his wife's virtue when he made sexual advances toward Louisa. In the letter he wrote to Helen before they got married, he explicitly stated that she would find many of his sexual requests monstrous and not something a respectable lady would want to entertain. He needed to have a young enslaved woman on hand to engage in the vulgar and undignified sex that he professed to need and shield his wife from such degrading behavior. In other words, Louisa did not need to be protected from his vulgarity. He felt that because of her color and status, she was equipped to withstand his crudeness. The South's rape culture dictated that she was not entitled to his concern. Like many slave-owning men and pro-slavery advocates, Robert justified sexually exploiting enslaved women as an ideal way to safeguard white women's virtue.

When Robert Hamilton was confronted by his wife and various members of her family about having sex with their female servant, his inclination was to not take responsibility for the chaos he had created. Instead, he offered a myriad of excuses for why he had had sex with Louisa and placed the burden to forgive and forget his transgression on his family. According to Helen's mother, Robert walked out of Helen's childhood bedroom after Helen confronted him with the allegations and headed toward the parlor, where his mother-in-law was seated. He looked at her and asked, "Madam, can't you forgive a man for one sin?" According to Robert, that was all his sexual relations with Louisa were, just one sin, which he quickly attributed to his flawed nature. He offered the same refrain he told Helen before they were married— due to his nature, he was "not fit to be a husband to any woman." By framing his actions in this way, he could claim that his behavior was not a malicious or controllable act for which he should be held accountable but a sin, a flaw in his nature rather than his character that should be forgiven without question. As God forgave sin, so should his wife and mother-in-law; Robert skillfully placed the burden of reconciliation in their hands.[14]

To further release himself from responsibility, Robert then assumed an accusatory posture with his mother-in-law and said the predicament surrounding Louisa would never have happened had she and her husband permitted him and Helen to marry several years earlier, when Helen was seventeen. Although the reasoning behind this excuse is not totally clear, he could have meant that if he had married earlier, he would not have had the opportunity to experiment with and develop a taste for sex with Black women. To his friend and trusted physician, Martin Burton, Robert offered a completely different excuse for his behavior. He said that once Helen entered the second trimester of her pregnancy, her mother insisted that they refrain from sexual activity to safeguard her health and that of the baby. It was quite common, however, for men to seek sex outside their marriages during the last months of their wives' pregnancies. They referred to this time as their "gander months." Slave-owning men would venture to the slave cabins or call on enslaved women to have sex, with very little pushback from their wives, who lay in confinement.[15]

In essence, Robert Hamilton felt absolved from the pain he had caused because he had acknowledged himself as a flawed man who was weak in the face of his monstrous eccentricities, and he had never promised his wife he would be anything different. Although the Brookes, one of Virginia's most prominent slave-owning families at the time, feared public humiliation if word of Robert impregnating an enslaved woman spread through Richmond, Robert appeared unwilling to consider the magnitude of their concern. His primary position was that "his passions controlled his moral senses and [they] left him, and did not return," rendering him weak to resist Louisa. He was not the perpetrator of a bad act but a victim of temptation. This is what he reportedly told his father-in-law, Francis Brooke, when Francis forced him to explain why he had "destroyed the happiness of one of the happiest families in the world." In fact, he told his father-in-law that his reason for being so forthright about being the father of Louisa's unborn child was so that "it would reconcile his wife." Now it was up to her not only to forgive but to forget so that they could move forward with their lives.[16]

Like Robert Hamilton, many white men attributed their "illicit" sexual relations with free and enslaved Black women not to their character but to their flawed nature. The characterization of their nature as an affliction or state of being for which they had little to no control only reinforced the South's rape culture.[17] In 1813, William Kendall of Virginia wanted to emancipate and provide financial security for the mixed-race son he had fathered with an enslaved woman. He explained his predicament to the King George County court, declaring that "like many frail men, he hath fallen into a vice." He wanted to convey that under normal circumstances, he, as a respectable gentleman, would not have debased himself by mingling with enslaved women. Therefore, neither he, nor his son, should be punished for his actions during a moment of weakness. John Randolph of Roanoke, Virginia, went so far as to blame the devil for his sexual attraction to a Black woman. In a letter of desperation to his friend Henry Watkins, Randolph begged Watkins to visit and pray for him, "for the effectual fervent prayer of a righteous man availeth much." He claimed to be "in extremis," or on the verge of destruction, "because I am under the powerful influence of the Prince of Darkness who tempts me with a beautiful mulattress."[18]

Although interracial sex between white men and Black women, free and enslaved, was rather commonplace, men used the language of affliction and weakness to justify their conscious choice to have sex with Black women because preachers, politicians, and other moral torchbearers inundated the public sphere with rhetoric that denounced interracial sex. In theory, an honorable Southern gentlemen would not engage in interracial sex because it was considered debasing and a threat to the purity and supremacy of the white race. In his highly regarded publication *Notes on the State of Virginia*, Thomas Jefferson spoke extensively on what he believed to be African peoples' moral and biological inferiority, a position he articulated throughout his life. Thirty years later, he wrote to a neighbor that "amalgamation with the other color produces a degradation to which no lover of his country, no lover of excellence in the human character can innocently consent." Similarly, James Henry Hammond, former governor of South Carolina and noted pro-slavery advocate, denounced interracial sex to discredit a British abolitionist's reports of rampant sexual abuse of enslaved women by white male slave owners. Hammond argued that "this intercourse is regarded in our society as highly disreputable" and "if carried on habitually, it seriously affects a man's standing." And "he who takes a colored mistress . . . loses caste at once." Preachers of the gospel also warned their congregations that race mixing through interracial sex would lead to the corruption of their society. The Reverend J. D. Long of Maryland, a critic of the South's system of slavery, preached that "amalgamation" was increasing at a horrible rate throughout the slave states and that "one of the reasons why wicked men in the South uphold slavery, is the facility which it affords for a licentious life."[19]

Jefferson's and Hammond's pontifications on the ills of interracial sex did not match the realities of the South's rape culture. This rhetoric did very little to persuade white men from engaging in interracial sex, and those who did engage rarely suffered significant damage. During their lifetimes, both Jefferson and Hammond were engulfed by public scandal due to their own long-term sexual liaisons with enslaved women. This did little to diminish their political power or relevancy, even if it bruised their reputations for a short time.[20] Former bondman Lewis Clarke said that his slave owner, who also happened to be his grandfather, was considered a highly respectable man among his fellow slave owners. "It did not render him less honorable in their eyes, that he took to his bed Mary, his slave."[21]

White people's social commentary against interracial sex failed to change white men's behavior because the critiques were strategically accompanied by caveats meant to excuse interracial sex in certain instances. For example, white men and boys could conjure long-held beliefs in African women's hypersexuality and inherently seductive nature. Over centuries, Southern society became conditioned to accept that a white man could easily succumb to this seduction in a momentary lapse of judgment. Former pastor John D. Paxton, before a congregation of worshippers in Virginia, reasoned that the "rapid increase of mulattos" in the South was because vice and temptation prevailed. He argued, however, that respectable parents needed not fret over their sons' sexual experimentation with enslaved women because they "may trace the impiety and licentiousness and shame of their prodigal sons to the temptations found in the female slave of their own or neighbour's households."[22]

Enslaved women were rarely the seducers that Paxton and others claimed them to be. Yet the fact that white men could invoke weakness to explain away the rape and sexual exploitation of enslaved women speaks to the power they possessed in and out of the plantation household. Essentially, the South's public condemnation of interracial sex was a smoke screen. White men's status as slave owners and patriarchs afforded them considerable power over their dependents, Black and white. It is significant that Paxton referred to the South's young white men as prodigal sons. In the book of Luke, it is written that Jesus told a parable of a father who gave his two sons their inheritance before he died. One son squandered it, earning him the title of the prodigal, or wasteful, son. Despite his disgraceful behavior, he was forgiven by his father and welcomed back home, where a lavish feast awaited him. Like the father in Jesus's parable, Paxton publicly pardoned young men who were supposedly weakened by enslaved women's sexuality because he believed that the sinfulness and temptation were "found in the female slaves." Therefore, the South's prodigal sons should always be welcomed back into the graces of honorable society.[23]

James Henry Hammond, a formidable politician in antebellum South Carolina, is a perfect example of a figure who publicly helped generate a discourse of disdain for interracial sex, but who privately acted in ways that completely contradicted his public vitriol. As a public figure, he opposed interracial sex and the dilution of the white race primarily to preserve the white superiority on which his own power rested. As a man and a slave owner, however, he respected the rights of his fellow slave owners to do as they wished with their human chattel behind closed doors, and he expected the same consideration. It was only when his sexual relations with two female slaves became a major source of contention for his wife, tore apart his family, and threatened to cause irreparable damage to his political career that James began to consider the implications of his actions. For the most part, however, he looked for ways to deflect responsibility from himself for all the damage his behavior had caused.

On December 15, 1850, James, several terms removed from the South Carolina governor's office, opened his diary to write about what he called the "difficulties betwixt my wife and me." For his contribution to their marital problems, he wrote that although he intended to be a good husband, he was the victim of his flawed nature. "I have not been immaculate," he wrote. "I could not be. I tried it—oh, I tried it fully, fully and failed wholly."[24] He had a seemingly obsessive attachment to both the enslaved Sally and her young daughter, Louisa. In 1838, at the height of his political career—two years after serving in the US House of Representatives and four years before being elected governor of South Carolina—James purchased eighteen-year-old Sally and her daughter for $900, ostensibly for Sally to serve as his family's seamstress.[25] Once James brought Sally and one-year-old Louisa to his Silver Bluff Plantation in Barnwell, South Carolina, he began having sex with her. James's sexual exploitation of Sally continued for years and produced multiple children, although the exact number is unknown.[26]

James's wife, Catherine Fitzsimons Hammond, was born into a wealthy slave-owning family. The Fitzsimonses were regarded among South Carolina's elite and owned considerable property in the Charleston and Barnwell districts of the state. When Catherine's father died, she inherited several of his properties in Beech Island, a community in the district of Barnwell, just across the Savannah River from Augusta, Georgia, including the Silver Bluff Plantation that became Catherine and James's home. Her land holdings totaled over ten thousand acres, and she owned approximately 150 enslaved people.[27] When James married Catherine in June 1831, he hoped that these land and slave holdings would become his. Because Catherine's family considered Hammond a fortune hunter, they took extreme measures to keep all the property in Catherine's name, even after the couple married.[28] James and the Fitzsimons family had to enter into arbitration to settle the matter. The proceeding went in James's favor, and he earned full rights to Silver Bluff and the rest of Catherine's inheritance, finally placing him among the ranks of South Carolina's slave-owning elite. Now that James was the patriarch of his own household, he expected his wife to honor him and the decisions he made for their rapidly expanding family.[29]

Although James was the head of their household, Catherine did not approve of his sexual relations with Sally. Her ill feelings boiled over in 1850, when James started having sex with Sally's now twelve-year-old daughter, Louisa. Apparently Catherine could no longer contain her vitriol in the face of her husband simultaneously having sex with the enslaved mother and daughter.[30] For her, his behavior had finally crossed the line between tolerable and intolerable. She packed her bags and left James and Silver Bluff with their two youngest children, Catherine and Elizabeth, in tow. Since she did not take Sally or Louisa with her, her concern was not for their safety but for how her husband's behavior offended her. When James opened his diary in December 1850, he wrote, "My wife has been gone to Charleston for a week or more, when to return is uncertain."[31]

James was being sincere when he wrote that the date of his wife's return was uncertain. Catherine's departure started out as a short stay with family in Charleston. By June 1851, she still had not returned to Silver Bluff and was now living with family in the Sand Hills area near Augusta, Georgia. Although James purchased her a carriage horse as a peace offering and to persuade her to come home, her terms for reconciliation were clear: she would not return until he terminated his sexual relationship with Louisa and removed her from Silver Bluff. James wanted his wife to return, but he was unwilling to meet her conditions. In his diary, he wrote, "Concessions are demanded to which I am averse, because they involve injustice and cruelty to others concerned." Ostensibly, he did not want Sally and Louisa to suffer the pain of separation. But he also acknowledged that he continued to have an uncontrollable attachment to the mother and daughter. He explained that he loved his wife dearly and never intended to disrespect her. "As the mother of my children and mistress of my household I would not exchange for her any in the world, and I have never failed in kindness and respect for her." However, "God has given me tastes and appetites which she was not fitted to satisfy," he wrote. He told himself that he had no choice but to keep Sally and Louisa. His wife would have to grow to understand.[32]

While Robert Hamilton assumed his wife would be unwilling to fulfill his sexual "eccentricities," James argued that Catherine was not naturally suited to meet his "tastes and appetites." Just as Robert asked his wife to turn a blind eye to his extramarital affairs, James placed responsibility on his wife to accept his "defective" nature and reunite their family to avoid further humiliation and a public scandal. Although he offered explanations and excuses for why he needed to have sex with Sally and Louisa, he ultimately made the choices he did because he felt entitled to do so. Rather than give up this right of mastery—sexually exploiting the enslaved—to reunite his family, he put his efforts into convincing his wife to accept his excuses. He professed that he simply did not have the discipline to do what she asked. "I should fail were I to try it again," he wrote. "Shall I pretend to do it, knowing I cannot succeed?" he asked rhetorically.[33]

James was a son of the slaveholding South. The rape culture of the day dictated that his sexual liaisons with Sally and Louisa should have been inconsequential. They "seem to me venial and in others are generally so considered," he wrote. James also wrote about having a difficult time understanding why Catherine could not just accept him for the imperfect human he was. On May 25, 1851, he wrote in his diary, "No one, *not one*, exercises the slightest indulgence towards me. Nothing is overlooked, nothing forgiven. I am never spared." He asserted that *he* was the victim and not the creator of their marital strife. He agreed that he was not perfect, although he rationalized that he had "striven as hard as *any one* to be so." He did accept that his lack of discretion was a true shortcoming. "I have no *art* to conceal my faults," James declared. When Catherine first left their home, he declared, "I am wholly to blame, not so much, as I view matters, for what I have done as for what I left undone, for want of caution which led to discoveries." He was not wrong about the importance of discretion in regard to interracial sex. By his own estimation, however, his lack of discretion was the only excuse his wife could have had for abandoning him at Silver Bluff. What James failed to consider is that there were some actions that even his privilege and discretion could not excuse, at least as far as his wife was concerned.[34]

James was distressed to learn that Catherine had disclosed the details of his sexual liaisons with Sally and Louisa to her family. "My wife, who paralyzed me by her arrogance and violence at the critical moment in 1850 and who has ever since kept me in torment, has at last, managed to make our domestic difficulties apparent to the world, which of course throws all the blame on me," he wrote. When he wrote this entry in May 1852, Catherine had not lived with him at Silver Bluff for over a year and a half. Surely he did not expect that an elite family like the Fitzsimonses, who had a reputation of their own to protect, would not demand an explanation for why Catherine left her husband, a former governor of the state who still possessed plenty of political aspirations. Rather than showing remorse for her pain and humiliation, which had prompted her departure in the first place, he obsessed over the damage her disclosure of their marital problems might cause to his reputation and political prospects.[35]

In this moment, James, who had his hopes on winning a seat in the US Senate, chose to ignore his own prescribed duty to safeguard his reputation. In the event he suffered political consequences, he was prepared to blame Catherine and her family instead. He used any excuse he could muster. "What a fatal thing it was when I connected myself with that low-Irish family," wrote James. He condemned them for always seeing him as inferior; he attributed this to why they always showed such rage when he did anything to displease them. In his words, a family had an obligation to forgive one another and protect one another's character from outside attack, but the Fitzsimonses never extended these courtesies. "They have been mean and base enough to expose what families of real pride and proper tone would have concealed; and, in blind, vulgar fury, and a conceited idea of their own elevation, they have for petty revenge utterly sacrificed themselves to ruin me," he exclaimed.[36]

James's position that his wife and her family should have pardoned him without hesitation reveals the role that such excuse-making and entitlement played in fortifying the South's rape culture. The Fitzsimonses had good reason to look down on James with disdain. Almost a decade before, in 1843, the family had discovered that James, who was serving as governor at the time, had sexually molested his four nieces. They were the daughters of Catherine's sister Ann Fitzsimons Hampton and Wade Hampton II, who was a member of one of the South's most wealthy and largest slaveholding families, owning thousands of enslaved people. The revelation that James had sexually molested the teenage girls over the course of several years created a tremendous rift between him and the Fitzsimons and Hampton families. True to form, James assuaged his conscience then, too, writing that although he had been wrong in the matter, his actions were "the result of impulse, not design." In reference to the Hampton girls, he asked, "Is there a man, with manhood in him and heart susceptible of any emotions of tenderness, who could tear himself from such a clutter of lovely, loving, such amorous and devoted beings?"[37]

James convinced himself, if no one else, that he had no choice but to respond to what he called the Hampton girls' affections. "Here were four lovely creatures from the tender but precocious girl of 13 to the mature but fresh and blooming woman nearly 19, each contending for my love, claiming the greater share of it as due to her superior devotion to me," he wrote. According to him, they rushed into his arms and covered him in kisses every opportunity they had and *allowed* him to touch them. Having an excuse for his behavior, he fixated on Wade Hampton II's desire to ruin him socially and politically because of the assaults. According to James, the Hampton and Fitzsimons families "pursued and are still pursuing me with the bitterest persecution," which he claimed placed a strain on his relationship with the South Carolina state legislature during the last year of his term as governor in 1844. Two years later, when James failed to be appointed to the US Senate by the state legislature, he blamed the loss squarely on Wade Hampton. Still unable to take accountability for his actions, he charged his in-laws with a desire to "black ball me and to mortify me and mine by keeping us out of society," wrote James. Of Wade Hampton specifically, he declared, "I always thought him generous and magnanimous and for these qualities I loved him. I love him no longer. And from this source arises all the pain I feel in this affair."[38]

Although James had destroyed the bonds of trust within his extended family, alienated his wife from her sister and nieces, and lost an opportunity to serve in the US Senate, he was still not convinced that he should suffer any consequences for his sexual behavior. He could not humble himself enough to bear the full burden for sexually assaulting four white teenage girls. It is no surprise that James blatantly rejected his wife's indignation over his overt sexual relations with Sally and Louisa, who, as enslaved women, were not entitled to the same protections as the Hampton girls. Although his molestation of his nieces did cost him the 1846 Senate seat, his sexual ties to Sally and Louisa cost him very little politically. In 1857, seven years after Catherine's initial departure, he was finally elected to serve as the junior senator from South Carolina. He and Catherine had reconciled two years prior and remained together until his death in November 1864. James never gave up ownership of Sally or Louisa despite his wife's ultimatum. He continued his sexual liaison with both women and fathered children by both. The mother and daughter remained enslaved by the Hammond family until the end of the Civil War.[39]

SOME SLAVE-OWNING MEN felt no need to offer excuses or seek pardon for having sex with enslaved women. Rather, this group of men felt exempt from judgment and showed little sign of concern for the consequences that ensued as a result of their choices. They relished both their status as patriarchs and a rape culture that afforded them the prerogative to do as they wished. They could disregard the costs to themselves, their wives and children, and the enslaved women involved. This was certainly the case for Newman Roane, a planter from King William County, Virginia. According to his wife, Evelina, in the summer of 1823, three months after their marriage, he moved an enslaved woman named Biney and her two children by him into the home he shared with his wife. In her petition for divorce, Evelina reported that Newman made it abundantly clear that nothing and no one was going to prevent him from providing his enslaved mistress and children with the comforts of his home.[40]

Newman only adopted this audacious attitude toward Evelina once their marriage became official. Prior to getting married, he did everything in his power, including requesting one of Evelina's brothers, Dr. Fendall Gregory, to discredit any rumors the Gregory family may have heard about him having an intimate connection with an enslaved woman. Fendall had, in fact, heard rumors that Newman had a "kept" female slave and had fathered her two children; he demanded to know if there was any truth to the rumors. Newman assured him that no such illicit connection existed between him and the woman, and he even promised Fendall that he would sell the woman and her children as a sign of his sincerity.[41] But once he became Evelina's husband, things rapidly changed. Newman was a modest planter before his marriage to Evelina, owning around ten enslaved people. When they married, he acquired land and slave holdings that increased his status among the men in King William County. According to the 1820 federal census, Evelina's father, William Gregory, owned over eighty enslaved people. That same year, he acquired Elsing Green, a notable estate in the county, which meant that he was equipped to provide his daughter with a generous inheritance when the time came.[42] Empowered by his new wealth, Newman made it clear that he intended to run his household without interference or judgment.

Newman did not parse words when he told his wife of his intentions to bring Biney and her children into their home to live with them side by side. "He would bring the mother and her children home, and not permit them to suffer any longer," he said. Newman even said that their comfort was more important to him than hers and that he had no plans of hiding his affection for the enslaved woman or the children they had made together. He considered himself standing "upon principle." Evelina, however, considered herself an unfortunate woman who was bound to a husband with no restraint. In her petition for divorce, she stated, "He would often say to your petitioner that he did not care for consequences & that he felt no repugnance to the character of a man of violence and that the fear of consequences could not restrain him from the acts of assassin if prompted by his passions."[43] Of course, it is possible that Evelina exaggerated Newman's statements. She was petitioning for a divorce, and it served her to illustrate all the ways that her husband's interracial relationship eroded his character and threatened her reputation as a respectable white Southern lady.[44]

Newman was determined to assert absolute authority over his household and made it abundantly clear that he would not be intimated by any threats his wife's family might make. According to Evelina's brother Thomas Gregory, Newman became "much incensed and declared that no respect was paid to his feelings." He demanded that people respect his prerogative to provide Biney and his enslaved children with the lifestyle he desired for them to have and declared that "those who wished to get this negro woman from him—only sought the opportunity of sending her to the backwoods." He had once admitted to Evelina that he had only married her to gain access to her father's fortune. In this moment, however, he asserted that "he would not part with the woman for all the estate of his father-in-law and in particular that his father-in-law should have anything to do with her." He did not need anyone to approve of his relationship with Biney, and asserting his right to prioritize an enslaved woman over his wife was more important than any financial consequences he might face.[45]

Despite Newman's expectations for what his wife should tolerate, Evelina declared that sharing her home with Biney was too great of a concession. She petitioned the Virginia General Assembly for a divorce in December 1824, less than two years after their marriage. According to the divorce records, Biney and her children lived, ate, and slept within the Roane home. Evelina communicated that the enslaved woman's mere presence in her home was enough to drive her out of the marriage.[46]

Like Newman Roane, James Norman also wished to be uninhibited about his sexual relationship with an enslaved woman named Maria and was quite intolerant to anyone's objections. One of the Normans' boarders testified that James often invited Maria to sit at the dining room table. On one occasion, James's wife, Lucy Norman, decided to adamantly object to having the enslaved woman sit at the same table as her and her guests. Slave owners and the enslaved eating together at the same table would have been unthinkable in most plantation households. According to the witness, when Lucy attempted to enforce social decorum, "Mr. N. insisted that the said girl should be so seated & said to Mrs. N that if she broached her he would take the life of her Mrs. N." In the past, he had invited Lucy to leave their household if she did not like his rules. This time, he threatened to kill her if she continued to question his authority regarding Maria. James's ability to keep Maria close was wrapped into his overall authority as a Southern patriarch. He wished to maintain that power at all costs.[47]

John Burwell of Mecklenburg County, Virginia, was also known to exhibit brash behavior toward his family when questioned about his sexual relations with enslaved women. According to his wife, Lucy Burwell, when it came to John having sex with enslaved women, "the actual presence of his wife and children has been insufficient to control him." She explained that on a recent occasion, he announced in front of her and their children that he would not be sleeping in his usual bedroom with her that night but would sleep in a different room. Then he immediately requested that an enslaved woman, Lucretia, join him in his temporary sleeping quarters, where the two remained for the rest of the night. Lucy testified that "this girl has in this a few years past been the mother of two children, the off-spring of a white father, and your oratrix has every reason to believe and does believe they are the children of her husband." John and Lucy's son Thomas also testified that over the years, his father had frequently treated his mother "unkindly and harsh," and his habit of engaging in sexual relations with enslaved women in the presence of their family only added insult to injury. Convinced that his father's habits would not change voluntarily after twenty-three years of marriage, Thomas decided to confront him directly about Lucretia's presence in the family's home. He requested that his father "send off this servant girl Lucretia." In response, John demanded that his son leave his home, infuriated that he would dare to dictate his actions. John would not stand to be questioned about Lucretia, especially by his son.[48]

John Prince of Charleston, South Carolina, perhaps most clearly illustrated a blatant disregard for his family when he abandoned his wife of over twenty years, Eliza, and their seven minor children to live with a female slave, Jemmima Jones. As a result of his move, John left Eliza virtually destitute. Although he earned over $600 annually, he only occasionally sent a small sum of money for the maintenance of his lawful family. In the meantime, he purchased a new home where he could live openly with Jemmima and not have the burden of a wife or children. Determined to fulfill his own needs, he forgot his obligations to be a protective husband and father. When his own son Alwyn petitioned him for support on behalf of his mother and siblings, he threatened him with physical violence, claiming Alwyn's real intentions were to interfere with Jemmima and her children. John Prince was no longer Eliza's husband, nor Alwyn's father. He was a man who wished to live openly with an enslaved woman. Fortunately for John, as a slave-owning man in the antebellum South, he did not need the consent of his dependents—his wife, his children, or Jemmima—to do so.[49]

WHILE SOME SLAVE-OWNING MEN tried desperately to offer excuses for their sexual relations with enslaved women, others altogether rejected the idea that they needed to provide justification for their behavior. Across the board, these men were never willing to assume full responsibility for the consequences their sexual behavior caused their families, enslaved communities, or even themselves. Although they reveled in their responsibilities and privileges as patriarchs—the trusted protectors of and providers for their families *and* the enslaved—they often prioritized their own needs and wants, sometimes to the detriment of their households and familial relationships. Although wives, children, and neighbors were expected to forgive or feign ignorance entirely, they were not always able or willing to do so. And unfortunately for enslaved women, because the South's rape culture mostly allowed these men to dodge responsibility and escape legal prosecution for acts of sexual violence, they remained as vulnerable as ever to sexual exploitation.

CHAPTER FIVE

A Licentious Master and a Jealous Mistress

Upon her arrival to the Georgia slave plantation owned by her husband, Pierce Butler, Frances Kemble quickly learned of the exploits of the Butlers' plantation overseer, Roswell King Jr. Apparently King was notorious for his sexual assault of the Butlers' enslaved women, a fact her husband knew, which left her feeling that much more disgusted.[1] Kemble, an English-born actress, was quite ignorant to the workings of plantation slavery before her husband, who owned a substantial swath of the Georgia seacoast, brought her to the slaveholding South for the first time. Her curiosity led her to make connections with the enslaved men and women whom her husband owned, and she began chronicling their encounters in detail in her journal. She recounted the story of an enslaved woman named Judy who suffered greatly at the hands of King. Judy revealed that King had frequently "forced her" to have sex and "flogged her severely for having resisted him." She even became pregnant as a result of the rapes. She gave birth to a child named Jem, "her first born, the son of Mr. King," she told Kemble. On one occasion, after beating her for resisting him, King sent Judy to a remote and swampy section of the Butler estate known as Five Pound as further punishment.[2]

Kemble characterized Judy's life as "a miserable story" under "Mr. King's overseership." Yet Judy's suffering did not begin and end with King. In addition to navigating the physical and psychological trauma of being raped, Judy also had to contend with King's wife, Julia Maxwell King. Having just given birth to another of King's children, Judy was recovering from labor alongside another female slave, who had also just given birth to a baby fathered by King, when she was confronted by Julia. It was during this visit to the plantation's hospital ward that Julia learned of the paternity of both women's babies. She became enraged by this discovery and, with no regard for their delicate condition, ordered that they both be "severely flogged," an act she "personally superintended," noted Kemble. Her husband had simultaneously impregnated these two enslaved women. He was the one who had engaged in interracial sex outside their marriage. He was the one who had earned a reputation for sexually assaulting enslaved women. Nonetheless, Julia set her eyes on these two enslaved women and determined that they would bear the burden of her wrath.[3]

Julia King was no stranger to slave management and concocting punishments for the enslaved, owning over fifty slaves in her own name. When she decided that she was not satisfied with a flogging alone, she further ordered that Judy and the other bondwoman be transported to Five Pound—ironically, one of her husband's favorite punishment spots—where an enslaved driver was to "flog them every day for a week." Julia appeared to be convinced that by being flogged every day for a week, these women would learn or perhaps try harder to avoid future sexual encounters with King. But as an experienced slave-owning woman who had shared a lifetime of experiences with her husband, that level of naivete was unlikely. What chance did these enslaved women have to curtail Roswell King's notorious abuse when Julia's own anger, frustration, and open disapproval had done very little to curb his "illicit" behavior over the years?[4]

From Judy's ordeal, Kemble learned that enslaved women's trauma was not always caused by their sexual assailants alone. Enslaved women were often caught between the "passions of their masters and mistresses," declared Kemble.[5] When slave-owning women learned of white men's sexual relations with female slaves, they sometimes directed their anger and frustration toward the enslaved women. As their subordinates, enslaved women were the convenient target. Just as white Southern patriarchs reinforced their authority over the enslaved through the perpetration of sexual violence against enslaved women, they also assumed guardianship over white women, rendering them legally and socially subordinate in the public and private sphere.[6] It was to white women's chagrin that white men could and did engage in interracial sex with virtual impunity.[7] However, white women were not completely powerless. As household managers and slave owners in their own right, slave-owning women wielded much power over the enslaved people in their charge. While their subordination to white men perhaps placed limitations on how they could confront them regarding sexual relations with enslaved women, slave-owning women's authority over the enslaved enabled those who were so inclined to persecute enslaved women for these acts instead.[8]

According to testimony by enslaved people, white men's sexual relations with enslaved women brought out the worst in the slave-owning woman. Yet in truth, slave-owning women responded to this behavior in a variety of ways. Many women chose or felt compelled to remain silent about their discontent, acquiescing to expectations of submission and gentility. Some used gossip and private correspondence to generate private and public discussions about their dissatisfaction with white men's sexual behavior with female slaves.

Others turned to violence and spite. Armed with the authority of owner-ship, these women inflicted physical and psychological abuse, negotiated the sales of women and children, and intensified already hostile environ-ments through harassment and derision. To this end, slave-owning men and women were "each alike armed with power to oppress and torture them," said Kemble.[9]

FROM THE AUCTION BLOCK to the plantation household to the slave quar-ter, white women were exposed to and even participated in the sexualiza-tion and reproductive exploitation of enslaved women. They frequently encountered enslaved children of mixed race, the irrefutable evidence of white men's sexual exploits with enslaved women — sometimes in their own households — and at times came face-to-face with the cries and pleas of en-slaved women hoping to gain refuge from rape and sexual assault. Slave-owning women were very aware that few spaces in the South went untouched by what they deemed white men's illicit intercourse with en-slaved women.[10] Regarding this behavior, Georgia plantation mistress Ella Gertrude Clanton Thomas said, "I know that this is a view of the subject that is thought best for women to ignore," but how can we "when we see so many cases of mulattoes commanding higher prices, advertised as 'Fancy girls.'" Similarly, Mary Boykin Chesnut, a prominent slave-owning woman from South Carolina, declared that all a white woman of good standing need do is walk through any town square to witness Black women on auc-tion blocks being purchased for sexual purposes by lusty-eyed men. Of one such occasion, she said, "I saw today a sale of Negroes — Mulatto women in silk dresses." Although she perceived one of the enslaved women to be looking "coy & pleased" at a bidder, she knew immediately that the bidders intended to make this woman a sexual servant. Shifting her attention away from the auction block to the plantation household, she said, "Our men live all in one house with their wives & their concubines, & the mulattoes one sees in every family exactly resemble the white children."[11]

Just as enslaved girls were taught and learned through observation that with sexual maturity they became vulnerable to rape, sexual coercion, and harassment at the hands of white men and boys, young white girls of the slaveholding South were similarly indoctrinated to white men's sexual rela-tions with enslaved women. For example, former bondwoman Harriet Jacobs said that "the white daughters early hear their parents quarrelling about some female slave." And the most curious, Jacobs said, would "soon learn the cause." These young girls would hear accusations of their father having sex with certain female slaves. Some girls would even learn that they had been "attended by the young slave girls whom their father has corrupted." The same enslaved girls who served as their first playmates and personal body servants, on whom they themselves had first practiced and honed the skills of mastery, were now the subject of their parents' marital discord. Most importantly, said Jacobs, they came to know that "woman slaves are subject to their father's authority in all things."[12]

From generation to generation, white women, especially of the planter class, issued warnings to their daughters, raising their consciousness to the prevalence of white men's interracial sexual relations. When Mary Boykin Chesnut married James Chesnut Jr. of Camden, South Carolina in 1840, her mother-in-law, Mary Cox Chesnut, warned her not to send enslaved women into town unsupervised. She argued that they were easily tempted and led astray by white men eager to have sex with them. The elder Chesnut said that the same advice had been given to her when she was a young bride, and although she was "very particular" in heeding the advice, she found her own efforts to be in vain. The younger Chesnut confessed that these conversations with her mother-in-law made her ruminate on the temptations to which her own husband might succumb. Chesnut correlated her cultural realities to the biblical figure Jacob, who was forced to marry Leah although he desired to marry her more attractive sister, Rachel. "So it is—flocks & herds & slaves—& wife Leah does not suffice. Rachel must be added, if not married," she wrote in her journal. Although Chesnut's metaphorical musing about Leah and Rachel helped her make sense of her station as the wife of a powerful, elite slave-owning man, she came to know that it would, in fact, encapsulate her family's real lived experiences. Her father-in-law had a "Rachel" of his own, an enslaved woman with whom he fathered multiple children. Struggling with this revelation and what it could mean for her own life, she asked, "Can I honor what is dishonorable? *Rachel*—& her brood—make this place a horrid nightmare to me."[13]

Although white women like Mary Chesnut expressed disapproval of white men's sexual relations with enslaved women, they often tolerated and, at times, accommodated these sexual relations across the color line. Some even had sexual relations with Black men, free and enslaved, although at much greater risk of public shame and consequence than their male counterparts. In her testimony, Harriet Jacobs asserted that their inclination for tolerance and accommodation was also learned behavior, passed down from one generation to another, even if unwittingly. Jacobs argued that a young white girl's exposure to the quarrels between her parents over one enslaved woman or another and her mother's outbursts of anger and jealousy was a significant part of white women's preparation for the realities of a culture shaped by racialized sexual violence and exploitation. But even though white girls might have learned to be displeased with white men's consorting with enslaved women, the fact that they did not see their mothers and aunts and sisters fleeing these relationships in droves taught them that begrudged tolerance was perhaps the slave-owning woman's lot in life. When these young impressionable girls became women, they mimicked the actions of their mothers before them in the presence of their own daughters, generating a cycle that bolstered rather than disrupted the South's rape culture.[14]

SILENCE WAS A FREQUENT RESPONSE of slave-owning women to white men's sexual relations with enslaved women. For many women, there was consolation in silence. Their disapproval did little to preclude white men's behavior. There were virtually no legal measures to prosecute white men for raping, coercing, and sexually harassing enslaved women, or even cohabiting and engaging in long-term liaisons with them. The social consequences were also few. As a result, silence served as a useful tool to maintain peace within their households and the plantation community at large.[15]

Sixty steps separated Robert Newsom's plantation house and the private cabin he assigned to his enslaved housekeeper Celia. She could anticipate Robert regularly making the sixty-step journey from his house to her cabin to sexually assault her. The house on the other side of those sixty steps was bursting at the seams with members of the Newsom family. Robert's wife had died in 1849, a year before he purchased Celia, and it was around this time when his oldest daughter, Virginia—who was married with three children—moved back into the house. It is unclear whether she had been widowed or had become estranged from her husband, precipitating this return to her father's home. Newsom's son Harry also lived in the house at that time but left around 1852, when he remarried and settled into a place of his own. Newsom's youngest children, a son named David and a daughter named Mary, were teenagers in 1850 and still very much dependent on their father. David moved out in 1855, when he married, but Mary remained behind. She was unmarried and likely assisted Virginia in her duties as the lady of the house.[16]

As Virginia and Mary were charged with overseeing the daily operations of their home, this placed Celia, the Newsoms' house servant and cook, under their direct supervision. The moments when Celia was cooking or cleaning the Newsoms' house might have been the few occasions when she felt some modicum of protection. Every time she returned to her cabin, however, she became more vulnerable. It is possible that Virginia and Mary, along with Newsom's sons, were unaware of their father's routine sexual assaults on Celia in her cabin. Celia *did* testify that Newsom usually came to her cabin around 10:00 P.M., after his family went to bed. However, despite any efforts put forth by Newsom to create a veil, there were too many clues that pointed to Newsom's illicit relationship with Celia for them to go completely unnoticed by his daughters. If Virginia and Mary did claim ignorance to their father's behavior, their ignorance would have been quite willful.[17]

Virginia and Mary were, in fact, confronted with concrete evidence of their father's attacks on Celia. According to the Newsoms' neighbor, William Powell, Celia said that she had told members of Newsom's family that he had been hurting her and that she would hurt him in return "if he did not quit forcing her." And if this testimony was not enough, Virginia and Mary would have surely noticed when Celia gave birth to a child of mixed race, possibly even assisting or supervising her during childbirth. Once Celia issued her fervent petition to Virginia and Mary Newsom, requesting that they protect her from their father's sexual assaults, the Newsom daughters could no longer claim in good faith to be unaware of their father's actions. Yet according to Celia, they did not speak up on her behalf.[18]

Although Virginia and Mary likely had more intimate contact with Celia than Newsom's other children, they would have had many reasons not to respond to her pleas and intervene on her behalf. For one, questioning their father about his sexual activities would have been seen as improper or, at the very least, uncomfortable. Also, Virginia was either estranged from her husband or widowed, and Mary was unmarried, making them both dependent on their father. Under the legal and social conventions of coverture, women were regarded as the dependents of their fathers, husbands, or brothers. Under their guardianship, they received financial support as well as social respectability. There were women of the slaveholding class who owned land and enslaved people in their own name and experienced varying degrees of economic independence. But as most women experienced at least some financial and social dependency on men, they would have been hesitant to challenge the authority of the very men upon whom they relied.

In addition to the fear of financial instability, fear of physical retaliation also solicited silence from some women. For example, a former bondman from Georgia said that his owner's wife raised no visible objections when he bought a "real pretty young gal" to be his sexual servant because she, along with their slaves, "knew better" than to question his actions. When her husband demanded that the enslaved woman work and sleep in their home, she was expected to remain silent. When the enslaved woman's womb began to swell with her husband's child, she was still expected to remain silent. According to the former bondman, his owner's dominance within the home meant that the "wife nor nobody else didn't say nothing about it."[19]

In some instances, slave-owning women and enslaved women were unified in their fear of violent husbands and owners. Virginia Shepherd of Virginia told of a slave owner named Gaskins who owned a housemaid named Diana. It was Gaskin's routine to send Diana to his barn to shell corn and "cage her in the barn so she couldn't get out" when he wanted to sexually assault her. Shepherd said that Gaskin's wife had genuine empathy for Diana, but she knew she too would face consequences if she intervened. "He would beat her if she tried to meddle," said Shepherd. He had even pulled out his wife's hair on a previous occasion.[20]

In some instances, it is unclear whether a slave-owning woman's silence or inaction in response to an enslaved woman's pleas signified callousness or indifference or simply reflected a sense of powerlessness to compel a different outcome. According to Annie Young, when her enslaved aunt retreated into the woods to escape being raped by her owner, she was eventually hunted down by his bloodhounds and brought back to his house, where he "knocked a hole in her head and she bled like a hog, and he made her have him." When her aunt told her mistress about the episode and pleaded for protection, the mistress told her she better submit to him because otherwise he would likely kill her. Similarly, Jacob Manson told of an enslaved woman who lived on a neighboring plantation who also appealed to her mistress to save her from her husband. According to Manson, the woman looked at her and said, "Well go on, you belong to him." As if to wash her hands of this woman and her plea, this slave-owning woman not only failed to provide the enslaved woman with refuge but failed to give her a meaningful solution to her problem. Her urging the enslaved woman to concede to her owner's demands perhaps reflected her own frustrations or even fear of being married to a man who would engage in that sort of behavior.[21]

In the case of Virginia and Mary Newsom, it is reasonable to conclude that they may have felt that silence was their only option. Nonetheless, their silence had a significant impact on Celia's life. By not sounding the alarm when Celia came to them for help, they did nothing that might have deterred their father from entering her cabin at night and forcing himself on her. Unable to secure the support of Newsom's daughters, Celia argued that she had no choice but to physically harm Newsom to save herself from another rape. On the night of June 23, 1855, Celia reportedly struck Newsom on the head with a wooden stick when he barged into her cabin, as he had done so many nights before. Although she claimed she only wanted to hurt him, the blows to his head and body ended Newsom's life, along with his sexual assaults.[22]

To maintain their silence, Southern white women often bargained with themselves, asserting that they could ignore what they did not see. In fact, for the slave-owning woman, this was more of a directive than a natural inclination. When writing about one man's "midnight doings in the quarter," Mary Chesnut said his wife and daughters, "in the might of their purity and innocence, are supposed never to dream of what is as plain before their eyes as the sunlight." In order words, these women had an active role to play in inducing their own ignorance.[23]

In many ways, Southern society required that slave-owning men and women both partake in the delicate dance between discretion, ignorance, and silence. Former slave W. L. Bost acknowledged that his plantation mistress's ability to feign ignorance of her husband's sexual behavior was very much contingent on his master's discretion about his interracial relations. If a mistress was forced to confront the fact that her husband was having sex with enslaved women, "she raised a revolution," said Bost. Ideally, the slave-owning wife would never find out. At minimum, these women expected their husbands to be discreet and save them from the details. Discretion was tantamount to honorability according to the South's social contract of honor and respectability. Per historian Bertram Wyatt-Brown, "The mother's honor was to be protected from the grossness of manhood, the lustiness that was both deplored and celebrated by the men themselves." Bost said, while "plenty of colored women have children by the white men," slave mistresses "hardly find out," because "the white men not going to tell and the nigger women were always afraid to." All enslaved women could do was "just go on hoping that things won't be that way always."[24]

When slave-owning men failed to be discreet, some slave-owning women felt freed from any expectations of silence. This opened a door for them to air their grievances, even if in the most passive ways. Mary Reynolds grew up enslaved on a large plantation in Concordia Parish, Louisiana, which was owned by Dr. Andrew R. Kilpatrick, a noted physician. While Mary and her fellow slaves knew of their owner's frequent sexual relations with enslaved women, their mistress appeared to be unaware of her husband's notorious behavior until she investigated the faces of two enslaved children who closely resembled her own children. Such unawareness would have taken real effort on her part. According to Mary, Kilpatrick "took a black woman as quick as he did a white and he took any on his place he wanted and he took them often." As a result, he fathered many children who he also held in bondage. One enslaved woman, Aunt Cheyney, claimed to have given birth to four of Kilpatrick's children.[25]

Kilpatrick took extra measures to keep one enslaved woman, Margaret, separate from not only his wife but his other slaves as well. Kilpatrick purchased Margaret while on a trip to Baton Rouge. When he returned home with the woman, who Mary described as a "yellow gal dressed in fine style," he immediately began building her a cabin that was set apart from the rest of the slave dwellings. For his other enslaved people, the placement of the cabin was a clear signal that he wanted privacy to have sexual relations with Margaret away from the gaze of them and his wife and children. Their suspicions were confirmed when Margaret became pregnant. When the birth of that child was quickly followed by the birth of another and then another, Mary concluded, "This yellow gal breeds so fast and gets a mess of white younguns."[26]

Kilpatrick's placement of his slave cabins, and Margaret's in particular, "up the hill back of the big house," allowed for Margaret's children and the other enslaved children he fathered to go relatively unnoticed by his white family in the main house. But the veil, however thin, was forcibly removed from his wife's eyes when she witnessed a confrontation between her own children and two enslaved children. According to Mary, Mrs. Kilpatrick called down from her window to ask her sons why they were playing with the two enslaved children. Her son explained that they were not playing but chastising the two children for playing with their dollhouse. Her son then pointed to one of the children and said, "He says that our daddy is their daddy." The enslaved child responded by saying that not only was Kilpatrick their daddy, but they call him daddy when he comes to visit their mother. With this enslaved child's utterances, Mrs. Kilpatrick was ushered from a place of darkness to light, providing her with concrete information that she could not pretend to ignore.[27]

The Kilpatrick's house servants reported that when Kilpatrick returned home that evening and greeted his wife, "his wife says howdy to him but she don't say it so nice — or just like he thinks she ought to." According to Mary, she spoke to Kilpatrick about Margaret and her children with an accusatory tone. Apparently Margaret's light skin tone had not gone unnoticed by Mrs. Kilpatrick. She, like whites and Blacks across the South, knew that white men were particularly fixated on enslaved women with light skin tone and loosely curled hair. Many enslaved women of mixed race were sold as sexual servants in a niche market called the fancy-girl trade in cities like

New Orleans and Baton Rouge. When the enslaved children identified Kilpatrick as their father, Mrs. Kilpatrick instantly thought of Margaret, signaling that she already knew that her husband had purchased the "yellow" woman in Baton Rouge to carry out a long-term sexual liaison. Enslaved witnesses said that she further explained to her husband that it seemed too coincidental that these two slave children had the same kind of hair and eyes as her own children and that they both had his nose. Up to this point, she had clung to the pretense of ignorance as a coping mechanism. By not addressing the rumors or her own suspicions, they could remain just that — suspicions — and not reality.[28]

While coming to terms with her new reality, Mrs. Kilpatrick threatened to leave her husband and their marriage. She reminded him that she could return to her father's home and live quite comfortably. While he assured her that she could not trust the talk of little children, he felt compelled to extend a peace offering. According to Mary, he went out and bought her a "new span of surrey horses." Although she did not follow through with her threat to leave, she created a new dynamic between them. The household servants who were privy to the most intimate aspects of their lives reported that prior to the confrontation, a new Kilpatrick baby had been born in frequent intervals. Afterward, Mrs. Kilpatrick was no longer cordial to her husband, and she had no more children. Outside observers might have been unaware of their marital discord, but within the walls of the Kilpatrick home, discontent was alive and well.[29]

Similarly, Betty Snead caused a fuss with her husband, Ben, after she caught him in the act of having sexual intercourse with their female slave Fannie. Over the years, Betty had noticed that her husband treated Fannie differently from the other slaves and that her children were "white" and bore a striking resemblance to her husband, yet she remained silent. But now, having witnessed her husband having sex with Fannie, she felt free to say that she knew he had been having sexual relations with her all along and that Fannie's three children looked just like him. Although Betty had felt unable to express her anguish prior to this moment, she seized the opportunity, and like Mrs. Kilpatrick's, her response had lasting consequences within her household. She continued to express her fury, and Fannie was sold the following week.[30]

This bargain — silence in exchange for discretion — served the needs of slave-owning women not only within the confines of their own homes but in the public sphere as well. For elite slave-owning woman especially, presenting a clean, well-managed, and respectable household was of the utmost importance. Although men were heads of the household, a woman's value and reputation, in public as well as in private, rested heavily on the appearance of a spiritually sound, well-managed, and happy home. Often unable to seek education outside the home or hold public office, slave-owning women embraced the fact that to a certain extent, the plantation household served as a vehicle for exercising authority and garnering attention and recognition from one's peers and larger community. Despite the prevalence of interracial sex, having one's husband or son openly engaging in sexual relations with Black women chipped away at the veneer of the idealized plantation household.[31]

Henry Ferry's female owner took surprising measures to keep her home's reputation intact. Henry told of the time when his owners' preacher came to visit and mistook an enslaved child named Jim—whom his owner had fathered by his female slave Martha—for his mistress's child. The child's nearly white skin, coupled with his strong resemblance to his owner-father, gave the preacher no reason to believe the child was born of anyone other than his female parishioner. He remarked that although the child favored its father most, in his eyes, which were the looking glass of the soul, he could see that "he's his mother's boy." In the moment, Henry's mistress "never did let on it wasn't her chile." Rather, she simply "shooed de child away an' took de preacher inside." For the white and Black occupants of this plantation household, it was no secret that the mistress despised her husband's sexual behavior and the mixed-race children it produced. If she had had her way, she would have never had to lay eyes on Jim. Unfortunately for her, her husband gave him full access to their home. During the preacher's visit that day, she felt compelled to maintain her composure and even acquiesce to his presumption that the child was hers to preserve the respectability of her household in the eyes of this outsider. Once the visit ended, however, she took on a different posture. Those who lived within the confines of this plantation saw her anger swell and noticed that she "never would let dat boy in de house no mo'."[32]

For Isabella Kelly, her husband's refusal to exhibit discretion eroded her patience for silence and any desire she might have had to keep their marital discord private. In an 1859 divorce petition before the Alabama chancery court, she charged her husband, Edwin Kelly, with having "constant and undisguised" sex with a female slave named Matilda, with whom he had two children. There is no certainty that Isabella would have stayed married to Edwin if he had in fact chosen to be less conspicuous in his actions. Yet the grounds for which she filed for divorce suggest that it was not solely his sexual acts that brought them to this precipice but that his sexual behavior was constant and "undisguised." Like Henry Ferry's slave mistress, Isabella resented her husband for not even attempting to feign adherence to the social mores that condemned adultery as well as interracial sex. But unlike Henry's mistress—and many other women in the same position—Isabella did not contain her grievances to her household.[33] In his response to the court, Edwin Kelly denied his wife's charges, accusing her of having unfounded suspicions of every female slave he had ever purchased. For Edwin, blame lay not in his behavior but in his wife's paranoia. Unfortunately, there is no record of the court's judgment regarding Isabella's petition for divorce. But Isabella's petition is a glimpse at the more assertive ways in which slave-owning women responded to interracial sex.[34]

ALTHOUGH LIMITS WERE PLACED on white women's engagement in the public sphere, they used their speech within private spaces to offer powerful critiques against interracial sex and even hoped to deter it. While many white slave-owning women were hesitant to acknowledge the possibility of interracial sex between white men and female slaves taking place under their own roofs, they were eager to point out the immoral sexual behavior of their neighbors and acquaintances. According to Mary Chesnut, when these women convened among themselves, sipping tea or eating freshly baked biscuits with jam, gossiping about these matters was one of their favorite indulgences. Although gossip was considered a lowbrow form of communication, it allowed these women to reinforce their moral disdain for white men's infidelity and interracial sex with enslaved women. And by doing so, it not only served as an indictment but enabled some, if only for a moment, to ignore or distract others from the sins that might be taking place within their own households. "Every lady tells you who is the father of all the mulatto children in everybody's household, but those in her own, she seems to think drop from the clouds, or pretends so to think," said Chesnut. According to historian Kathleen Brown, elite planter women defined themselves by the opinions of their female peers. What their friends, neighbors, and families thought and said about them mattered. It was at these intimate gatherings in one another's homes that women negotiated their status by analyzing the lives of others and passing the appropriate judgment. Although Chesnut claimed to despise gossip, confessing that at times it made her disgust boil over, she found no fault in these women for taking part in the activity. Rather, she pitied them for their connection to immoral men. "They are, I believe, in conduct the purest women God ever made," she said. To her mind, it was not *their* behavior that should be judged but that of white men who indulged in sexual relations with female slaves.[35]

In 1864, Laura Jones Gresham, a member of the Virginia slave-owning elite, engaged in this kind of gossip when she wrote a letter to her husband, Dr. Henry Gresham, concerning her uncle's recent death. She opened with the following quip: "Now how do you think he made his will? Don't get nervous & disappointed as to the result." Her statement, coated in facetiousness, was not so much a question but a way of signaling her husband to draw what she considered an obvious conclusion. Her uncle, Anderson Scott, was known to have had a long-term sexual liaison with an enslaved woman, so it was no surprise to Gresham that he had left most of his estate to "his mulatto negroes." In her letter, she underlined her description of her uncle's benefactors, "mulatto negroes," a clear demonstration of her irritation. Her irritation appeared to be twofold. Not only did her uncle live a life of scandal by living openly with an enslaved woman and their children, but he also bequeathed his property to them rather than to those whom Gresham considered to be his "legitimate" family. For these and other reasons, Gresham thought very little of her uncle, stating, "I only regret he should have wasted his talents, and led such a poor, unprofitable life."[36]

As Anderson Scott's niece, Gresham knew that her opinion mattered very little. However, this did not prevent her from forming an opinion, and writing this letter gave her an opportunity to share it. She told her husband that there was a possibility that her uncle's will might be contested. After all, his stated beneficiaries were enslaved. Their legal status would surely be a hurdle in their efforts to collect their inheritance. She noted that even if they gained their freedom, they might not be permitted to stay in the state of Virginia, as the law required all formerly enslaved persons who were freed after May 1, 1806, to leave the state or petition the local courts to remain.[37] Knowing her own limitations as a woman and a distant relative, she said, "I have ceased building 'castles in the air' as regards future wealth and do not anticipate any accession to my worldly estate from the old gentlemen's possessions." Yet the confidential and intimate nature of a personal letter permitted her to openly express her disgust over her uncle's choices to her husband. She also informed her husband of her general intolerance of interracial sexual relations, communicating consciously or unconsciously that she would be similarly dissatisfied if he ever chose to follow the same path.[38]

When not engaging in salacious gossip with others, slave-owning women speculated by themselves over the illicit happenings in other people's households. Many mused over the parentage of the "mulatto," "yellow," or

a fortnight ago - Now how do you think he made his will? I don't
get nervous & disappointed as to the result - It is just what I
always anticipated - About an hour before he breathed his last
a lawyer was sent for and he disposed of his property thus: $1000
One thousand dollars was bequeathed to Mrs Smith in consideration
I suppose of her kindness & attention during his last illness
the remainder to his _mulatto negroes_, whom he desires that
they shall be liberated and remain on his farm - Not one
cent to any relative in the world - No doubt Mrs Smith has
long ago extinguished the little spark of interest he may
have felt towards those nearest him - & perhaps aroused
strong prejudices - Mr Hoard informed Brother Aubrey of it
a few days since but says moreover that he has presented
a copy of the will to several lawyers and they all agree that
there is a flaw in the will and they doubt whether it can
be established. The negroes of course cannot remain
at "Greenway" unless Va should become a free state - in
that event they may be allowed to stay - but on the other
hand if we gain our independence I doubt whether the
state will allow any more negroes to become free - if so they
will have to become slaves and the property divided amongst his
relatives - but I have ceased building "castles in the air" as
regards future wealth, and do not anticipate any accession to
my worldly estate from the old gentleman's possessions - Peace to
his ashes, say I - I only regret he should have wasted his
talents, and led such a poor, unprofitable life - what reward
can he have unless repentance came upon him - with the
heavy weight of misfortune that this war has laid upon him
I had a letter from Aunt Mary Saunders last mail, she says
Grandmama's health is still very feeble and often wishes to
see the children & myself - I have some forebodings that I shall
never see her again, the old of our land are dropping away
like the withered leaves of Autumn - the chilling blasts of age
and sorrow are crushing many down to the grave - and
as she must be fully 75 - we cannot expect her to last much
longer -

A page from Laura Gresham's letter to her husband, Dr. Henry Gresham. Here she expresses disgust over her uncle Anderson Scott's decision to leave a sizable portion of his estate to his enslaved children. She underlined the words "mulatto negroes" for emphasis. Gresham Family Papers, Virginia Museum of History and Culture.

light-skinned children who occupied their communities. In her diary, Ella Gertrude Clanton Thomas recalled an instance when a slave girl came to her door to deliver some jackets that were made by her mother, a seamstress owned by Thomas's neighbor, Mr. Towns. Thomas described the girl's mother as a "coloured woman, a very bright mulatto." What started as a mundane event—Thomas receiving a delivery from this enslaved girl—evolved into an opportunity for Thomas's imagination to run wild. In the pages of her diary, she deliberated on whether Towns could possibly be the father of the girl. "The child is very bright & there was only one inference," said Thomas. She then quipped that Towns might not be the father after all, as the little girl "bears too strong [a] resemblance to someone else." She could not definitively state who the father was; however, she knew for sure that the father was a white man. While Thomas put considerable thought into the paternity of this enslaved child, she conceded that perhaps the exercise was in vain, as white men's interracial relations were "so common as to create no surprise whatever."[39]

Pen and paper provided white women like Thomas a certain degree of freedom to articulate themselves more openly and honestly about wrought subjects like interracial sex. They turned to their diaries and journals and wrote intimate letters to close family and friends to issue indictments about white men's sexual proclivities and enslaved women's presumed hypersexual nature. On paper they could offer seething critiques of white men's unseemly behavior with less risk of creating chaos in their marriages, households, or communities or pulling at the threads of patriarchy and white supremacy that bound Southern society. "God forgive us, but ours is a monstrous system," wrote Mary Boykin Chesnut in one of her many diaries. Here Chesnut lambasted white men's sale and purchase of enslaved women as sexual servants. "Who thinks any worse of a Negro or Mulatto woman for being a thing we can't name," asked Chesnut. Rather than point fingers at the enslaved women who were indeed the victims of this legalized sexual exploitation for which they did not reap the spoils, Chesnut pointed instead to Southern patriarchs who delighted in the sexual servitude of enslaved women and forced their wives, children, and "concubines" to live together without consequence. Questioning the fate of Southern morality, she referred to the practice as a "wrong" and an "iniquity." She then said, "Perhaps the rest of the world is as bad." In her diary, Ella Gertrude Clanton Thomas expressed similar anxieties. Like Chesnut, she feared that white men's interracial sexual behaviors compromised the "standard of morality" in homes across the antebellum South.[40]

In the pages of her diary, Frances Kemble emphasized the hypocrisy of slaveholders who insisted "vehemently upon the mental and physical inferiority of the blacks" yet frequently engaged in sexual relations with enslaved women. According to Kemble, although they condemned the degenerate nature of the enslaved, their sexual behavior suggested that they were "doing their best, in one way at least, to raise and improve the degraded race" by creating a "bastard" population with forms and features "they derive from their white progenitors." White men professed that it was unnatural and repugnant for white people to form alliances with Black people, but it was widely known that "almost every southern planter has a family more or less numerous of illegitimate colored children." Kemble knew firsthand the prevalence of this sort of behavior, having met several female victims of her family's own overseer.[41]

Kemble also wrote in her journal that while she and her husband were touring their plantation, she was eager to discuss the possible parentage of a young enslaved man named Bran, who served as one of the Butlers' enslaved drivers. Observing that Bran was "himself a mulatto," Kemble concluded that he very likely was the son of their overseer, Roswell King Jr. Turning to her husband, Kemble asked, "Did you never remark that driver Bran is the exact image of Mr. King," wishing to know if her husband also noticed the strong resemblance. According to Kemble, Butler replied that Bran was very likely King's brother, confirming their likely familial relationship yet refusing to directly implicate King or his father, Roswell King Sr., in fathering a child by an enslaved woman. Kemble, annoyed by her husband's overall nonchalance about the matter, stated that it made her uncomfortable to think that such relationships were "accepted as such a complete matter of course." This only served to heighten her and her husband's irreconcilable differences over the merits of slavery. She resolved to refrain from future conversations with her husband regarding the subject and "said no more about who was like who." She relied on her diary instead to chronicle her bewilderment with these Southern cultural norms to which she could never grow accustomed.[42]

DESPITE HOW ROUTINE or predictable white men's sexual relations with enslaved women became, some slave-owning women's emotional responses did not lessen in their intensity. An enslaved man named Aaron relayed a story of a slave owner who "cut up with his female slaves more than he did with his wife," and as a result, "his poor wife was almost crazy." Former slave Savilla Burrell revealed that his South Carolina owner fathered multiple children with the enslaved women on his plantation, and his ongoing involvement with these women caused his wife "so much grief." Her pain was exacerbated by the fact that rumors of her husband's "mulatto" children had circulated throughout their community. To silence the neighbors' gossip, he got in the habit of selling these children away. Despite these efforts, his wife remained vocal about her frustrations. Whether it was her husband's relations with the enslaved women or the neighborhood gossip, she would cry routinely.[43]

Many of these women found release in directing their ire toward enslaved women. Former slave Peter Still recounted that whites and Blacks alike on the McKiernan plantation knew McKiernan "was extremely fond" of the women he enslaved, and they became "victims to his unbridled passions." In addition, the "heavy hatred of their mistress" fell upon them as well. He described Mrs. McKiernan as an impassioned woman who turned to alcohol to dull the pain she felt over her husband's sexual relations with enslaved women. "The demon of intoxication fanned the fires of hatred that burned within her," and with each passing year, "her jealousy ran higher, till at length reason seemed banished from her mind, and kindliness became a stranger to her heart." On one occasion, Mrs. McKiernan walked in on her husband sexually assaulting an enslaved girl named Maria. She was thirteen years of age and said to be "a bright mulatto, and uncommonly pretty." Despite Maria's young age and the high probability that Mr. McKiernan had forced himself upon her, Mrs. McKiernan did not express sympathy for the young girl. Rather, "All the fierceness of her nature was aroused," and she "seized the trembling child and put her in a buck." For his part, Mr. McKiernan immediately left the scene, "mounted his horse, and rode off to escape the storm," leaving Maria behind to face the full impact of Mrs. McKiernan's wrath. He knew well that his wife's "full fury would fall upon the young head of his victim." As a result, he never had any incentive to stop assaulting enslaved women and girls. As predicted, his wife placed blame for his "illicit" transgression at the feet of the young Maria, who was the more convenient target for her frustration.[44]

As Maria's slave-owning mistress, Mrs. McKiernan had authority to discipline her as she saw fit. Armed with such authority, Mrs. McKiernan could disguise her cruel intentions toward Maria as effective slave management. Walking this blurred line between discipline and vengeance, she declared it her responsibility to teach the young slave to avoid sexual contact with her master. "After I've done with her, she'll never do the like again through ignorance," she said. What Mrs. McKiernan proposed as punishment for Maria was nothing short of torture. According to Peter Still, Mrs. McKiernan "whipped her till she was tired." After a short rest, she whipped her again "till she had exhausted her own strength," and then locked the young girl in the brick smokehouse, where she would stay for two weeks. Maria and the other women on the McKiernan plantation were caught between a slave master, notorious for assaulting enslaved women and girls, and a slave mistress, committed to directing all her frustrations on his victims. If they resisted Mr. McKiernan's sexual assaults, they risked harsh punishment; if they were unable to escape his grasp, they risked receiving Mrs. McKiernan's punishment. For the enslaved women on the McKiernan plantation, there was no way to win.[45]

As a feature of the South's rape culture, the plantation household was a site of rape, harassment, and assault for enslaved women. For slave-owning women, the plantation household simultaneously was a site of empowerment, restriction, respectability, and sometimes shame. The convergence of these features made the plantation household a hostile terrain to navigate for both groups of women. Unlike enslaved women, however, when slave-owning women came to battle over the ways in which their husbands' interracial sexual relations disrupted their households and troubled their psyches, they were armed with much more than just their feelings. Their feelings of anger, betrayal, and even jealousy were buttressed with the power and authority of slave ownership.[46]

Historians have long conceived of sexual exploitation as white men's crime against enslaved women, in which they used their authority of slave ownership to procure limitless access to enslaved women's bodies. It is equally important to recognize the ways in which slave-owning women exploited their own powers of slave ownership to victimize these enslaved women. When Frances Kemble said that enslaved women were indeed caught between the passions of their masters and their mistresses, even as a nineteenth-century observer she articulated the importance of acknowledging slave-owning women's power and authority over the enslaved. They oversaw enslaved people's labor, brokered their sale, and were known to inflict violence against enslaved people for the most trivial of offenses. In Kemble's experience, these women did not hesitate to exploit this power in order to resolve their personal feelings of shame, anger, and jealousy, as well as the damage these interracial sexual relations inflicted on their marriages and the soundness of their households. These women knew on a conscious level that their husbands were the driving force behind sexual encounters with enslaved women. They also knew, however, that their own power over the enslaved was stronger than any authority they could ever assume over their husbands. Thus, when confronted with white men's sexual relations with enslaved women, slave-owning women used their authority to inflict physical violence and impose harsh sanctions on enslaved women and encouraged the sale of certain enslaved women and children as a way to redress their pain and hopefully discourage future sexual encounters.[47]

In his prolific autobiography, Solomon Northup provides one of the most compelling descriptions of a slave-owning woman employing violence in this way. Northup spent the better part of his twelve years of enslavement as the property of Edwin and Mary Epps of Avoyelles Parish, Louisiana. Originally from North Carolina, Edwin settled in Avoyelles, where he leased a plantation from his wife's family and grew cotton. Northup described Edwin as a "large, portly, heavybodied man" whose behavior was repulsive and coarse, especially when he drank alcohol, which he frequently abused. According to Northup, his wife, Mary Epps, twelve years his junior, was a cultured and well-educated woman from the well-respected Roberts family of Holmesville, Louisiana. This changed, however, when the mother of four became possessed by what Northup called the devil of jealousy. The Eppses owned an enslaved woman named Patsey whom Northup said Mary once loved and treated kindly. But when her husband began to routinely rape and harass Patsey, Mary developed misplaced contempt. Like Frances Kemble and Harriet Jacobs, Northup articulated that enslaved victims of rape and harassment could find themselves the victims of both "a licentious master and a jealous mistress."[48]

According to Northup, Mary would have been content with disposing of Patsey through sale or even death, but because her husband refused her request to sell Patsey, she resorted to violence and harassment instead. It was not uncommon for her to throw broken bottles or pieces of wood at Patsey's head. Mary Epps also solicited the help of others to do her bidding, launching a multifaceted assault on Patsey. Northup spoke of Patsey trembling with fear because when Mary would "work herself to the red-hot pitch of rage," Edwin would quietly appease her by promising to whip Patsey, since he had no intentions of selling her. Northup said that Mary even tried to coax him to kill Patsey and secretly "bury her body in some lonely place in the margin of the swamp."[49]

In her slave narrative, Octavia Albert described how her former mistress succeeded in killing her eighteen-year-old slave Ella. Knowing that her husband had sexual relations with Ella, she "had no more feelings for her than she had for a cat" and found all sorts of ways to punish her for her husband's transgressions. The woman often tied Ella up by her thumbs, which was her favorite form of punishment. One day, however, having tied Ella up earlier in the day, she came back to find her dead. The woman claimed she had not intended to kill the girl; she "only wanted to punish her." Ironically, the couple "did not live good after she killed Ella."[50]

Many slave-owning women looked contemptuously at their husbands' or any white man's children by enslaved women. According to Moses Roper, his slave-owning mistress had months to anticipate his birth. Although his paternity was not certain, she had long suspected that her husband had been having sex with Moses's mother and that the baby might be his. When news came that the baby had arrived, Mrs. Roper sent one of her female slaves to check on the status of the mother and child. Her only inquiry was whether the child was "white or black." When the young enslaved woman returned, she reported that the child "was white, and resembled Mr. Roper very much." Dissatisfied with this report, Mrs. Roper grabbed a "large club-stick and knife" and stormed down to the birthing room that housed the child and mother. According to Moses, Mrs. Roper was intent on killing him. Wise in these matters, Moses's grandmother was prepared for the unexpected. Mrs. Roper "was going to stick the knife into me," but his grandmother "caught the knife and saved my life," reported Moses. While Mrs. Roper was unsuccessful in bringing about Moses's demise, she was successful in bringing about the sale of the mother and child. Although Moses said that his white slave-owning "father" sold him and his mother shortly after her confinement, there is little doubt that Mrs. Roper was a major broker in the transaction. Moses was fortunate to escape the Ropers with his life intact. Nonetheless, Mrs. Roper significantly altered the course of his and his mother's life. When they were sold, they were ripped away from Moses's grandmother, as well as the only semblance of kinship they had ever known.[51]

In his 1818 petition for divorce, Henry Norrell alleged that the only way he could relieve his wife's feelings of jealousy toward their enslaved women was to sell them. He said that shortly after they married, his wife Delia became convinced that he was "having illicit intercourse" with one of his slaves. To appease her, he sold the woman "at a very reduced price, & at great sacrifice." For Henry and Delia Norrell, however, the sale of the enslaved woman did not quell their problems. Henry was forced to sell yet another enslaved woman "for the same reason," he claimed. He assured the court that her accusations were unsubstantiated, but he had agreed to sell the enslaved women to demonstrate his faithfulness to her and their marriage. He argued that despite his efforts, her charge that he was having "illicit connection[s] with other women" put an irreparable strain on their marriage. They did "not lie on the same bed nor have any connection as man & wife" due to her suspicions. For this reason, he appealed to the court to grant him a divorce. Henry and Delia Norrell had suffered irreparable damage to their marital relationship. Yet this archive of the Norrell's divorce proceedings provides no meaningful details on the sufferings of these enslaved women. We have no way of knowing whether Henry had "illicit intercourse" with them. But we can extrapolate that they suffered the pain of being separated from their enslaved community and of being a disposable prop in this couple's marital disputes.[52]

As previously noted, when white women acted out against their female slaves, they were motivated by a variety of emotions. Whereas historian Victoria Bynum argued that white men's sexual exploitation of enslaved women created "twisted strands of resentment and empathy" within the hearts of white women, interracial sex created a more complex braid. There were strands of resentment, jealousy, self-pity, and a desire to seek vengeance against enslaved women.[53] From the testimony of both the enslaved and slave-owning women themselves, expressions of empathy are much harder to see. While some white women expressed empathy for the enslaved woman's plight, they still saw themselves as very much removed from the enslaved woman's condition, very rarely acting to shield enslaved women from these abuses. Most were preoccupied instead with their own suffering.

Slave-owning women's repeated demonstrations of jealousy, anger, and contempt toward enslaved women illustrate that they saw enslaved women and their sexuality as a threat. They were forced to reconcile their beliefs in enslaved women's inferiority with their visions of these women as viable competitors for their husbands' time and attention who could provoke feelings of jealousy and threaten the integrity of their marital households. As Harriet Jacobs wrote, "Slaveholders' wives feel as other women would under similar circumstances."[54]

Enslaved women had many hard battles to fight, said former bondman Richard Mack, but white women's jealousy was one of the hardest. Harriet Jacobs argued that although her slave-owning mistress, Mary Norcom, should have protected her from her husband's constant sexual harassment, Mary had no other feelings toward her but jealousy and rage. It was not uncommon for Jacobs to wake in the middle of the night to find Mary standing over her, watching her sleep. Many household servants were required to sleep on makeshift straw or moss-filled mattresses at the foot of their owners' beds so that they could be readily available to fetch a glass of water or revive the flames of a dwindling fire. Mary forced Jacobs to sleep at the foot of her bed, however, to outmaneuver her husband, James Norcom, who had previously proposed that Jacobs sleep in his bedroom. James had concocted a plan to have his and Mary's child sleep in his room at night. As the young child would need a nurse to attend to him in the middle of night, Jacobs would have to sleep in his room as well. Over the years, Mary had witnessed plenty of her husband's indiscretions with female slaves. Just as the Norcoms' enslaved people knew that James had fathered numerous children by enslaved women on their compact urban plantation, Mary would have known as well. Jacobs's own tenure in the Norcoms' household had been punctuated by constant sexual harassment and innuendo. It is hard to imagine that Mary never caught a glimpse of her husband whispering in Jacobs's ear or heard him direct Jacobs to come to his study at night. The physical walls of her home that sheltered her and her children also facilitated her husband's predatory behavior toward enslaved women like Jacobs. When she learned that her husband wanted to use *his* bedroom as a site for sexual relations with Jacobs, she determined to use *her* bedroom as a site of resistance.[55]

In essence, James and Mary Norcom's household became a battleground in the fight for control over Jacobs's body and mind. As such, Mary welcomed the opportunity to scrutinize Jacobs's every move, even while she slept. Her motivations were not to protect Jacobs. Rather, she was in search of concrete proof that her husband had already engaged in sexual intercourse with Jacobs. While Jacobs slept, she would assume a man's voice and whisper softly in Jacobs's ear, "as though it was her husband who was speaking," to see how Jacobs would react. Mary wanted proof not only that her husband was sexually pursuing Jacobs but that Jacobs was a willing participant in his scheme. Perhaps she needed to believe that Jacobs was, in fact, in collusion with her husband to justify her intense feelings of jealousy and rage toward this young, enslaved woman who was casted as her subordinate in every measurable way. For this, Jacobs suffered greatly.[56]

Mary Norcom's nightly schemes were much more than harassment; she became a sexual perpetrator in her own right. With her words and her body, which hovered closely over Jacobs's frame, she waged a sexualized attack on Jacobs's defenseless body and psyche. Jacobs said she began to fear for her life and struggled to articulate how terrifying it was to "wake up in the dead of night and find a jealous woman being over you." Mary Norcom knew she held a position of power and privilege over Jacobs, yet she was tortured by the ideological illogicality that Jacobs, an enslaved Black woman, was a formidable and beautiful young woman — a possible counterpart — at least in the eyes of her husband. This raised Mary's insecurities about her own attractiveness, said Jacobs, and her ability to maintain the fidelity within her marriage and household.[57]

What reason would a woman like Mary Norcom have to harbor jealousy toward an enslaved woman? Ideological assertions of Black inferiority and Black women's immoral, seductive, and monstrous nature had long existed in the minds of white people on both sides of the Atlantic.[58] Mary was of the elite, slave-owning class in Edenton, North Carolina. She was born into a profitable slave-owning family, and when she married James Norcom, a prominent doctor, she brought her family's prestige, money, land, and slaves to their union, including Jacobs, who was a "gift" from her mother's sister. She was charged with managing their in-town plantation household, the domain in which she wielded the most control. However, she could not control her husband; his past indiscretions with enslaved women were evidence of that. She had had little to no success in diverting his attention away from Jacobs. At every turn, she found herself having to undermine his efforts to be alone with Jacobs—most notably his plans to move Jacobs into his bedroom and build her a private cabin several miles away from their in-town plantation. When it came to capturing her husband's attention, Mary concluded that in this instance, Jacobs held the mantle.[59]

White women were especially jealous of enslaved women who were deemed beautiful. While beauty may have been a source of pride for some enslaved women, Jacobs contended, "If God has bestowed beauty upon her, it will prove her greatest curse." While beauty affords white women respect and admiration, it only "hastens the degradation of the female slave" at the hands of both white men and women, said Jacobs.[60] White women shared in enslaved people's cultural understanding that white men were especially fond of enslaved women with certain physical attributes. Jacobs herself was described by James Norcom as a "bright, mulatto girl," with "dark eyes, and black hair inclined to curl; but it can be made straight," features that were common among enslaved people with African and European ancestry.[61] People classified as "mulatto" were often noted for having "bright" or light-colored skin, loosely curled or straight hair, thin noses, and slight lips, and these characteristics were frequently hailed as beautiful by Black people and white people alike.[62] As white men's sexual relations with and sexual abuses of enslaved women were systematic, these features were not an aberration but a fixture throughout the geographic North and South. Free communities of color were largely made up of people of mixed race, and mixed-race enslaved people were tangible markers of the South's rape culture.

White women learned to be suspicious in the face of enslaved women who embodied these traits, even questioning their husbands' intentions for purchasing or interacting with such women. Enslaved people testified to their inclination to give off "antagonistic feeling" in the face of "beautiful" women and children.[63] When Jack Maddox's owner, Judge Maddox, brought home a new woman he had recently purchased, who was described as a "pretty mulatto gal," his wife was instantly displeased. After taking one look at the woman's light skin and "long black straight hair," she asked, "What did you bring that thing here for?" with obvious discontentment. Judge Maddox explained that he had purchased the woman to serve as her seamstress and do her fine needlework. According to Jack, Mrs. Maddox quickly dismissed this explanation and outwardly showed doubt about the sincerity of his stated intentions. The moment Judge Maddox left the home and Mrs. Maddox could secure some time alone with their new female slave, she picked up a pair of scissors, grabbed the woman by the hair, and cut her hair at the roots. Knowing that this woman's hair was likely one of the reasons her husband had made this particular purchase, she wanted to rob this woman of her sexual appeal with each snip of her scissors.[64]

Rebecca Hooks was the grandchild of her owner William Lowe and inherited his large brown eyes and long dark hair, just as his white family members had. Disturbed by the likeness, Lowe's wife insisted that her hair always be cut very short. According to Hooks, she finally rebelled against having her hair cut, a move that only intensified her mistress's dislike. Pierce Cody recalled that on the plantation where he lived, when a child was born with "a beautiful suit of hair," it was mandated that their hair be "cropped very short," even if they were born to two enslaved parents.[65]

Enslaved people also found that jealousy and contempt went hand in hand. Harriet Jacobs witnessed a fellow enslaved woman suffer great pain due to complications after childbirth. Her pain was compounded by the contempt her mistress displayed toward her after she gave birth to a child who was "nearly white." The mistress, clearly convinced that her husband had fathered the child, showed no sympathy for the woman. According to Jacobs, she looked at her like an "incarnate fiend." In a mocking tone, she said, "You suffer, do you? . . . I am glad of it. You deserve it all, and more too," reported Jacobs. Her contempt settled on the newborn child as well. When the baby died shortly after birth, the mistress exclaimed that there was no heavenly reward "for the likes of her and her bastard."[66]

According to Harriet Jacobs, white women devoted just as much energy to self-pity. Ella Gertrude Clanton Thomas flirted with the idea of going public to draw attention to the Southern white woman's plight, which she defined as their contention with inherently seductive Black women. According to Thomas, these women easily captured the attention of weak men and thus diminished white women's sexual appeal as well as their standing in good Southern society. In January 1865, she drafted an open letter to the wife of William Tecumseh Sherman, a lead general in the Union army during the Civil War. Although she considered publishing the letter, she settled for inscribing her thoughts on the pages of her diary instead. The letter informed Ellen Sherman of her husband's own alleged dealings with "coloured" women and stated that she and the security of her household were not safe from the influence of Black women, something that had plagued Southern white women for generations. "Enquire of Gen Sherman when next you see him who has been elevated to fill your place . . . Did he tell you of the Mulatto girl for whose safety he was so much concerned that she was returned to Nashville when he commenced his vandal march?" wrote Thomas. She stated to Ellen that this "mulatto" woman was not simply sharing in her husband's attention but could eventually replace her altogether. She conveyed that other "negroes" already referred to the woman as "Sherman's wife." Thomas warned that while Northern women like Ellen hoped for the "elevation of the negroes," they should be concerned that their "husbands are amongst a coloured race whose reputation for morality has never been of the highest order." Thomas only implicated Black women for causing these interracial liaisons, not acknowledging the position of authority that white men, Northern or Southern, held over Black women, free or enslaved, before and during the Civil War. Rather, she welcomed her Northern "sisters" to share in Southern white women's concerns regarding the Black woman. In closing she said, "I will only add that intensely, Southern woman as I am, I *pity you*."[67]

WHEN REFLECTING ON THE PRESENCE of the "white children of slavery," Ella Gertrude Clanton Thomas argued that female slave owners had this "inborn earnestness" to teach enslaved women to circumvent sexual relations with white men—or, in the words of Thomas, to "do right." Yet she found this impulse to be quite problematic. She asked why her contemporaries were so eager to combat interracial sex through the discipline of their slaves, when the abolition of slavery would eliminate these concerns altogether. She wondered why they did not devote their energy to that cause. "Southern women are I believe all at heart abolitionists but there I expect I have made a very broad assertion," said Thomas. Surely Thomas was not alone in thinking that the abolition of slavery would solve a multitude of life's problems, including the sorrows of having to deal with the "white children of slavery." Thomas argued that "the institution of slavery," coupled with white men's immoral sexual behavior, "degrades the white man more than the Negro and oh exerts a most deleterious effect upon our children."[68]

Although few and far between, there were in fact women who were compelled to tackle white men's illicit interracial relations from the top down, setting their sights on the white male perpetrators. The slave-owning woman's boldest retort was to file for divorce or separation to seek redress for white men's sexual intercourse with enslaved women. The South's rape culture was largely able to thrive, however, through the subjugation and silencing of enslaved people, slave-owning women, and even the better part of Southern society. Although white Southerners may have disapproved of interracial sexual relations in general and illicit intercourse with slaves specifically, most were ultimately coaxed into cultural reconciliation.

For slave-owning women, the tenets of patriarchy placed limits on their ability to curtail white men's sexual behavior. And at times they curbed their own reactions to interracial sex between slave-owning men and enslaved women, opting to turn a blind eye, suppress their feelings, or express their discontent through gossip and the written word. When it came to the enslaved, however, slave-owning women did in fact garner a lot of power. Their authority as slaveholders provided them amble space to lash out, negotiate sales, and inflict violence on enslaved women. This authority served as a tool for expressing the emotional turmoil they experienced—be it jealousy or anger—as a result of white men's sexual relations with enslaved women. Some sought revenge in secret, while others conducted public displays of violence to serve as a warning to other enslaved women. And their positions as household managers permitted them to inflict these punishments, all under the guise of legitimate plantation management.

Slave-owning women's varying responses to white men's sexual relations with female slaves illustrates that these women had a complex role to fill that included occupying the spaces between finer womanhood and mastery and between gentility and cruelty—paradoxes created by the very system of enslavement from which they benefited. The enslavement of human beings by its very definition is cruel and unjust, and it is no wonder that slave-owning women adopted gruesome strategies to subjugate and punish the enslaved for what they found offensive. Slavery was a brutal system, and the South's rape culture brought out the worst in slave-owning women and men.

CHAPTER SIX

Petitions from Jealous and Discontented Wives

In October 1814, Ellen Shields Dunlap wrote to the Virginia House of Delegates asking for a divorce from her husband, Robert, after just two years of marriage. She must have had confidence in her complaints to request that the legislative body pass a private act granting her a divorce, something it did infrequently and with great hesitancy although it received many such requests.[1] In her petition, she explained that although she had just given birth to her first child, a daughter, she had no choice but to leave her husband because he had become "criminally, unlawfully, and carnally intimate" with an enslaved woman named Milly. She further attested that Robert's sexual activity with Milly "eventuated in a total neglect and despret [sic] treatment to your petitioner." Bold in her delivery, Ellen explicitly stated how disgusted she was with her husband for having sexual intercourse with an enslaved woman. She peppered her petition with words like "criminal," "diabolical," and "carnal," even describing his actions as "unpardonable" and "not only against the law of God and man, but against the sound dictates of a good conshious [sic]."[2]

While Ellen appeared unafraid to display her anger and disgust, she could not afford to lose sight of her audience. In 1814, Virginia's House of Delegates was composed entirely of white men, most of whom were slave owners like her husband. Colonels Andrew Anderson and Robert Doak were the elected delegates from Augusta County, where Ellen and Robert resided. According to the 1810 US Census, Anderson and Doak—veterans of the Revolutionary War and retired military officers—owned ten and eight enslaved people, respectively. Among the men of the house of delegates were undoubtedly some who raped, coerced, and forced enslaved women to sexually reproduce new generations of bonded people.[3] However, a consistent feature of the South's rape culture was that while political, community, and religious leaders—like Anderson and Doake—denounced interracial sex, they understood white men having sex with the enslaved to be among the powers and privileges of mastery.[4] Many of these legislators would have considered it Robert's prerogative to have sex with Milly and respected his right to do so without scrutiny. Legislative bodies and courts across the South were disinclined to dissolve marriages on these grounds alone, as to do so would have weakened white men's patriarchal authority within the plantation household, the foundation on which the South's slave societies had been built.[5]

Ellen's strategy for capturing the attention of Virginia's delegates and eliciting their sympathy was to hone in on how indiscreet her husband had been about having sex with an enslaved woman. She said, "The crime with which the said Robert Dunlap stands charged are peculially [sic] and dubley [sic] aggravated when we reflect on the public and daring manner in which he perpetrated his diabolical design."[6] For Ellen, he compromised his honor and respectability, as well as hers, when he made a spectacle of having sex with Milly. Honor and respectability were the pillars on which Southern men cultivated their reputations and status and asserted their authority within the public and private spheres. If Ellen could turn their attention to her husband's lack of discretion and the brazen way in which he flaunted his relations with Milly in front of Ellen's family and others outside their household, she might convince them that his actions were "unpardonable."

To corroborate Ellen's charges, several witnesses—including members of her extended family—testified to Robert's propensity to speak openly and shamelessly about his sexual liaison with Milly. The witnesses drew particular attention to the fact that Robert made these outward declarations in Ellen's presence. They considered this especially disrespectful and felt it added to Ellen's humiliation. In an accompanying affidavit, Ellen's brothers, James and Thomas Shields, said that they "both heard him the said Robert Dunlap say in the presents [sic] of his wife Ellen and several others who were present that he had carnal knowledge with a negroe [sic] woman named Milly whom he got by intermarrying with the said Ellen." They reported that Ellen was compelled to leave her and Robert's household due to his ill treatment of her and his public "acknowledgement to the illicit knowledge and criminal intimacy with the said negroe [sic] Milly." Other family members testified that they had also heard Robert's confession "in the presents [sic] of his lawful wife Ellen" and that he "had repeatedly [had] carnal knowledge of her the said negroe [sic] woman [Milly]." They also testified that Robert had taken Milly "in his own wife's bed and there carryed [sic] his licenshious [sic] designs into operation." Although they gave no report on Milly's emotional state, they made sure to note that she subsequently "delivered of a mulatto child."[7]

Ellen's claim that Robert did not even attempt to keep his sexual intercourse with Milly a secret was supported by the testimony that accompanied her petition. He did not even insist that it remain an unspoken truth between husband and wife. Many couples during the antebellum period kept such secrets to appear respectable and maintain well-ordered households. In Ellen's case, not only did her husband have sex with Milly in her bed, but he made public declarations about it, allowing others to witness her humiliation. In asking the Virginia legislators to reflect on how public and daring Robert was, Ellen hoped this body of men would at least concede that her husband had forsaken an unspoken agreement among white Southern gentlemen and, by extension, white Southern ladies. Like other slave-owning women, Ellen was expected to look the other way and resign herself to white men's indulgences, but this was contingent on Robert upholding his end of the bargain through discretion. She contended that by making his sexual relations with Milly a topic of public discussion, he placed irreparable shame on her. After his public and daring behavior was denounced, the very next request was "that your honorable body . . . take her case into consideration and pass a law granting your petitioner a bill of divorcement and thereby rendering null and void the said marriage contract."[8]

Ellen's appeal to the Virginia House of Delegates illustrates that the South's rape culture permeated many facets of Southern life, including the marital relations of white people. Even in a society where rape of the enslaved was commonplace, coercion was normalized, and the presence of enslaved people of mixed race made a mockery of Southern "honor" and "respectability," it was still possible to go beyond the pale. Divorce petitions like that of Ellen Shields Dunlap reveal the thin line between tolerable and intolerable. Yet how white women articulated these distinctions mattered. For example, Ellen could publicly accuse her husband of engaging in sexual relations with an enslaved woman and even label it "criminal intimacy," but she could not build her case on that alone. Her argument could not merely be that interracial sex was wrong or that her husband engaging in sex with an enslaved woman made her feel betrayed, hurt, or even jealous. And she certainly could not speak to the greatest tragedy of all—that enslaved women and enslaved communities suffered grave physical harm and psychological distress due not only to instances of rape and sexual coercion but also to the ever-present threat of sexual violence and exploitation. White men having sex with enslaved women, especially ones they owned, and inflicting physical or psychological wounds on the enslaved were neither intolerable nor illegal; these were rights of slave ownership over which most legislators and jurors would not dissolve a marriage.

Divorce petitions show that white women's public complaints against interracial sex were most potent when they illustrated that "illicit intercourse" threatened white supremacy and patriarchal authority, which undergirded the South's slave societies and empowered both white men and white women in and out of the plantation household. Ellen Dunlap clearly had no patience for her husband's sexual relationship with Milly. But by emphasizing how her husband's behaviors threatened the respectability and social standing of her household, she revealed what she believed an all-white male delegation and, by extension, Southern society would find unpardonable behavior that could weaken rather than strengthen the position of the slaveholding South. For Southern white women, stoking such fears was a worthwhile strategy for escaping abusive husbands, protecting their economic interests, and avenging perceived wrongs.

Through their legal arguments, white women also illustrated what they understood their positionality and power to be within the South's rape culture. They could assert that there should be some bounds to which men confined their sexual behavior. However, it was to their detriment to suggest dismantling the South's rape culture and the power that white men derived from it. Whether consciously or unconsciously, white women were complicit in upholding the South's rape culture every time they turned a blind eye to enslaved women's sexual exploitation or appeared unmoved by tales of their male family members' interracial liaisons. After all, they, too, were financial and social beneficiaries of the systematic rape and sexual reproductive exploitation of enslaved women. Their petitions were rarely motivated by enslaved women's trauma. Rather, they were most inclined to raise concerns about white men's interracial relations when their own social standing and financial security were threatened.

ELITE SOUTHERN WHITE WOMEN like Mary Boykin Chesnut and Ella Gertrude Clanton Thomas, who were cultural and moral arbiters of their time, harshly critiqued the South's rape culture. They expressed a particular vitriol for white men who shamed their wives by engaging in long-term liaisons with enslaved woman and fathering enslaved children, especially when done inside or near the plantation household. Yet in neither their published nor their unpublished commentaries did they declare divorce as the answer to the problem of white men's "illicit intercourse" with enslaved women. What, then, would compel a Southern woman to go beyond the boundaries of the plantation to expose that such sexual transgressions were taking place in her household? Better still, what picture would she have to paint to dissolve the bonds of matrimony and the patriarchal power inherently embedded in the institution of marriage?[9]

At the dawn of the nineteenth century, obtaining a divorce in the Southern states was not simply uncommon or undesirable; the process for getting divorced was still not fully defined and appeared in different stages of development from state to state. In part, state legislatures were slow to develop the legal infrastructure needed for couples who wished to sever ties because most white Southerners continued to cling to traditional Anglican attitudes regarding the sanctity of marriage, which called for the resolution of marital conflict. When delegates met for the first state constitutional conventions across the South, none put forth any statutory measures addressing divorce. Consequently, individuals seeking divorce had to petition their state legislatures to pass private acts granting them either a divorce *a vinculo matrimonii*—an absolute divorce—or a divorce *a mensa et thoro*—a legal separation without permission to remarry. Absolute divorce was typically reserved for extreme circumstances, such as insanity, impotence, bigamy, and consanguinity. People seeking divorce on grounds of adultery, cruelty, or desertion could expect a legal separation at best. In Virginia, most people who appealed to the general assembly for divorce were told to remain married for the "common good of society." Privileging marriage over individual happiness, legislators believed that divorce not only threatened Christian values but endangered the health of Southern slave-owning society, which they argued was built on and sustained by white patriarchal authority and the cohesion of the plantation household.[10]

As Southern legislatures became more and more overwhelmed with divorce petitions in the first few decades of the nineteenth century, they began to extend power to chancery, district, and superior courts to adjudicate divorce petitions. This shift was to the detriment of the South's nonelite. According to historian Jane Turner Censer, the South's judicial system was more responsive to elite white women. They could afford legal counsel to represent them before the court, and they symbolized virtues of domesticity and submissiveness that elite white male jurists valued. However, legislative divorce, which entailed writing a petition to the respective legislative body to ask that a private act be passed to grant the divorce, offered a "cheaper and more egalitarian venue" for the Southern majority, who were not part of the elite slave-owning class. By 1850, most state legislatures made constitutional provisions to bring legislative divorce to an end, relinquishing complete responsibility to the judicial system. South Carolina, from its founding, never conceded to demands for divorce law and refused to issue divorces of any kind until after the Civil War, when it passed its first divorce law in 1872. The state did grant married women the right to petition for alimony on grounds like abandonment and extreme cruelty. Although divorce was prohibited, this did not deter marital problems. While other state legislatures waded through divorce petitions, South Carolina's general assembly had to grapple with its fair share of alimony petitions.[11]

Southern white women seeking divorce had many challenges to face. Historian Stephanie McCurry argues that nowhere was the South's commitment to "the subordination of women so plainly articulated as in the matter of marriage and divorce." Based on a representative sampling of divorce petitions across urban and rural spaces in all Southern states during the antebellum period, most white women who filed for divorce were from the slave-owning class.[12] These women had the financial means to retain lawyers and pursue divorce suits when their marriages were beyond repair. In contrast, the South's poor were more apt to practice "self-divorce." Unable to afford legal counsel or perhaps distrustful of the legal system, husbands and wives forwent filing divorce petitions and went their separate ways, sometimes remarrying other people. However, no woman—wealthy or poor—would have initiated a divorce frivolously during the antebellum period. Slave-owning women risked great social and financial loss if their marriages fell apart. To secure a successful judgment, complainants had the burden of not only proving their spouses' guilt but demonstrating their own innocence and devotion. According to historian Loren Schweninger, divorce was, indeed, an adversarial process. The law required that petitions "be supported by persuasive arguments of domestic turmoil and proven by verifiable charges of violation of the marital bond, a process that entailed a thorough and unsparing look into the domestic lives of those suing for divorce." For many, however, opening their lives to public scrutiny would have been a lesser concern than the potential financial impact.[13]

Most women of the slave-owning class who brought enslaved people, property, and other assets into their marriages did so knowing that, per laws of coverture, legal ownership of their property transferred to their husbands. These laws also prohibited married women from working outside the household, operating businesses, or signing contracts. Once married, even women born into significant means were dependent on their marital ties to their husbands to reap the economic benefits of what they brought to their marriages. When requesting that their marital ties be severed, women asked for a variety of financial protections, including alimony, legal ownership of enslaved individuals, and proceeds from the sale of land, chattel, and slaves. Slave-owning women who were born into elite families that owned twenty or more enslaved people might have had the option to return to their childhood homes and reclaim the financial and social protection of their fathers' guardianship. Those outside the elite class had much invested in their petitions to gain spousal support and control of assets they brought to the marriage or that were acquired during the marriage. Aside from money, their children were the most significant things women risked losing when they filed for divorce. Under coverture, fathers' custody rights to children superseded those of mothers. Unless a mother could prove that the father was incapacitated or severely mentally impaired or had abandoned the family, she ran a high risk of losing her children in pursuit of a divorce. With so much at stake, Southern women had little room for error when crafting their divorce petitions.[14]

For Southern white men, accusing their wives of committing adultery with Black men proved to be a winning formula. The aforementioned sampling of divorce petitions shows that most men filed for divorce on grounds of adultery. Of that group, 75 percent charged their wives with having sex with Black men. In Virginia, the general assembly sided with most of these men, granting divorces to 70 percent of men who charged their wives with having interracial sex. Despite the frequency with which white men had sex with Black women, the South's rape culture dictated that the consequences for having sex across the color line were not universal. Black men having sex with white women threatened white men's position at the top of the social hierarchy. It not only called into question their ability to protect white women's "virtue," and thus white racial purity, but suggested that Black men were on par or even superior to white men when it came to fulfilling white women's sexual desires. Also, when a married white woman committed adultery with a Black man and gave birth to a child of mixed race, she provided her husband with just the kind of irrefutable evidence that legislators and jurists desired in divorce cases. It is worth noting that most of these white men who charged their wives with having interracial sex were not of the slave-owning class. It is impossible to say whether slave-owning women were less likely to engage in sexual relations with Black men than were non-slave-owning women. But it is true that slave-owning men and women had many incentives, both financial and social, to maintain their marriages, even in the face of adultery.[15]

In contrast, Southern white women were far less likely to cite adultery as their primary reason for divorce. Less than 40 percent of white women cited adultery in their divorce petitions, and the charge was usually accompanied by others, such as cruelty, neglect, or abandonment. Of that 40 percent, only 50 percent accused their husbands of interracial adultery, which was significantly less than their male counterparts. The majority were from the slave-owning class, and they characterized their husbands' interracial sexual relations in the bleakest of terms. Historian Thomas Buckley argues that due to the South's "double standard" for men's and women's sexual behavior, "run-of-the-mill male infidelity, even across the color line," did not merit divorce. He contends that women typically had to couple interracial sex with other charges, because legislators and judges were "more moved" by descriptions of cruelty and physical abuse than by interracial sex with enslaved women.[16]

It is true that white male leaders were less interested in their brethren's sexual misdeeds, especially those involving enslaved women. However, placing this—along with white men's sexual behavior and white women's responses to it—within the framework of the South's rape culture adds more nuance to our understanding of the relationship between sex and power in the antebellum South. White male leaders stood to lose credibility and thus power and influence by judging too harshly how other white men exercised their "right" to sexually exploit the enslaved. Southern white women, as well as their legal counsel, were not ignorant to this fact. This chapter sheds light on how white women seeking divorce strategically placated to their all-male audiences, who they knew would not be invested in toppling the very rape culture that afforded them power over both white and Black women.

I contend that Southern white women, especially of the slave-owning class, consciously and out of necessity told grisly tales of physical abuse and abandonment, perhaps even false ones, to accompany their charges of adultery. They understood the importance of framing these accusations in a way that legislators, judges, and juries could not afford to ignore. When they chose to invoke interracial sex in their divorce and alimony petitions, they did not simply charge their husbands with adultery across the color line but asserted that their husbands' sexual relations with enslaved women subverted white women's social status and authority within the plantation household. They further contended that these threats to their authority and the stability of their households were a threat to white men's power and authority by extension. They knew that white men also viewed the plantation household as essential to maintaining the South's slave economy and that it served as the centerpiece of Southern respectability politics. In essence, any subversion of white power was a threat to white supremacy as a whole. In petitioning to be freed from men who threatened the Southern values of honor, virtue, and domesticity, they also appealed for financial support, sometimes even requesting that they legally regain control of the enslaved and other physical assets that they brought to the marriage. If they could not have the ideal plantation household, they at least wanted to restore and protect their and their children's economic and social standing.

In these petitions, Southern white women made charges of white men having sex with enslaved women that were surely some combination of truth, lies, and gross exaggerations. What emerges is a set of tropes that can be seen repeatedly in the archival record across the antebellum South. Accompanying almost every one of these tropes were lamentations over the sinfulness and criminality of their husbands' actions and the shame, humiliation, and dishonor that befell their households as a result. The four prominent tropes that I will discuss in this chapter are *lack of discretion*, *withdrawal of affection*, *neglect of duty*, and *acting like a wife*. First, petitioners frequently accused husbands of demonstrating a lack of discretion when engaging in sex with enslaved women. For wives, this represented their husbands' lack of character as well as their failure not to bring shame on their wives and families. Second, wives hurled complaints of how their husbands deteriorated their marital bonds by withdrawing affection, showing preference for enslaved women, and having sex with enslaved women in their homes and even their marital beds. Next, women emphasized how their husbands neglected their patriarchal responsibilities to their legitimate families by providing support for enslaved women and their enslaved progeny. In the most extreme cases, husbands reportedly abandoned their households altogether, sometimes to live with an enslaved woman, leaving their wives to struggle financially to care for their children and households. Last, women accused husbands of treating enslaved women as wives or allowing enslaved women to "act" like white women. Petitioners were especially keen to report when their husbands' sexual servants asserted authority over household matters, displayed impertinence over obedience, or inflicted physical harm on them or their children, essentially claiming the privileges of whiteness and the authority of slave ownership that these white women claimed for themselves.

It was not uncommon for petitioners to use more than one of these tropes to craft a compelling petition narrative. Their petitions illustrate in detail how one behavior could serve as a gateway to others. For example, a husband charged with withdrawing his affection from his wife, preferring to direct his attention toward an enslaved woman, might have also been accused of shaming his family by failing to be discreet and then bringing the enslaved woman into the household and treating her like a wife. Due to this overlap, certain women's names will appear in more than one section of the chapter.

Just as these women knew what strategies would prove effective in court, they also understood that they were treading on delicate ground. When invoking these tropes, women were careful not to call for an outright public denouncement of interracial sex. Unsurprisingly absent from almost all these petitions was any acknowledgment of remorse for the rape and sexual coercion of enslaved women. Rather, white Southern women underscored their own sufferings and their dutifulness in trying to keep their marriages and households intact. Their true leverage lay in revealing the consequences that could emerge for the white slave-owning class when white men veered too far outside the boundaries within which the South's rape culture permitted them to play. They hoped to pique interest, stoke fear, and garner sympathy from the legislative and court-appointed officers who held the power to grant them a divorce and secure their financial support.

Lack of Discretion

When Ellen Dunlap humbly begged the Virginia House of Delegates in her divorce petition to "reflect on the public and daring manner in which he [Robert Dunlap] perpetrated his diabolical design," she was daring them to uphold the very cultural prescriptions regarding interracial sex that they helped reinforce. As described by historian Bertram Wyatt-Brown, interracial sex between white men and Black women, free or enslaved, did not generate an ethical dilemma for Southern communities as long as men followed the rules. They were to be discreet and not let their interracial relations make them "derelict about civic duty or work." The South's rape culture thrived due to the ubiquitous understanding of these cultural prescriptions. Some women were spurred to go before courts and legislative bodies when their husbands did not take heed and made their interracial indiscretions public.[17]

Like Ellen Dunlap, these women staked their arguments not on their revulsion for their husbands' actions but rather on their husbands' failure to stay within society's boundaries regarding discretion. They understood that therein lay their best chance to gain favor. Petitions showcase the array of colorful descriptions these women used to describe their husbands' imprudence. The common thread was that their husbands' actions were "open" and "undisguised," whether they took place within the family home or in separate accommodations. Sarah Smith in Talladega, Alabama, said her husband was "living utterly estranged from Oratrix in undisguised acts of adultery" with an enslaved woman. Eliza Prince described her husband as living in "open and unconcealed profligacy." Alzonuth Whitehead of Natchez, Mississippi, and Caroline Dungan of Port Gibson, Mississippi (just northeast of Natchez), used practically identical language, emphasizing the "open" and "notorious" ways their husbands conducted their interracial affairs.[18]

For Lucy Burwell, a proper husband would have, at least, been discreet about having sex with an enslaved woman, especially in front of the children. She told the Circuit Court of Mecklenburg County, Virginia, that when she and John Burwell first got married, he was kind and affectionate. When he began abusing alcohol, though, he developed a quick temper that was impulsive and violent, and he became "unkind and tyrannical in the management of his children." Her mission, however, was to convey that these abuses paled in comparison to how indecently he carried on his sexual liaison with an enslaved woman, Lucretia. His violence toward their children was not "by any means the greatest evil resulting from this sad change in her husband's habits and disposition." According to Lucy, "So unrestrained has he become in the indulgence of this illicit and adulterous intercourse" that the presence of his wife and children had become "insufficient to control him." She was horrified on the day when John announced in front of their sons and daughters his intentions not to sleep in their bedroom but to spend the night in a different room, where he ordered Lucretia to attend to him for the night.[19]

In his written response to Lucy's charges, John admitted that "some unpleasant occurrences" had taken place between him and his wife. Knowing the court could harshly judge his wife's account of his relations with Lucretia, he unequivocally denounced her recollection of events. According to John, on the night in question he was suffering from a terrible headache. He had asked his wife to press her hand on his forehead to provide relief, as she had done many times before, but she refused. He was "mortified at such refusal" and told his wife that if she would not do it he would make a servant do it instead. He then said that he did not occupy a private room with the house servant Lucretia but took rest in a passage that had folding doors, "being the last place about the house that would have been selected for the purpose charged." John Burwell did not deny ever having sexual relations with Lucretia, but he rejected any accusation that he would have perpetrated the scene his wife described in front of his children.[20]

Both Lucy and John demonstrated before the court their understanding that discretion was sacrosanct. Lucy testified that in the previous years, Lucretia had given birth to two children, "the offspring of a white father." She said she had every reason to believe they were her husband's children. Yet she chose not to characterize his years of engaging in sexual relations with Lucretia and fathering enslaved children as his "greatest evil." It was the humiliation, his "disreputable intimacy," and his failure to shield their children from her humiliation that she found unforgivable. While Lucy honed in on his lack of discretion within their household, John was reportedly preoccupied—even before his wife petitioned the court—by how his wife's accusations could damage his reputation if they spread beyond the walls of their home. When deposed, Charles G. Feild, a family friend, testified that John had begged Lucy "not to give their difficulties publicity," especially because it could "fix a stigma upon the character of his children." According to Feild, John asked for Lucy's forgiveness. He even promised to sell Lucretia, but Lucy would not consent to her sale.[21]

Although Lucy's strategy in her divorce proceedings was to emphasize her husband's lack of discretion, deposition testimony reveals that her children were not naive about their father's sexual relationship with Lucretia. Lucy and John's twenty-two-year-old son, Thomas, who was residing in Norfolk, Virginia, at the time of the divorce proceedings, testified that "there was a negro woman in the house named Lucretia with whom I have reason to believe my father was intimate." He said that the previous summer he had even asked his father to "send off this servant girl Lucretia." His father responded by ordering him to leave his house. While two other sons, Armistead and J. E., testified to not knowing whether their father had been intimate with Lucretia, their fourth son, John, testified that his father slapped him when he reported that Lucretia had been "impertinent" to his mother. He also stated how attentive his father was to Lucretia when she was pregnant, visiting her almost daily. Based on this testimony, the degree to which John practiced discretion is debatable. Two of the couple's sons validated their mother's charges. The other two might not have had any knowledge of a sexual relationship between their father and Lucretia, or they could have been employing discretion to compensate for their father's failure to do so. The Burwell family was at odds, but they nevertheless understood the relationship between discretion and respectability.[22]

Mary Garrett of North Carolina told the Guilford County Court of Equity that in addition to being neglectful and harsh, her husband Edward had begun a sexual relationship with an enslaved woman. At the time, her life was especially "intolerable" and "burthensome" because they lived in the same house with her mother in Greensboro. Her complaint was that "his conduct & intimate connection with said slave was so open and undisguised." At the behest of their friends and family and having received Edward's promise to reform, she returned to her mother's house for the sake of their child. Edward, ostensibly in an act of good faith, left home with the unnamed enslaved woman to sell her. Mary was shocked when her husband returned with "another female slave, adorned in fine dress and jewelry." Mary saw the woman's attire as a signal that Edward planned to have sex with her as well. In her petition, Mary suggested that her husband never intended to stop having sexual relations with enslaved women and sold the first woman for the sake of appearances. According to Mary, he abused her and hurled accusations, "alleging that she had accused him publicly—that she had disgraced him," when she would not aid him in his scheme. Like Lucy Burwell, Mary Garrett requested a divorce in part because of her husband's lack of discretion. And like John Burwell, Edward Garrett was less concerned with his actual behavior and more concerned about his wife drawing the public's attention and tarnishing his reputation.[23]

Some wives told tales of husbands who cared nothing of their public persona, reporting that their husbands declared it their patriarchal prerogative to have sex with enslaved women in whatever fashion they desired. These wives made certain to capture their husbands' bold neglect or outright rejection of discretion in their petitions, illustrating that the men had betrayed both spoken and unspoken agreements with their wives and society writ large. When Evelina Roane married Newman Roane on March 6, 1823, on her father's Elsing Green estate in King William County, Virginia, she had no idea the extent to which her husband spurned the idea that he should hide his sexual liaison with the enslaved woman Biney or his adoration for the two children they shared. He did not care about what anyone thought of it, least of all his wife. Evelina would build her case for divorce on his flagrant disregard for propriety and discretion. Newman's sexual liaison with Biney predated the marriage, and when he brought Biney and their two children to live in the house he shared with his wife, he quickly established their position of importance and priority, most notably through violence. In her petition to the Virginia General Assembly, Evelina described her situation with her husband as perilous. He enjoyed torturing her for his sake and theirs. Newman's "practice of tutoring his mulatto child . . . to abuse her was very early commenced & regularly continued." If she dared to rebuke him, he would "instantly kindle into wrath & threaten her life or that he would give her the severest punishment if she struck the child." Evelina pleaded that if her happiness and safety were dependent on her husband's character, then she had "no security" whatsoever. He was not deterred by threats or looks of shame from her father and brothers or their friends and the greater community. According to Evelina, "He would often say to your petitioner that he did not care for consequences & that he felt no repugnance to the character of a man of violence and that the fear of consequences could not restrain him from the acts of assassin if prompted by his passions."[24]

Regardless of whether their husbands cared about their reputations, most wives were intent on keeping their own reputations intact. Their petitions served as vehicles for retaining or restoring respectability. In Bertie County, North Carolina, Mary Hassell told the state's general assembly that her husband Benjamin had "lost sight" of "every principle of honor & respect" by making a "wife & companion" of an enslaved woman. His conduct was so "dishonorable & disreputable" that she was convinced she was now "looked upon as disgraceful, and discountenanced by every upright & virtuous member of civil society." She felt he had also been "stigmatized by every honest member of the community." Not wanting to suffer the same fate for behavior in which she did not engage, she wished to "relieve herself from the odious embrace of a man so entirely destitute of all the finer feelings of sensibility."[25]

Although faced with similar fears, Sarah Strickland vowed before the North Carolina Superior Court of Wake County that despite her husband's tawdry list of offenses, "her own reputation for chastity and indignity as well before marriage as since stands among all her acquaintances unimpeached & unimpeachable." She boldly told the court that she was still a young, healthy, and industrious woman who, if granted an absolute divorce from her husband, Nathan, could still be a dutiful and affectionate wife to a worthy respectable Southern gentleman. She explained that it was not until her wedding night that she discovered that she and her husband were unequally yoked. He told her "he was afflicted with a certain venereal disease which he intended to give her" and that he and another man had struck a bargain "to exchange wives every alternate night" and thus she would "be compelled to sleep with this stranger every other night." Nathan's questionable habits also included having "criminal intercourse with one of Mr. Ellington's negro women." These were among the most notable reasons why she needed to end her alliance with "a profligate & worthless husband." Court records do not indicate whether Sarah was granted an absolute divorce or even a legal separation. Even if unsuccessful, divorce petitions afforded women like Sarah the opportunity to publicly display their faithfulness to society's rules, even if their husbands refused to stay within the limits.[26]

Withdrawal of Affection

When Emily Manning crafted her divorce petition for the Honorable Joseph W. Lessene, she labeled her husband Moses's indiscretion as well as several other behaviors as degrading and "so regardless of the laws of society." Not only was her husband disgraceful and indiscreet, but he forced her to watch as he "exhibited openly his fondness and partiality" for an enslaved woman, Epsey. Southern white women knew that white men might have sex with enslaved women, but they were not supposed to prefer Black women. Southern white women understood themselves to be culturally and morally superior to free and enslaved Black women. White men prioritizing the needs and wants of enslaved women over their own not only was demoralizing but contradicted and threatened the social hierarchy of the slave society. Emily described how brazenly Moses carried on with Epsey despite her objections, even threatening her with violence if she got in his way. She claimed to be distraught to learn that her feelings and expectations for what their marriage should look like did not matter. Regardless of whether Moses withdrew affection, Emily understood that her husband was not supposed to willfully alienate her and strain their relationship by having sexual relations across the color line. By pointing out another way in which he violated society's laws, she hoped to gain the court's favor.[27]

To further appease judges, legislators, and juries, women like Emily Manning emphasized how they could have satisfied societal expectations and overlooked their husbands' sexual relations with enslaved women if they had not brought these women into their homes, paraded them in front of their faces, and withdrawn their affection, both physical and emotional, in the process. Emily told the court that at the beginning of her marriage, she silently endured Moses leaving their marital bed in the middle of the night to walk to Epsey's cabin in their yard, where he would stay in her bed "till near day, when he would return to his own bed." After about three months, Moses left their bed completely to sleep in a separate bedroom, where "he might with less restraint carry on his criminal intercourse" with Epsey in their house. She was careful to articulate that despite her husband indiscriminately having "adulterous intercourse" with Epsey in their home, she continued to remain committed to them having a marriage that included intimacy and passion. Proclaiming that her devotion had not been enough to save her marriage, Emily told the court that she eventually had no choice but to leave her home and seek refuge in her father's house because "all hope had vanished of ever enjoying the affections of her husband." Moses had been explicit in favoring Epsey over her. In fact, she decried that he "had made the theatre of low and degrading debauchery." She recounted how after she left their home, she learned that her husband's interracial relations extended beyond their household. He had also been engaged in a "liaison" with a free "mulatto" woman named Venus. Her charge to the court was that her husband destroyed their marriage and household because he preferred Black women, both enslaved and free, over a lasting intimate relationship with his wife.[28]

In her petition to the Virginia General Assembly, Evelina Roane said that she, too, had been forced to watch her husband play the doting lover to an enslaved woman in her own home. Before Evelina married Newman Roane, her family had heard rumors that Evelina's husband-to-be had long engaged in a sexual liaison with an enslaved woman named Biney. While Evelina and others dismissed the rumors, her brother Fendall Gregory confronted Newman directly. In his affidavit for the general assembly, Fendall said that upon learning that the enslaved woman Biney lived in Newman's household, he made Newman promise to "dispose" of Biney to put an end to the rumors and so that his sister would not be subjected to her presence once they were married. Newman agreed to oblige and even solicited help from Evelina's other brother, Thomas, asking him to help dispel the rumors regarding the bondwoman and clear his name. After eighteen months of marriage, Evelina filed for divorce, asserting that the rumors of her husband's sexual relationship with Biney were true and that he even confessed to fathering two children with Biney. She further learned that he had never sold Biney, as he had promised her brother, but had merely sent her and their children to live with his brother. She told the court that when she objected to Newman's plan to bring Biney and the children to live in their house, he said, "If he had not supposed her father would give her a fortune, he would never have married her; that he had two mulatto children then at his brother's who were much more comely and hansome [sic] than any she would ever have." He went on to say that despite her objections, "he would bring the mother and her children home, and not permit them to suffer any longer." Their happiness was paramount, and Newman welcomed them with much affection.[29]

In addition, women provided accounts of husbands having sex with enslaved women in their beds, sometimes forcing them to watch. By evoking the marital bed as a symbol of the sacredness of the marriage covenant and detailing the ways in which their husbands willingly violated that space, these women hoped to convey that their husbands caused irrevocable damage to their marriage ties. Bringing enslaved women into this sacred space was beyond the pale. In her petition, Sarah Ann Simpson of Fairfield, South Carolina, likened the experience of her husband having sex with an enslaved woman in her bed to being tainted by the stench of shame and disgust. She probably would have been angered had her husband committed adultery with any woman in her bed, but because it was an enslaved woman, her subordinate, it was a grave insult. She said she had been confronted "with the pollution of her bed, in a manner the most offensive to the feelings of the wife—the disgusting intercourse of her said husband with his own slave."[30]

Ruthey Ann Hansley reported that her husband also operated quite stealthily to bring an enslaved woman into their bed. In the beginning, Samuel Hansley began disappearing at bedtime. For weeks at a time, he would "absent himself from the petitioner during the whole night," she said. Ruthey later learned that he was spending this time having sex with an enslaved woman named Lucy. She said she tried to endure "as long as it was reasonable for any wife to endure the conduct of her husband." When Samuel eventually moved Lucy to their bedroom, this left no more room for reason. According to Ruthey, Samuel "would, at night, compel the petitioner to sleep in bed with said negro Lucy." She testified that because they occupied the same bed, she was forced to watch him have sex with Lucy, or, as she phrased it, watch him "treat the said Lucy as a wife." Next, she declared that "she was afraid to resist or to decline so occupying the same bed with her husband and the said negro woman."[31]

Lucy Norman illustrated for the court why white women had a difficult time protesting the presence of enslaved women in their beds. Although the marital bed was considered a sacred space that symbolized intimacy and familial ties, it still existed within the patriarchal paradigm of the plantation household. Slave-owning women wielded power as managers of enslaved people and household operations. However, men highly valued their role as head of the household. In that vein, when husbands' and wives' ideals regarding the sanctity of the marital bed did not align, women often found their preferences and objections ignored. Lucy said that when her husband, James, began living a life of "licentious immorality," he did not hesitate to bring an enslaved woman into "the chamber occupied by your petitioner." Her response was to remonstrate against this "earnestly & feelingly." James not only spurned her objections but told her that "if she did not like it she might look out for other quarters." He declared their bed to be his domain, and his will superseded the interests, comfort, and values of all involved. She could stay or go. Regardless, he intended to have his way.[32]

During Sopha Dobyns and Jonah Dobyns's divorce proceedings, Jonah was characterized as being quite proud of having had sexual relations with an enslaved woman in the bed he shared with his wife. When deposed, Stephen Terry, a neighbor, reported to the Virginia General Assembly that he was not surprised by Jonah's outlandish behavior. He and presumably others in their Bedford County community knew Jonah to be a man who "drank freely of spiritous liquors, became remarkable turbulent & arbitrary (which is his character in his family)," he said. On one occasion, he heard Jonah boast to Sopha that "he had taken one of his own negroe [*sic*] women into her bed." According to Terry, Jonah then told his wife that "he would do it again whenever it suited him," punctuating his indifference to the supposed sanctity of their marital bed. Sopha and her counsel had to be pleased with her neighbor's testimony. The legislators were left with an image of Sopha grappling with not only her husband engaging in sexual acts with their bondwoman in her bed but also the shame brought on by his lack of discretion. The general assembly rejected two-thirds of all divorce petitions. For Sopha, they drafted a bill for divorce.[33]

Neglect of Duty

One of the most potent strategies that white women used in divorce petitions was to show how their husbands neglected their duties as fathers, providers, and guardians of their households in order to engage in sexual relations with enslaved women. Some painted pictures of men abandoning their legitimate families altogether to provide for enslaved women and their enslaved progeny—compromising the South's principles of white supremacy and Southern honor—and neglecting their obligations to nurture the next generation of Southern patriarchs and dutiful wives and mothers. These women understood that society would excuse a Southern man for having sexual relations with enslaved women. However, at least in principle, a white man shirking his responsibility to provide for and protect his family in favor of an enslaved woman was unnatural and threatened the health of the South's slave societies. In essence, it made him less of a man.[34] In her divorce petition, Harriet Laspeyre decried that she and her children faced financial ruin because of her husband Bernard's relations with enslaved women. From the very beginning of their marriage, Harriet reported, her husband took all she had and used it for his own benefit. She brought what she described as a little amount of property to their union. Within weeks, she realized that her property, "trifling as it was, had been the primary object of his warmest affection." According to Harriet, her husband was dishonorable in every sense of the word. Not only was he in the habit of having sexual relations with enslaved women, but he violated "every law human or divine" by doing it in their house without reservation. Although Bernard proved to be selfish, squandering their money on himself, and thought little of parading enslaved women in front of her and her children, she still expected that she and her children would be supported financially. When she petitioned the North Carolina General Assembly for a divorce, she spoke of her husband's audacity to spend the money that was generated by *her* enslaved people's labor on his enslaved "mistresses" rather than his own family. These profits, "which ought to have been appropriated to the support and education of her children," she argued, were "wantonly lavished on his black and mulatto mistresses."[35]

Evelina Roane said that after her husband, Newman, moved Biney and their two children into the Roane household, he insulted her by saying not only that Biney's children were more handsome than any she would ever have but also that they would garner more love and privilege than her children would. According to Evelina, he explicitly said that "he meant upon principle, to do more for them, than for his lawful children." She had no reason to doubt his word. Even before she had children of her own, she witnessed her husband dote on the two enslaved children. She recalled how he showered the eldest child with "every act of familiar intercourse" and lovingly placed the child on his knee. All who testified in the case agreed that Newman's commitment was to Biney and their children above anyone else. John Gregory, Evelina's father, offered to purchase Biney and the children from Newman and "give him negroes in their place" for the sake of his daughter's happiness. Newman refused his offer, declaring, "The fidelity of the woman was essential to him and he felt for her & his children what was natural." Newman further threatened that if his feelings were not more respected, he would sell his estate, abandon his wife and child, and move to Ohio with Biney and their children.[36]

Some men walked away from their families to carry on sexual liaisons with enslaved women and never looked back. Eliza Prince of Charleston, South Carolina, had been married to John Prince for twenty-six years before she finally decided to file a petition for alimony in 1837. Eliza testified that four years prior, John had completely abandoned their family, which consisted of ten children. At the time, seven of the children, one in its infancy, were still dependent minors. According to Eliza, John left to finally live in "open and unconcealed profligacy with his slave and concubine," a woman named Jemmima Jones. In doing so, he left his family "dependent for support on their own exertions." John's sexual liaison with Jemmima had been going on for almost fourteen years, more than half of John and Eliza's twenty-six-year marriage. Eliza said that from the start of John's liaison with Jemmima, he began neglecting and ill-treating Eliza and their children. He deprived them of "the comfort of his company and assistance, bestowing most of his time and attention upon said negro woman." Eventually, he disregarded his obligations as a husband and a father altogether, "spending most of the means which should have been devoted to the support of his family" on the "maintenance of the said negro woman Jemmima."[37]

When John first initiated his liaison with Jemmima, he was not her owner, but he rectified this by purchasing her several years later. Eliza said she felt "mortification and distress" when Jemmima became a permanent fixture in and around her household. Nevertheless, Eliza claimed that she continued to endeavor by "all proper means in her power to secure the affections of her husband." It is impossible to know if she did so out of obligation or because she truly loved him. Regardless, Eliza continued to be sexually intimate with her husband, giving birth to at least four more children while her husband continued his liaison with Jemmima.[38]

Eliza said that she decided to stay with her husband to "preserve him from the evil and dishonourable courses into which he had fallen." It was one thing for her to scrutinize his character and declare him dishonorable. To have people in the city whispering about how he had abandoned her bed to have a sexual liaison with an enslaved woman was an entirely different matter. Eliza had many reasons for not wanting to be the subject of her peers' salacious gossip. Although she said she wanted to protect John from the consequences of his scandalous behavior, on a more practical level she knew what was at stake for her if she ceased to be John Prince's wife. She and her children were financially dependent on her husband under the laws of coverture. According to the 1830 census, Eliza and John already had five children together when John began having sex with Jemmima. Even if Eliza had wanted to separate from John at that time, it would have been a logistical quagmire. Because South Carolina did not grant legal divorces, the best Eliza could have hoped for was alimony to support her and her children. She was not guaranteed to regain ownership of any enslaved people or other property that she brought to the marriage, nor would she be permitted to remarry. Eliza decided to press on and lived as husband and wife with John Prince until he abandoned their family in 1833 and never came back.[39]

When Eliza petitioned the Charleston County Court of Chancery four years after her husband had left, she asked that he be ordered to pay alimony for "the maintenance of herself and her children." According to Eliza, John and Jemmima were living in "comparative ease and comfort" while she and her seven minor children were left "suffering the privations of poverty." John had purchased a house in the northern part of the city called Charleston Neck, where he and Jemmima could live in what Eliza called "open contempt of the laws of God and man." Although only a few miles separated John from his wife and children on Charleston's narrow peninsula, he had made a clear and very public statement on where his priorities lay. Eliza told the court that he occasionally sent her a small portion of his salary, which amounted to six to eight hundred dollars annually and was "altogether inadequate" to support their large family. Eliza singularly attributed the financial, emotional, social, and physical breakdown of her household and family to John turning his back on his family for Jemmima. Even if the judge ruling in her case did not care that John was engaged in an interracial liaison, Eliza hoped he would be troubled by John leaving his household without a proper guardian to establish a new household with an enslaved woman, creating a financial burden for his family, friends, and the greater Charleston district.[40]

Eliza and her children lived separately from John for four years before she filed a formal petition for alimony and familial support. Although she called his financial contributions up to that point inadequate, she and her children had not fallen into poverty during those four years. If their conditions had neared destitution, she likely would have petitioned for alimony years before. When she did decide to petition for alimony, she did not want an arbitrary sum of cash. She specifically requested to receive the appraised value of Jemmima and her two sons as well as any profits gleaned from their labor. She had been unable to stop her husband from prioritizing Jemmima over her family, but she could still exert control over Jemmima and benefit financially from her enslavement. In her original petition filed in June 1837, Eliza asked that the court prohibit her husband from departing the court's jurisdiction and "selling, disposing of or removing the said negress Jemmima and her two children Edward and Sam from the State." In a court-ordered appraisal of John's assets, it was determined that John earned $300 per annum and that Jemmima was worth $750 to $900; her son Edward, a carpenter, was worth $1,000 to $1,300; and her younger son Sam was worth $700. John's annual salary in addition to the interest earned on the appraised value of Jemmima and her sons was reported as $471.50 per annum. The appraiser's recommendation to the court said that due to Eliza's advancing age and her large number of "helpless children," she should receive half of John's annual income, equaling $235 per annum. Never losing sight of the fact that a price could be placed on Jemmima's head, Eliza turned her husband's betrayal into an opportunity to benefit from Jemmima's commodification.[41]

Like Eliza Prince, Anna Allen of the Columbia district in South Carolina went to great lengths to contrast her dutifulness as a wife with her husband's decision to abandon her and their seven children to live in "disgraceful illicit &

criminal intercourse" with an enslaved woman. In her petition to the Court of Equity, she said she "always conducted herself with strict propriety & fidelity towards her said husband, both before and since his said separation from her." Despite almost twenty years of marriage, John Allen refused to return, "wholly forsaking his family & unmindful of the duties which his character of father & husband impose upon him." Prior to his departure, Anna said they had lived in peace and harmony for many years. One day, however, it was "her misfortune to discover him in the act of having an illicit & criminal intercourse with a negro wench, a slave of her said husband in a remote & secluded spot." Refusing explanation or reconciliation, John expressed irritation with her and left their home to establish residence at his mill that was half a mile away. According to Anna, he took the unnamed bondwoman with him and lived there with her for many years.[42]

Anna recounted the many ways she tried to reunite her family over the eight years her husband lived at his mill. She said that "at her earnest entreaty," several of their neighbors called on her husband to return to his family. They suggested that he sell the enslaved woman or at least send her away so he could devote his attention to the maintenance of his family. When asking John to return home did not work, Anna even suggested that she and the children move to the mill so that they could reside together. She did not specify whether she demanded that her husband sell or at least send the enslaved woman away as a condition of her proposal. Either way, she said he treated all her propositions with contempt and "declared that if she went to the mill he would beat her away." With this testimony, Anna punctuated her charge that her husband willfully tarnished his character, choosing illicit and criminal intercourse over duty. That her husband abandoned his responsibilities as a husband and father was clear. Yet she never insinuated that what he had done was unforgivable. By law and by custom, he had not committed a crime against his enslaved woman. Anna did not concern herself with this either way, at least not in her presentation before the court. His crime had been against her and their children; yet even in her request for separation, Anna appeared willing to reunite with her husband if he agreed to come home and resume his position as a respectable husband and father.[43]

Acting Like a Wife

Ruthey Ann Hansley told the Superior Court of New Hanover County, North Carolina, that first her husband Samuel moved the bondwoman Lucy into their home and marital bed. Within a matter of weeks, he had deprived Ruthey of "control of all those domestic duties and privileges connected with the house which belong to a wife, and placed the said Lucy in the full possession and enjoyment of those privileges and duties." She told the court that per her husband's order, she had been stripped of the authority to manage her household and the enslaved laborers who lived and labored within it. More importantly, Samuel had bestowed on Lucy the authority he had taken from Ruthey, and now she was required to "give place to the said negro." Ruthey expressed resentment over the fact that not only was her husband having sex with Lucy but he had subverted the power dynamic between her and the enslaved woman in furtherance of the sexual liaison. Ruthey reported that this reversal of roles—her loss of power to an enslaved women within her own household—was an assault on her rightful position as a slave-owning white woman.[44]

Perhaps the most damning charge that white women made in their divorce petitions was that their husbands threatened white supremacy and white womanhood with their sexual relations with enslaved women. They hoped that their descriptions of white men treating enslaved women like white women and Black women playing the part of household managers and indulging in the privileges of whiteness would conjure up white slave-owning societies' greatest fears—Black domination and the collapse of the plantation household—and secure the favor of courts and legislative bodies. It was within the plantation household that young white boys were groomed to be guardians of their own households one day. It was where white girls learned that although men were the head of the household, they were to ensure that the household was a well-managed, respectable domicile for the sake of their husbands and children. This required that they raise a household full of well-mannered children and supervise or, in some cases, work alongside enslaved laborers to ensure the proper execution of cooking, cleaning, and child-rearing. Southern slave-owning women took this responsibility seriously, and they coveted the power they were afforded to perform their assigned duties. Their reputation and place within the cult of domesticity depended on it. Because enslaved women made up most of the labor force in the majority of plantation households, white women viewed their deference as imperative. Their need to feel intellectually, physically, and culturally superior to Black women was equally important for maintaining their position within the South's gendered and racialized hierarchy. When a husband's sexual relations with an enslaved woman disrupted a woman's position in her household, it felt like a threat to her standing in society at large.[45]

In reading divorce petitions, some historians have interpreted white women's complaints of enslaved women "acting like wives" to mean that enslaved women like Lucy capitalized on their sexual connections to white men, even using resultant marital turmoil, to assert power over white women and assume authority over household matters.[46] Archival evidence does reveal that some enslaved women lived as pseudo-free and were even recognized as "wives" within white men's households. Some were formally emancipated; others received trinkets, finer clothes, or private cabins as a result of their sexual connections to white men. While it is important that we acknowledge enslaved women's agency and the ways in which they strategized and seized opportunities to improve their lives, to take white women's characterizations of enslaved women's behavior in these divorce petitions at face value minimizes the power white women held over the enslaved. Further, it places too little emphasis on how white women like Ruthey, with the help of legal counsel, carefully crafted their petition narratives to elicit outcomes most beneficial to them and their families.[47]

When reading these sources, the truth is not always clear. It is reasonable to conclude that some enslaved women behaved just as these slaveowning women described. But it is necessary to recognize that in addition to acting in their own best interests, these white women were assessing enslaved women's behavior through a lens colored by white supremacy and the power of slave ownership. They had incentive and opportunity to lie or exaggerate about enslaved women's behavior to capture the attention of white male audiences. On the contrary, enslaved women had no platform to rebut, confirm, or modify these women's accusations. White women almost never wrote about enslaved women who were terrorized by sexual violence. They rendered enslaved women's fears, pain, and trauma insignificant, making them virtually invisible in this archival space.

In their divorce petitions, white Southern women sought to reveal the multitude of ways in which they felt their husbands had elevated their sexual servants to act out the privileges and responsibilities that were "rightfully" theirs. When Evelina Roane outlined her husband's sins in her petition, she was sure that the "humane & dignified assembly should feel the imposition of her aggravated wrongs and sufferings." At the time of their marriage, her husband, Newman, had hidden away an enslaved woman named Biney and the two children they shared at his brother's house. After the dust settled on their marriage, he brought Biney and the children to live in their home. This arrangement—a wife living alongside a domestic servant with whom her husband had a long-term sexual liaison—was not unprecedented among the

South's slave-owning class. Evelina's family had heard the rumors that New-man "kept" an enslaved woman, and it was even suggested that this was a source of contention in his first marriage. According to Evelina, Newman did more than dote on Biney and their two children. From the moment Biney and the children arrived, Newman "rejected his unhappy wife and made her the victim of a worthless competition with a negroe [sic]." In addition to plac-ing her in competition with an enslaved woman, Newman "adopted this woman as the more eligible companion & wife."[48]

Evelina Roane's and Ruthey Ann Hansley's use of the word "wife" to characterize the enslaved women in long-term sexual liaisons with their husbands was significant then, just as it is in the present. Slave-owning women were prepared to anticipate that their husbands might have sexual relations with enslaved women. They were not prepared, however, to be anything other than the ladies of their households and to hold tightly to the authority afforded them. In fact, their express power over enslaved people—most notably those who labored in the plantation household—was their most formidable tool for expressing discontent or exacting re-venge for the interracial sexual relations that were taking place around them.[49] Having their husbands leave their beds to venture to the slave quarters was one thing. To be in competition for their social position as married white women was altogether an unfathomable matter. By claim-ing that her husband rejected her and embraced Biney as his wife, Evelina conveyed the extent to which this long-term sexual liaison robbed her of the power and privileges she was entitled to assume when she became a wife. From the beginning, she claimed, her husband intended for her to be a Roane in name only. She told the court that he said, "The name of a Roane was enough for your petitioner." He wanted Biney to be the lady of his household instead.[50]

For the court, Evelina and her family painted a provocative picture of Eve-lina performing hard labor and Biney waiting to be served. Evelina said that after her husband moved Biney into their home, she was "quickly reduced to the situation of a slave who for some unpardonable offense, was constantly under the frowns of its master." She alleged that she was ordered to bring tubs of waters from the spring or cook breakfast and dinner for the enslaved people working in the fields, the exact tasks a house servant like Biney would be responsible for doing. When deposed, Evelina's brother Thomas Gregory claimed to have never seen Biney do any work: "She was always idle, and her eldest child very generally at Mr. Roane's heels, and constantly fed in the house, very much humoured and spoiled." Mary Gregory, Evelina's sister, testified that her sister told her "this negro was at liberty to go where she pleased and was not held to any species of labour."[51]

Similarly, Elizabeth Clubb said that while her husband, David, ate his meals with his enslaved woman Polly and "whilst the negro was idle in the house," she was forced to work in the field. Her husband was so devoted to Polly that he became violent and abusive and "drove your petitioner from his house & forbade her return" when she "remonstrated" him for his sexual conduct, she said. Elizabeth and David's marriage was quite complex. During the divorce proceedings, they both accused each other of sex crimes. Elizabeth's primary focus, however, was to "prove to them that defendant took into his house a negro woman & treated her as a wife." To counter his wife's allegations, David turned the spotlight on her sexual past. He testified that shortly after their marriage, "he discovered that his wife had communicated to him the venereal disease" that his doctors described as the "Pox," a term for syphilis at that time. He claimed she contracted the disease while living as a "common prostitute" in South Carolina. At the end of his answer, he said that Elizabeth's charges concerning Polly were "utterly untrue." Although his wife had accused him publicly of reducing her to a servant and treating an enslaved woman as his wife, this was the whole of his defense.[52]

Evelina Roane reported that once her position was swapped with Biney's, she found that her and her child's needs were made secondary to the needs and whims of Biney and her children. Biney now received the personal attention to which any slave-owning woman of substantial means would have grown accustomed. Evelina said that even after just giving birth, her husband denied her care from the enslaved servant who was responsible for attending to her and "relieving the wants and necessities of her helpless babe." Per Newman's orders, the servant was "made to wait & attend upon his favorite negro woman, who was sick at this time." As a result, Evelina was "forced to rise from her bed in the night to administer to the comfort of her infant." Even when her family and friends offered financial relief and material supplies to compensate for her husband's neglect, "what was offered by her friends was often taken from her and given to the two mulatto children & their mother," Evelina declared.[53]

Evelina made the case that Biney's new elevated status emboldened the servant to act insolent toward her. Evelina's sister Mary said that whether at the behest of her brother-in-law or on her own accord, Biney was impertinent to her sister, and Newman "paid her no respect in the presence of this negro." Although Biney's status loomed large in Evelina's imagination, she was still required to perform the typical duties of a household servant. But even when Biney was cooking or cleaning, Evelina perceived her as having the upper hand. In fact, she suspected that Biney wished to poison her, a fear she expressed to her whole family. According to Mary, Evelina refused to eat the food Biney prepared when Newman was away from the house. On these occasions, she requested that her sister bring her food to eat, as "it was her condition not to eat of the food cooked in the kitchen until she saw her husband first partake of it."[54]

Other women made similar claims, charging enslaved women with infractions that ranged from the use of crude language to physical violence. Sarah Carter of South Carolina's Columbia district said that when her husband, Benjamin, "attached himself to one of his own female slaves," he began treating her with "great rudeness" and even beat her with a cowhide whip. Next, he allowed and even encouraged "the said slave to treat your oratrix with such rude opprobrious language as to render your oratrix situation most unpleasant and disagreeable." Elizabeth Cline, who had been married to Daniel Cline for more than twenty-five years, said that after her husband began to "bed & cohabit" with an enslaved woman, "the said negro woman hath beaten your petitioner at different times with great cruelty" without her husband's interference.[55]

Although these women's disgust with enslaved women was palpable, most understood that these enslaved women's violent actions were often an extension of their husbands' authority. They were sure to emphasize their husbands' roles in permitting and even instigating the enslaved women's displays of power. Elizabeth Pannell told the Virginia General Assembly that her husband, Edmund, and an enslaved woman, Grace, abused her in ways that ran the gamut. Elizabeth was offended by her husband's infidelity in general with women, Black and white, but especially with Grace. When Elizabeth became ill after consuming fried chicken, she was convinced that "poison had been put by the said Edmund, or by a negro woman Grace at the insistence of said Edmund." Elizabeth claimed that Edmund "encouraged the said negro woman Grace to use not only the most insolent language, but even to inflict blows upon said Elizabeth." Elizabeth said that she eventually had to abandon her home and seek the protection of friends. She claimed that if she remained under the power of Edmund—and Grace by extension—"her life would be put in jeopardy." Anne Wilson of Burke County, North Carolina, informed the court that after thirty years of marriage, her husband, William, moved an enslaved woman named Silva into their home and began "indulging himself in sexual intercourse with her." Next, he made her "suffer" at the hand of Silva, "whom he ordered to inflict blows on her person without any conviction on his part or the least rebuke." She argued that the consequences of William and Silva's liaison were great. She suffered not only emotionally but physically as well.[56]

There were women who contended that their husbands derived pleasure from watching enslaved women inflict violence and be disobedient to them. It was as if they were orchestrating a game, pitting their wives against their sexual servants. When their wives attempted to rebuke these enslaved women's behavior, that was their signal to join the game and further chastise their wives with abusive language and behavior. In Virginia, Barbara Pettus wrote to the general assembly that her slave-trading husband, Hugh Pettus—notorious for his "kept mistresses"—would "actually promote their insolence" toward her. Per court testimony, Hugh reveled in flaunting his sexual liaisons with enslaved women, almost as if these women were a testament to his virility and power. William Johnson, an employee of Hugh, testified to walking in on Hugh in the act of having sex with one of his enslaved women in his barn. Further, Johnson "frequently saw them together at other times in habits of intimacy and his belief was that for a length of time he kept said girl as his miss in his house." According to Barbara, Hugh garnered pleasure not only from parading women in and out of her house like it was a harem but from watching them disparage her. He neglected to "retrain" them to act like proper servants, she said. When she responded to their crudeness by making a "placid effort" to restore the balance of power in her home, Hugh "inflicted upon her person the most cruel violence." Similarly, when Anna Allen complained to her husband that the enslaved woman for whom he abandoned her "took occasion to beat and ill treat" her children, he armed himself with a stick and beat her with it, she said. Anna told the court that rather than the enslaved woman receiving punishment, she was unjustly punished instead. He chose to protect the enslaved woman's interests over hers, and together they made the powerful front that Anna and her husband were supposed to be.[57]

WHITE MALE JUDGES, JURIES, AND LEGISLATORS, the South's arbiters of justice, undoubtedly experienced discomfort over images of enslaved women striking white women and children and white women laboring in fields while enslaved women enjoyed the comforts of the slave-owning class. This was especially true when they heard instances of enslaved women assuming almost the entire breadth of white slave-owning women's responsibilities and privileges. In 1816, Harriet Laspeyre of New Hanover, North Carolina, generated anxiety for members of the North Carolina General

Assembly when she reported that her husband, Bernard, permitted the household servant with whom he was having sex to "exercise all the rights and authorities of a wife." Consequently, Harriet was "divested of her keys, deprived of the authority of a mistress, her negroes forbidden to obey her orders under penalty of the severest punishment." According to Harriet, her husband only married her to acquire the enslaved people she owned. To add insult to injury, "the profits arising from the labor of her slaves, which ought to have been appropriated to the support and education of her children, she had the extreme vexation to see wantonly lavished on his black and mulatto mistresses." She made the case that she literally had been stripped of every meaningful facet of her identity as a white slave-owning woman in the antebellum South while Bernard betrayed his responsibilities as a husband and an honorable protector of white supremacy and slave society. Her reported injustice resonated with members of the general assembly. They granted her request for separation and to retain the property, enslaved and otherwise, she had brought into the marriage.[58]

Bernard was so shocked by the general assembly's decision to grant Harriet's request for separation that he filed his own petition a year later. His complaint with Harriet's accusations and the legislators' decision was twofold. First, he claimed that his wife's accusations were motivated by her "fits of jealousy" and not the truth. In her petition, she committed "virulent and infamous libel," which humiliated him "publicly in the street." Second, because of the separation, his wife was permitted to send all his children out of the state and remove "from his service, all his negroes," which violated their initial marriage contract, he argued. In essence, he had now been stripped of his authority as a husband, father, and slave owner. Bernard told the assembly that they had made a grave mistake by indulging the petty jealousies of a woman. Other Southern women were "now on the tiptoe of expectation to see the issue of this petition," he said. He warned that "before long the tables of Both houses [will be] covered with Petitions from Jealous and discontented Wifes."[59]

Bernard neglected to realize that his wife crafted her petition narrative about his sexual liaison with an enslaved woman and the consequences their family suffered in such a way that no reasonable legislator would dismiss her claims as petty jealousy. Harriet understood that the South's rape culture required her to turn a blind eye if her husband acted with discretion and did not threaten the social and economic stability of their household and the system of enslavement. Like Bernard, she knew that jealousy over his interracial sexual relations would not be sufficient grounds for a divorce. Although her husband underestimated her, she knew that how she characterized her husband's "illicit intercourse" mattered. In navigating the South's rape culture, women like Harriet learned to discern for them themselves as well as from their legal counsel which behaviors judges and legislators would find tolerable and intolerable. Showing that her husband betrayed the South's most coveted tenets—white supremacy, Southern honor, and absolute authority over the enslaved—offered her the best pathway to success.

In Harriet's case, she described a household turned upside down by her husband's long-term liaison with a household servant. She spoke to how her husband stripped her of all the authority she was entitled to within the household and bestowed it on the enslaved woman with whom he was having the sexual relationship. By allowing this enslaved woman to usurp her power and authority, her husband showed an utter disregard for his responsibilities as an honorable Southern patriarch. White women repeatedly employed similar tropes—their husbands' lack of discretion, preferential treatment of enslaved women, and neglect of patriarchal duties—in their divorce petitions, which did not simply vilify white men's interracial sexual relations but stoked fears about the waning of Southern honor and respectability, patriarchal authority, and white supremacy. Exposing their husbands as sexually depraved and dishonorable and accusing enslaved women of acting like white women—seizing power and exercising authority within the plantation household—were shrewd and provocative strategies for obtaining divorces and alimony. Much was at stake. Separating themselves from disgraced men and securing ownership of property and alimony was how they could best maintain or restore their social standing and provide financial stability for themselves and their children. In this process, they did not directly place white men's sexual exploits of enslaved women on trial. Their intentions were not to protect enslaved women; rather, they were most invested in their own interests as white women, mothers, wives, and slave owners and hoped to secure their place within the plantation household.

Epilogue

Six years before the Civil War ended and emancipation came to the more than four million enslaved people in the United States, Mary Walker laid bare her greatest fears. She was afraid that her daughter Agnes, just on the cusp of womanhood, would be raped or sexually exploited in some form if she remained in bondage. She regretted the distance that lay between them. Walker was living as a free woman in Boston, but her daughter remained enslaved in North Carolina, which meant she was unable to protect her or educate her about remaining vigilant in a society where dangers lurked everywhere. In the final days of the war, Walker was finally reunited with her daughter and her youngest son. One can only imagine the joy and relief Walker felt when she embraced her children once again. Her daughter was now a woman, and they would be able to navigate the path toward freedom together. For Walker and millions of other enslaved and formerly enslaved people, the end of the war and the promise of emancipation from chattel slavery generated hope. In his classic text *Black Reconstruction in America*, W. E. B. Du Bois declared the enslaved as "willing almost in mass to sacrifice their last drop of blood" for freedom and citizenship. The promise of emancipation "sent them into transports of joy and sacrifice," and they were filled with boundless faith. In his words, "It was the Coming of the Lord."[1]

Black people had their minds set on the rights of citizenship, education, economic independence, and control over their own bodies. They were especially hopeful that the systematic rape and sexual exploitation of Black women would end. The formerly enslaved Reverend P. Thomas Stanford expressed confidence in the Black woman's future. The Black woman was "the mightiest moral factor in the life of her people," declared Stanford. He proclaimed that just as the imprisoning walls of one-room slave cabins were "passing away" with freedom, the Black woman "is no longer the easy victim of the unlicensed passion of certain white men." Unfortunately, Stanford's declaration proved to be more aspirational than accurate.[2]

From the start of the Civil War through Reconstruction, Black women continued to face threats of sexual violence both old and new. While the Civil War and the Thirteenth Amendment to the US Constitution formally ended chattel slavery, Southern white men were determined to reconstruct and maintain a caste system defined by white supremacy and Black subjugation. As they did during slavery, they turned to sexual violence to affirm their "racial and sexual power." As Black women asserted themselves as citizens, white men used rape and sexual violence to punish and threaten "black women's bodily rights as citizens."[3]

As the nation engaged in civil war, enslaved people seized opportunities to flee plantations with the hope of reaching free states or finding refuge behind Union army lines. Enslaved men joined all-Black regiments in the Union army by the thousands. However, this rupture of plantation communities resulted in an escalation of violence against enslaved women. White overseers seized on the absence of enslaved men as well as their employers to sexually assault enslaved women who remained under their control.[4]

Black women were also raped, sexually coerced, and harassed by Union officers and soldiers in Union-occupied spaces. According to historian Leslie Schwalm, because enslaved women were seen as "legitimate prey of lust," sexual assault of enslaved women became endemic on Union-occupied sea islands like Beaufort, South Carolina.[5] Elsewhere, Black women faced similar threats. Rose Plummer, a Black laundress for the Union army at Fort Jackson in Louisiana, confessed to Brigadier General William Dwight that she was, in fact, engaged in a sexual relationship with one of his captains. Assaults had become so rampant in their camp that even Dwight acknowledged that Plummer had engaged in the sexual relationship in exchange for protection from fellow officers.[6] Although most Union soldiers were not slave owners, these men's perceptions of Black women were informed by racist assumptions like those of their Southern counterparts. Specifically, they believed that bondage had destroyed Black women's "sense of morality and sexual restraint." In Beaufort, Union army general Rufus Saxton defended the accused men under his command to the American Freedmen's Inquiry Commission, testifying that "the colored women are proud to have illicit intercourse with white men," which caused "great difficulty in keeping the soldiers away from the women."[7]

When the Civil War ended, Black men and women across the South embarked on constructing a new, free world. They built churches and schools, established businesses, and engaged in leisure, partying in dance halls, drinking in saloons, and hanging out on street corners. Angered by the sight of Black people exercising and enjoying their rights of citizenship, Southern whites inflicted violence and destruction on Black communities to reinforce white dominance. They burned churches, schools, and businesses and threatened Black men who dared to exercise their constitutional right to vote.

They raped and harassed Black women for "a range of perceived transgressions," from "participating in Republican Party politics, to engaging in interracial sex, to challenging white authority." Some white men raped and sexually harassed Black women, especially domestics like laundresses and housekeepers who worked in their homes, for the sole reason of proving they still possessed racial and sexual power.[8]

In 1866, Memphis police officers attacked a group of Black soldiers who had served with the federal troops that occupied the city. Angered that these Black men wore uniforms, carried weapons, and assumed authority over Memphis's white population, the police, along with white businessmen, led a three-day insurrection on the city's Black community. At least forty-eight Black people were killed and over seventy more were injured. The rioters raped at least five Black women whom they believed to have intimate or familial ties to Black soldiers to underscore their message. Similarly, in 1871, Alabama night riders raped at least four Black women in Meridian, Mississippi, while rioting through the city. The violence was in retaliation of Black Meridians who had organized a street march to protest previous acts of white vigilante violence against Black citizens.[9]

While Black women continued to be plagued by the threat of rape and sexual violence, as freedwomen, they challenged white men's sexual power in ways that were previously unavailable to them. During the Civil War, Black women used military courts to file charges of sexual assault against their attackers. Unlike Southern state laws, military codes acknowledged the rape of Black women as a crime. Armed with legal protection for the first time, Black women entered military tribunals and testified against white men. After the war, Black women reported sexual assaults to the Freedmen's Bureau and asserted themselves as citizens, filing charges of rape in criminal courts for the first time. After the riots in both Memphis and Meridian, Black women testified to being raped and sexually harassed by night riders and Klansmen before congressional committees, which contributed to the passage of unprecedented federal legislation, such as the Ku Klux Klan Act of 1871. According to historian Hanna Rosen, Black women testifying before bodies of white men about how they were terrorized and assaulted was a radical act in the context of a cultural and legal tradition that had previously "negated the possibility that black women could be raped."[10]

As a result of continued sexual violence, Black people maintained their consciousness of Black women's vulnerability to rape and sexual exploitation in the post–Civil War and Reconstruction eras. They learned from their mothers, grandmothers, and members of their communities about the horrors of slavery. They witnessed or experienced how white men contin-ued to use sex to assert racial and sexual power over Black people in the decades that followed. In 1937, May Satterfield, born enslaved in Virginia, recalled her mother telling her that during slavery, enslaved women had no choice but to have sex with their enslavers. "He would take one down in de woods an' use her all de time he wanted to, den send her on back to work." She told her interviewer that "now it's diffunt"; however, Black women "gotta whole lot yet to go through." Seven decades removed from slavery, Satterfield reported that Black women's challenges had not drastically changed from enslavement: "De white man still atter 'em. An' ef she ain't got grit in her craw, he git her."[11]

This consciousness, however, evolved to accommodate the evolving rape culture of post-slavery America. This evolution was poignantly articulated by the formerly enslaved anti-lynching advocate Ida B. Wells. In 1892, Wells embarked on a one-woman campaign for anti-lynching legislation on the heels of the tragic lynching of her friends—three Black men who owned the successful People's Grocery Company in Memphis, Tennessee. White people justified the lynching of Black men by arguing that Black men lacked sexual control, and therefore, white women needed to be protected from their predatory nature. In her self-published pamphlet, *Southern Horrors*, Wells contended that lynching was the result of white men's perverse belief that Black men's desires for economic and political equality were really a de-sire for sexual equality—namely, sexual access to white women. For Wells, the irony of this Black male rape myth was that it was merely a reflection of white men's historical record of raping and sexually harassing Black women. According to Wells, white men are "notorious for their preference for Afro-American women."[12]

Just as the rape and sexual exploitation of enslaved women had implica-tions for enslaved women *and* men, Wells understood that lynching was just as much about the sexuality of Black women as it was about the sexuality of Black men. Wells argued that while a group of white people lynched a Black man to "protect their wives and daughters," a "white man was in the same jail for raping . . . an Afro-American girl," yet the white man remained un-harmed. To combat Black women's sexual exploitation, Wells joined the Black women's club movement, which was dedicated to the strategy of racial up-lift, accomplished through a politics of respectability. For Wells, however, a politics of respectability had never protected Black women from white men's sexual aggression. She argued that respectability would not be enough, seeing that white men had been permitted since slavery to project myths of hypersexuality and promiscuity onto Black women to justify their rape.

In the 1890s, Wells recognized that the lynching epidemic inherently tied whites and Blacks together. White men's and women's efforts to police both Black men's and women's sexuality were motivated by their desire to reaffirm their long-standing authority over Black people. In the aftermath of slavery, the tools of oppression—rape and lynching—remained virtually the same, and a rape culture continued to affect the lives of the oppressors as well as the oppressed. By moving the rape and sexual exploitation of enslaved women from the periphery to the center of enslavers' and enslaved people's experiences, we learn how significant white men's sexual power was to the founding of the nation and the success of slavery and how significant it continued to be long after slavery's end. Yet in contemporary discussions of patriarchy, sexual violence, and American culture, scholars and pundits alike often fail to foreground the history and experiences of Black women. The denigration of Black women's sexuality to reinforce white supremacy and patriarchal power was and continues to be a feature of American culture. It is my hope that scholars and activists will more actively and explicitly foreground the exploitation of Black bodies in the analysis of rape culture in a historical and contemporary context. If we are to better understand rape culture in the present, we must begin with slavery and the role that the systematic rape and sexual exploitation of Black people, especially Black women, played in the founding and perpetuation of the nation's political, economic, and social landscapes.

Notes

Introduction

1. Frederick Douglass, *My Bondage and My Freedom*, 175; Douglass, *Narrative of the Life of Frederick Douglass*, 33. Frederick Douglass was born in Talbot County, Maryland, in 1818 and was owned by a small-scale slave owner named Aaron Anthony. Douglass's family was originally owned by Richard Skinner, whose family was among Talbot County's slaveholding elite. When Skinner's granddaughter, Ann Catherine Skinner, married Anthony in 1797, she transformed the poor, landless overseer into a slave owner when her personal slaveholdings became his as a result of their marriage. Among the enslaved people Ann inherited were Douglass's grandmother, Betsey Bailey, and his mother, Harriet Bailey. For more on Douglass's early life, see Preston, *Young Frederick Douglass*.

2. Douglass, *My Bondage and My Freedom*, 175. Frederick Douglass spells his aunt Hester's name differently in his three autobiographies. In his first published autobiography, *Narrative of the Life of Frederick Douglass*, he refers to her as Hester. In his two subsequent autobiographies, he refers to her as Esther. For consistency, I refer to her as Hester and, for clarity, put the name Hester in parentheses when Douglass uses the alternative spelling.

3. Douglass, *Narrative of the Life of Frederick Douglass*, 18–20; Douglass, *My Bondage and My Freedom*, 175–77.

4. Douglass, *Narrative of the Life of Frederick Douglass*, 18; Douglass, *My Bondage and My Freedom*, 179. Saidiya Hartman referred to the passage through the blood-stained gate as "an inaugural moment in the formation of the enslaved." She noted the significance of Douglass placing this "terrible spectacle" at the very beginning of his genealogical narrative. Hartman, *Scenes of Subjection*, 3.

5. Douglass, *My Bondage and My Freedom*, 179.

6. Douglass, *Narrative of the Life of Frederick Douglass*, 19.

7. Douglass, *Narrative of the Life of Frederick Douglass*, 18.

8. In *Scenes of Subjection*, Saidiya Hartman warned scholars against making a spectacle of the pain of the enslaved to create opportunities for "self-reflection." In fact, she chose not to recount Douglass's testimony of Hester's assault in her book. In writing this book, I grappled with Hartman's profound arguments, as her work has so greatly influenced my own. I determined that for me, recounting some parts of Hester's experiences was important, not merely for self-reflection but for a better understanding of how these women navigated this cultural landscape. This history is, in fact, a part of my own genealogical narrative. My paternal great-great-grandmother, Sarah Hutto, was held in bondage by the Hutto family of Barnwell County, South Carolina. After the Civil War, Sarah worked as a housekeeper for Montgomery Eaves, a member of the Hutto family. During her postwar tenure as the Eaves's housekeeper,

she gave birth to two children by Montgomery Eaves—Joseph Syrus Eaves and Rosa Eaves. Joseph Syrus Eaves is my great-grandfather. Though I don't know the exact nature of Sarah Hutto and Montgomery Eaves's sexual relationship, I do know that as a white man in the pre—and post–Civil War South, he held authority over her, first as a slave owner and then as an employer.

9. Douglass, *Narrative of the Life of Frederick Douglass*, 18. For more on enslaved women and sexual exploitation, see, for example, White, *Ar'n't I a Woman?*; A. Y. Davis, *Women, Race and Class*; Jennings, "'Us Colored Women Had to Go though [*sic*] a Plenty,'" 45–74; Painter, "Soul Murder and Slavery"; Hartman, *Scenes of Subjection*; Baptist, "'Cuffy,' 'Fancy Maids,' and 'One-Eyed Men'"; J. Morgan, *Laboring Women*; King, "'Prematurely Knowing of Evil Things'"; D. Cooper Owens, *Medical Bondage*; E. Owens, *Consent in the Presence of Force*.

10. My conception of rape culture as a collective sense of "knowing" was inspired by my dissertation adviser Dr. Heather A. Williams and her work *Help Me to Find My People*, which engaged the concept of "emotion" in a way that I wished to speak about consciousness. While serving as the Race and Gender Postdoctoral Fellow at Rutgers University, I was encouraged by Dr. Deborah Gray White to revisit Williams's book, and this proved to be the breakthrough that I needed. Dr. Richard Godbeer was the first person to tell me that what I was describing in my work was a rape culture and that I should explore that as an analytical framework. These scholars were instrumental in shaping my overall approach to this work.

11. Griffin, "Rape: The All-American Crime," 34. See also Griffin, *Rape: The Politics of Consciousness*.

12. For a discussion on secondary victimization, see J. E. Williams, "Secondary Victimization." On Southern patriarchy, honor, and violence, see, for example, Faust, *James Henry Hammond and the Old South*; Wyatt-Brown, *Southern Honor*; Wyatt-Brown, *Honor and Violence in the Old South*; McCurry, *Master of Small Worlds*; Glover, *Southern Sons*.

13. Collins, *Black Sexual Politics*, 224, 58.

14. Irina Anderson and Kathy Doherty note that second-wave feminist scholars have emphasized sexual violence as central to the analysis of patriarchy. I assert that these scholars, many of whom have not significantly incorporated the experiences of Black women into their analysis, have failed to prioritize the intersection of patriarchy and white supremacy in American culture. In doing so, they would see that rape culture in America cannot be discussed without emphasizing the primacy of racialized slavery in creating present day rape culture. Anderson and Doherty, *Accounting for Rape*, 20.

15. Buchwald, Fletcher, and Roth, *Transforming a Rape Culture*, xi; Jordan and Swartz, *Culture*, 51.

16. J. Morgan, *Laboring Women*, 12–49; K. Brown, *Good Wives*, 108–10; Fischer, *Suspect Relations*; Jordan, *White over Black*; White, *Ar'n't I a Woman?*, 15.

17. Hodes, *White Women, Black Men*, 139; T. A. Foster, *Rethinking Rufus*.

18. Morris, *Southern Slavery and the Law*, 302–6; Block, *Rape and Sexual Power in Early America*, 65–71; Sommerville, *Rape and Race*; Brownmiller, *Against our Will*, 162.

19. State v. Mann, 13 N.C. 263 (1829). For a detailed description of the *State v. Mann* case, see T. Morris, *Southern Slavery and the Law*, 190–93.

20. Fannie Berry, interview, in Rawick, *American Slave* (hereafter Rawick, *AS*), 16.5 (Virginia), 2.

21. Block, *Rape and Sexual Power in Early America*, 65–71; Spillers, "Mama's Baby, Papa's Maybe," 65–81.

22. Pennington, *Fugitive Blacksmith*, 2:546; Jacob Manson, interview, in Rawick, *AS*, 15.2 (North Carolina), 97–98; Thomas, *Secret Eye*, 168; Chesnut, *Private Mary Chesnut*, 21, 42.

23. Jordan and Swartz, *Culture*, 49.

24. Glover, *Southern Sons*, 89–90, 126.

25. Fuentes, *Dispossessed Lives*, 144–47.

26. Chesnut, *Private Mary Chesnut*, 42.

27. Camp, *Closer to Freedom*, 6–7.

Chapter One

1. Keckley, *Behind the Scenes*, 24.

2. Morrison, "Unspeakable Things Unspoken," 387. Darlene Clark Hine also attributed Black women's silences to a "culture of dissemblance." Hine argued that Black women's systematic rape and sexual abuse influenced their development of behaviors and attitudes that "created the appearance of openness and disclosure but actually shielded the truth of their inner lives and selves from their oppressors." See Hine, "Rape and the Inner Lives of Black Women," 37.

3. Keckley, *Behind the Scenes*, 24.

4. Craft, *Running a Thousand Miles*, 3:902. There were exceptional cases in which enslaved men were accused of raping free women of color. For more on rape, the law, and enslaved women, see T. Morris, *Southern Slavery and the Law*, 302–6; Block, *Rape and Sexual Power in Early America*, 65–71; Sommerville, *Rape and Race*; Susan Brownmiller, *Against Our Will*, 162; Clinton, "Southern Dishonor," 65; Getman, "Sexual Control in the Slaveholding South," 135; D'Emilio and Freeman, *Intimate Matters*, 101; Bynum, *Unruly Women*, 109–18; Bardaglio, "Rape and the Law in the Old South," 749–72.

5. Frye and Shafer, "Rape and Respect," 340–42; Keckley, *Behind the Scenes*, 24.

6. On the Cameron family and their ownership of Mary Walker and her family, see Nathans, *To Free a Family*.

7. Lesley to Cameron, September 4, 1859, Cameron Family Papers, Southern Historical Collection (hereafter cited as SHC).

8. H. Jacobs, *Incidents*, 28; Wright, *Black Girlhood*, 6, 89; Gampel, "Reflections on the Prevalence of the Uncanny," 55.

9. Swartz and Jordan, *Culture*, 49, 63; Robben, "Assault on Basic Trust," 73; K. J. Brown, *Repeating Body*, 177.

10. Nathans, *To Free a Family*, 9.

11. H. Jacobs, *Incidents*, 28.

12. J. Brown, *Slave Life in Georgia*.

13. J. Brown, *Slave Life in Georgia*.

14. Shang Harris, interview, in Rawick, *AS*, 12.2 (Georgia), 117–25; W. Anderson, *Life and Narrative of William J. Anderson*.

15. Ellen Sinclair, interview, in Rawick, *AS*, suppl. Ser. 2, 9.8 (Texas), 3593–94; Hall, *Samuel Hall, 47 Years a Slave*; Campbell, *An Autobiography*.

16. J. Jacobs, "True Tale of Slavery," 208; J. Brown, *Slave Life in Georgia*.

17. Douglass, *My Bondage and My Freedom*, 175–77; Douglass, *Narrative of the Life*, 18–20.

18. Minnie Fulkes, interview, in Rawick, *AS*, 17 (Virginia), 11.

19. Testimony of Jefferson Jones and testimony of Virginia Wainscott (or Way-nescot), State of Missouri v. Celia, a Slave, #4496, Callaway County Circuit Court, Fulton (1855). Database of digitized and transcribed trial records for *State of Missouri v. Celia, a Slave* available at https://famous-trials.com/celia. See also McLaurin, *Celia, a Slave*.

20. Testimony of Virginia Wainscott, *State of Missouri v. Celia*; Camp, *Closer to Freedom*, 6, 12–13, 28–34. Susan Griffin argues, "Each girl as she grows into womanhood is taught fear." Griffin, "Rape: The All-American Crime," 33.

21. May Satterfield, interview, in Perdue, Barden, and Phillips, *Weevils in the Wheat*, 245; Loguen, *The Rev. J. W. Loguen*; Virginia Hayes Shepherd, interview, in Perdue, Barden, and Phillips, *Weevils in the Wheat*, 257.

22. H. Jacobs, *Incidents*, 53.

23. H. Jacobs, *Incidents*, 42; testimony of Jefferson Jones and testimony of William Powell, *State of Missouri v. Celia*. On Southern honor, interracial sex, and reputation, see Bardaglio, *Reconstructing the Household*, 4, 49; Rothman, *Notorious in the Neighbor-hood*, 134; Bynum, *Unruly Women*, 36; Glover, *Southern Sons*, 126; Wyatt-Brown, *Southern Honor*; McCurry, *Masters of Small Worlds*.

24. Mattie Curtis, interview, in Rawick, *AS*, 14.1 (North Carolina), 220.

25. Case of Peggy, Patrick, and Franky, Executive Papers—Pardon Papers, box 316, May–September 1830, Library of Virginia. See chapter 3 for a detailed account of Francis's murder and Peggy and Patrick's murder trial.

26. Harry McMillan, interview, in Blassingame, *Slave Testimony*, 382.

27. For more on the destruction of "basic trust," see Robben, "Assault on Basic Trust," 76.

28. H. Jacobs, *Incidents*, 42; Mrs. Bird Walton, interview, in Perdue, Barden, and Phillips, *Weevils in the Wheat*, 301.

29. T. A. Foster, *Rethinking Rufus*, 34; Bibb, *Life and Adventures of Henry Bibb*, 2:365, 2:366–67; Ishrael Massie, interview, in Perdue, Barden, and Phillips, *Weevils in the Wheat*, 207; Jacob Aldrich, interview, in Rawick, *AS*, suppl. ser. 2, 2.1 (Texas), 28; Clarke, "Leaves from a Slave's Journal of Life." On enslaved men's constructions of masculinity, see Doddington, *Contesting Slave Masculinity*.

30. Victor Duhon, interview, in Rawick, *AS*, suppl. ser. 2, 4.3 (Texas), 1238; Shep-herd, interview, in Perdue, Barden, and Phillips, *Weevils in the Wheat*, 257; Ben Horry, interview, in Rawick, *AS*, 2.2 (South Carolina), 304–5.

31. Jack and Rosa Maddox, interview, in Rawick, *AS*, suppl. ser. 2, 7.6 (Texas), 2531; Craft, *Running a Thousand Miles*, 3:902. On the fancy-girl trade, see, for exam-ple, W. Johnson, *Soul by Soul*, 113–15, 154–55; Baptist, "'Cuffy,' 'Fancy Maids,' and

'One-Eyed Men,'" 1639, 1641–49; Clark, *Strange History of the American Quadroon*. On enslaved women, sexual economy, and prostitution, see Finley, *Intimate Economy*, 9–10, 44, 69–71, 93–95; Nunley, *At the Threshold of Liberty*, 88–93, 129–31, 135–58.

32. Jack and Rosa Maddox, interview, in Rawick, *AS*, suppl. ser. 2, 7.6 (Texas), 2531; H. Jacobs, *Incidents*, 18; Richard Macks, interview, in Rawick, *AS*, 16.3 (Maryland), 54.

33. Richmond County compilation in Rawick, *AS*, 4.4 (Georgia), 295; Clarke, *Narratives of the Suffering of Lewis*; Sis Shackelford, interview, in Perdue, Barden, and Phillips, *Weevils in the Wheat*, 250.

34. W. W. Brown, *Narrative of William Wells Brown*, 2:314–15; Richmond County compilation in Rawick, *AS*, 4.4 (Georgia), 295; Hattie Rogers, interview, in Rawick, *AS*, 15.2 (North Carolina), 230.

35. Andrew Moss, interview, in Rawick, *AS*, 16 (Tennessee), 6. James Calhart said his mother's owner also purchased her to serve as his wife's nurse. Once his wife died, he kept Calhart's mother as his housekeeper. During this time, she gave birth to Calhart. See James Calhart, interview, in Rawick, *AS*, 16 (Maryland), 34.

36. J. Morgan, *Laboring Women*, 83; Richmond County interview compilation, in Rawick, *AS*, 4.4 (Georgia), 295. For more on the inspection of enslaved women's bodies, see Schwartz, *Birthing a Slave*, 71–73.

37. T. A. Foster, *Rethinking Rufus*, 106; Simon Phillips, interview, in Rawick, *AS*, 6 (Alabama), 313; Willis Cofer, interview, in Rawick, *AS*, 12.1 (Georgia), 202–11; Rias Body, interview, in Rawick, *AS*, 12.1 (Georgia), 88; John Cole, interview, in Rawick, *AS*, 12.1 (Georgia), 226–30; Carrie Davis, interview, in Rawick, *AS*, 6 (Alabama), 107.

38. On slave courtship and marriage, see Sides, "Slave Weddings and Religion"; Blassingame, *Slave Community*, 156–70; Gutman, *Black Family*, 70–75; White, *Ar'n't I a Woman?*, 97–99; Stevenson, *Life in Black and White*, 226–57; J. Jones, *Labor of Love, Labor of Sorrow*, 31–33; West, *Chains of Love*; Fraser, *Courtship and Love*; Hunter, *Bound in Wedlock*; Parry, *Jumping the Broom*.

39. James Curry, speech, in Blassingame, *Slave Testimony*, 129; Marshal Butler, interview, in Rawick, *AS*, 12.1 (Georgia), 166; Angie Garret, interview, in Rawick, *AS*, 6 (Alabama), 133–36; Jacob Aldrich, interview, in Rawick, *AS*, 2.1 (Texas), 26.

40. Roper, *Narrative of the Adventures*, 1:70; H. B. Brown, *Narrative of Henry Box Brown*, 2:457.

41. Berry Clay, interview, in Rawick, *AS*, 12.1 (Georgia), 189–94; J. Brown, *Slave Life in Georgia*. Enslaved families were largely separated because of growing demand for slave labor in the expanding lower and western South. For more, see Gudmestad, *Troublesome Commerce*; Johnson, *Soul by Soul*; Tadman, *Speculators and Slaves*; Deyle, *Carry Me Back*; Rothman, *Ledger and the Chain*.

42. Kemble, *Journal of a Residence*, 245–46; J. Morgan, *Laboring Women*, 105.

43. K. J. Brown, *Repeating Body*.

44. Lesley to Cameron, September 4, 1859, Cameron Family Papers, SHC; Nathans, *To Free a Family*, 215–16; Stevenson, "Gender Convention," 171.

45. Mattie Curtis, interview, in Rawick, *AS*, 14.1 (North Carolina), 220.

46. Minnie Fulkes, interview, in Rawick, *AS*, 17 (Virginia), 13–14. See A. Davis, "'Don't Let Nobody Bother Yo' Principle.'"

47. Veney, *Narrative of Bethany Veney*; Olmsted, *Journey in the Seaboard Slave States*, 601–2, quoted in White, *Ar'n't I a Woman?*, 88. On enslaved women and infanticide, see Schwartz, *Birthing a Slave*, 207–11.

48. Mrs. Thomas Johns, interview, in Rawick, *AS*, suppl. ser. 2, 6.5 (Texas), 1973.

49. Keckley, *Behind the Scenes*, 24, 29.

50. Northup, *Twelve Years a Slave*, 328; Albert, *House of Bondage*.

51. Fannie Berry, interview, in Rawick, *AS*, 16.5 (Virginia), 2.

52. Testimony of Celia, testimony of Jefferson Jones, and testimony of William Powell, *State of Missouri v. Celia*.

53. Testimony of William Powell and testimony of Jefferson Jones, *State of Missouri v. Celia*.

54. Verdict [undated], *State of Missouri v. Celia*; McLaurin, *Celia, a Slave*, 102–15.

55. Northup, *Twelve Years a Slave*, 255.

56. Willie McCullough, interview, in Rawick, *AS*, 15.2 (North Carolina), 78; Mattie Curtis, interview, in Rawick, *AS*, 14.1 (North Carolina), 220.

57. Northup, *Twelve Years a Slave*, 255, 247, 269.

58. Clarke, "Leaves from a Slave's Journal of Life."

59. On free women of color in the slaveholding South, see, for example, Alexander, *Ambiguous Lives*; King, *Essence of Liberty*; Lebsock, *Free Women of Petersburg*; Myers, *Forging Freedom*; Spear, *Race, Sex, and Social Order*; Millward, *Finding Charity's Folk*; Milteer, *North Carolina's Free People of Color*; Milteer, *Beyond Slavery's Shadow*.

60. Rose Williams, interview, in Boykin, *Lay My Burden Down*, 160–62.

61. Williams, interview, 160–62.

62. Williams, interview, 160–62; W. W. Brown, *Narrative of William Wells Brown*, 2:330. On formerly enslaved people and marriage, see Hunter, *Bound in Wedlock*.

63. Kemble, *Journal of a Residence*, 245–46; Veney, *Narrative of Bethany Veney*. Before and after the Civil War, enslaved people held onto hope of reunification with their spouses and children. Enslaved men and women spent years searching for lost loved ones, using the Freedmen's Bureau and even placing advertisements to reestablish contact with family members. On family reunification and the search for lost loved ones, see H. A. Williams, *Help Me to Find My People*.

64. H. Jacobs, *Incidents*, 37, 39.

65. H. Jacobs, *Incidents*, 37, 54; Yellin, *Harriet Jacobs: A Life*, 27. For more on Jacob's relationship with Sawyer, see H. Jacobs, *Incidents*, chap. 10, "A Perilous Passage in the Slave Girl's Life."

66. H. Jacobs, *Incidents*, 42, 53–55.

Chapter Two

1. The title of this chapter is a quote from Octavia Albert, *House of Bondage*, 120.

2. Pierce Bailey will, September 1861, in George G. Cobb and Wife and James M. Jones and Wife v. Lawrence Battle, 34 GA 458 (1866) (hereafter *Cobb v. Battle*); 1850 US Federal Census of Warren County, Georgia, Slave Schedules, Bureau of the Census, National Archives and Records Administration, Washington, DC (hereafter cited as NARA).

3. The enslaved, slave owners, and even historians have assigned many names to enslaved women who had sexual relations with white slave-owning men—concubine, slave mistress, and kept woman, to name a few. I use the term "sexual servant" throughout because these enslaved women were required to have sex with their owners as a function of their enslavement.

4. *Cobb v. Battle*, 34 GA 458 (1866).

5. I have adopted the term "virtual freedom" from Amrita Chakrabarti Myers in *Forging Freedom*, 13. For more on enslaved women, sexual servitude, and material gains, see Rothman, *Notorious in the Neighborhood*; C. Kennedy, *Braided Relations, Entwined Lives*, 112–13; Myers, *Forging Freedom*; Schermerhorn, *Money over Mastery*; Stevenson, "What's Love Got to Do with It?"

6. In 1801, the Georgia legislature forbade slave owners from manumitting the enslaved without legislative approval. Owners who did so faced strict fines. An 1818 law overturned slave owners' right to free their enslaved people in their last will and testaments. On Georgia manumission laws, see Ford, *Deliver Us from Evil*, 195; Clayton, *Compilation of the Laws of the State of Georgia*; Lamar, *Compilation of the Laws of the State of Georgia*.

7. Northen, *Men of Mark in Georgia*, 124.

8. 1850 US Federal Census of Warren County, Georgia, Slave Schedules, Bureau of the Census, NARA.

9. Craft, *Running a Thousand Miles for Freedom*, 3:902; W. L. Bost, interview, in Rawick, *AS*, 14.1 (North Carolina), 142. Slave testimony reveals that slave owners' hearts were not often softened by sexual relations with enslaved women. Rape and sexual coercion of enslaved women were deeply entrenched in the culture of enslavement in the antebellum South. In addition, many male slave owners demonstrated the capacity to reap the benefits of their enslaved children's labor and even place them on the auction block with little to no reservations.

10. *Cobb v. Battle*, 34 GA 458 (1866). The state statutes of Ohio did not prohibit interracial marriage; however, it did prohibit cohabitation. According to chapter 86, section 1, of the Ohio statutes, Bailey could have taken Adeline into the state of Ohio as his servant, and she would have been permitted to settle in the township where Bailey brought her. See Swan, *Statutes of the State of Ohio*, 569, 610.

11. *Cobb v. Battle*, 34 GA 458 (1866).

12. In his seminal work, Eugene Genovese qualified the discussion of enslaved women's sexual exploitation by arguing that not all sexual relationships between white men and enslaved women were exploitive. According to Genovese, most white men "who began by taking a slave girl in an act of sexual exploitation ended by loving her and the children she bore." Genovese argued that most relationships between slave-owning men and sexual servants were benevolent. See Genovese, *Roll, Jordan, Roll*, 415.

13. A. Y. Davis, *Women, Race, and Class*; Hartman, *Scenes of Subjection*.

14. Stevenson, *Life in Black and White*, 241; Rothman, *Notorious in the Neighborhood*; C. Kennedy, *Braided Relations*, 112–13; Walker, *Mongrel Nation*, 45; Schermerhorn, *Money over Mastery*; Stevenson, "What's Love Got to Do with It?"

15. Schermerhorn, *Money over Mastery*, 108–10; C. Kennedy, *Braided Relations*, 112–13.

16. C. Kennedy, *Braided Relations*, 112–13.

17. Walker, *Mongrel Nation*, 45.

18. *Cobb v. Battle*, 34 GA 458 (1866).

19. Jack and Rosa Maddox, interview, in Rawick, *AS*, 7.6 (Texas), 2531.

20. Picquet and Mattison, *Louisa Picquet, the Octoroon*. Picquet's narrative was created from a series of interviews she did with Hiram Mattison.

21. Sis Shackelford, interview, in Perdue, Barden, and Phillips, *Weevils in the Wheat*, 250.

22. Women's work assignments confined them within the boundaries of the plantation and plantation household. This proximity, coupled with notions of Black women's hypersexuality, made enslaved women—especially those who worked and lived in the plantation household—vulnerable to sexual abuse. White, *Ar'n't I a Woman?*, 89–90.

23. Virginia Hayes Shepherd, interview, in Perdue, Barden, and Phillips, *Weevils in the Wheat*, 255–57.

24. Picquet and Mattison, *Louisa Picquet, the Octoroon*.

25. Picquet and Mattison, *Louisa Picquet, the Octoroon*.

26. Picquet and Mattison, *Louisa Picquet, the Octoroon*.

27. Picquet and Mattison, *Louisa Picquet, the Octoroon*.

28. Picquet and Mattison, *Louisa Picquet, the Octoroon*.

29. Stevenson, *Life in Black and White*, 240.

30. Willie McCullough, interview, in Rawick, *AS*, 15.2 (North Carolina), 78; Anthony Christopher, interview, in Rawick, *AS*, suppl. ser. 2, 3.2 (Texas), 719; Jacob Aldrich, interview, in Rawick, *AS*, suppl. ser. 2, 2.1 (Texas), 28; Hattie Rogers, interview, in Rawick, *AS*, 15.2 (North Carolina), 230.

31. Craft, *Running a Thousand Miles for Freedom*, 3:902–3.

32. W. W. Brown, *Narrative of William Wells Brown*, 2:314–15.

33. On perceptions of field work and housework within the slave community, see Blassingame, *Slave Community*, 249–51.

34. W. W. Brown, *Narrative of William Wells Brown*, 2:314–15.

35. Brown, *Narrative of William Wells Brown*, 2:314–15.

36. Virginia Boyd to R. C. Ballard, May 6, 1853, Rice C. Ballard Papers, Southern Historical Collection (hereafter cited as SHC).

37. In a letter to Rice Ballard, J. M. Duffield begged to buy an enslaved woman named Maria who was living under Samuel Boyd's control because of the cruel treatment she was enduring at the hands of Boyd. He wrote, "You will recollect the cruelties which you described to me once in confidence that had been perpetrated, by a certain person in whose power Maria is, and I recollect the horror you expressed of it. All these cruelties have been inflicted upon the feeble frame of that girl—and are frequently inflicted—she must die under them." J. M. Duffield to R. C. Ballard, May 29, 1848, Rice C. Ballard Papers, SHC.

38. Virginia Boyd to R. C. Ballard, May 6, 1853, Rice C. Ballard Papers, SHC.

39. Virginia Boyd to R. C. Ballard, May 6, 1853.

40. Scarborough, *Masters of the Big House*, 133, 213.

41. Virginia Boyd to R. C. Ballard, May 6, 1853; C. M. Rutherford to R. C. Ballard, August 8, 1853, Rice C. Ballard Papers, SHC.

42. Virginia Boyd to R. C. Ballard, May 6, 1853.

43. The Southern Claims Commission was formed because of congressional legislation to compensate Union loyalists for any personal property that might have been damaged or commandeered by the Union army during the Civil War. The SCC began its operations in 1871. Petitioners had to prove that they were loyal to the Union during the war and that their property had been, in fact, damaged or used by the Union army.

44. Susan Flowers petition, December 12, 1876, Claiborne County, Mississippi, Records of the Court of Claims, Record Group 123, NARA. Although Susan's petition started with the SCC, it was eventually appealed to the US Court of Claims, in whose records her petition can be found. SCC petitions can be found in the Records of the Southern Claims Commission, Record Group 217, NARA.

45. *Laws of the State of Mississippi.*

46. Du Bois, *Black Reconstruction in America*, 599–633; Foner, *Reconstruction*, 560–63.

47. Susan Flowers petition, December 12, 1876.

48. Susan Flowers petition, December 12, 1876.

49. Constitution and Ordinances of the State of Mississippi, 41st. Cong. (1869), 17.

50. Susan Flowers petition, December 12, 1876.

51. Susan Flowers petition, December 12, 1876.

52. According to the 1900 census taken in Claiborne County, Mississippi, where Susan and William Bryant lived, there was a Susan and William Bryant registered as husband and wife. Although the date of their marriage listed in the census — 1866 — is different from the 1875 date that Susan and William both gave the Bureau of Pensions, this is likely the same Susan and William Bryant, as the census noted that Susan was the mother of ten children. 1900 US Federal Census of Claiborne County, Mississippi, Bureau of the Census, NARA.

53. Susan Bryant petition, February 17, 1917, pension application no. 64590, Civil War and Later Pension Files, Department of Veterans Affairs, Record Group 15, NARA.

54. William Bryant form, Susan Bryant petition, February 17, 1917.

55. Steed commission report and deposition of Jack Brown, Susan Bryant petition, February 17, 1917.

56. L. C. Fischer deposition, Susan Bryant petition, February 17, 1917. According to the 1870 census, Thomas W. Brown was fifty years old and was still married and living with his wife, Ann M. Brown, who was forty-three in 1870. 1870 US Federal Census of Rocky Springs, Mississippi, Bureau of the Census, NARA; Susan Bryant petition, February 17, 1917.

57. Thomas Brown deposition, Susan Bryant petition, February 17, 1917.

58. Claim decision, Susan Bryant petition, February 17, 1917.

Chapter Three

1. The title of this chapter is a quote from Peter Randolph, *From Slave Cabin to Pulpit*, 175; Henson, *Truth Stranger Than Fiction*, 3.

2. On the vulnerabilities of slave marriages, see Gutman, *Black Family in Slavery and Freedom*, 52, 146–50; White, *Ar'n't I a Woman?*, 146–50; Stevenson, *Life in Black and*

White, 239–40; West, *Chains of Love*; Fraser, *Courtship and Love*; Hunter, *Bound in Wedlock*.

3. Lussana, *My Brother Slaves*, 5; Doddington, *Contesting Slave Masculinity*, 99, 102; T. A. Foster, *Rethinking Rufus*, 14, 34.

4. Henson, *Life of Josiah Henson*, 2:506. For white men, violence was the weapon of choice to assert authority. While white men could use violence to retaliate against the enslaved, the enslaved could not. According to Edward E. Baptist, enslaved men using violence to fight back against white men invited death. See Baptist, "Absent Subject," 137.

5. Cooper and McCord, *Statutes at Large of South Carolina*, 7:343, 389. For further discussion, see T. Morris, *Southern Slavery and the Law*, 267–68.

6. Henson, *Life of Josiah Henson*, 2:506.

7. Frances Foster argues that slave narratives were mostly written by formerly enslaved men who had joined the abolitionist movement. In their efforts to gain support for the abolition of slavery, they at times overemphasized enslaved women's sexual vulnerability to appeal to white sympathetic audiences. I acknowledge that these slave narratives were written to serve abolitionist purposes; however, I do not discredit these descriptions. There is plenty of evidence of enslaved women's vulnerability to sexual exploitation in criminal trial records, divorce petitions, and interviews of formerly enslaved people after emancipation. These sources are invaluable in that they reflect what formerly enslaved people found most important to report about the horrors of slavery. This speaks to their own understandings and captures some of what enslaved people shared from one generation to the next to survive. F. S. Foster, "Ultimate Victims," 845–54.

8. Stevenson, *Life in Black and White*, 195, 239–40.

9. Edwards, "Law, Domestic Violence," 733–70.

10. Because Pierce Butler—and his grandfather before him—preferred to live in Philadelphia and reap the benefits of slave ownership from afar, they relied on the experience of the Kings to oversee their plantations as if they were their own. For additional biographical information on the Butler family and Frances Kemble, see J. A. Scott, introduction.

11. Kemble, *Journal of a Residence*, 176.

12. Friend and Glover, "Rethinking Southern Masculinity," ix.

13. McCurry, *Masters of Small Worlds*; Edwards, *Scarlett Doesn't Live Here Anymore*, 3.

14. For example, article 1, section 6, of the South Carolina Constitution specified that "no person shall be eligible to a seat in the house of representatives, unless he is a free white man." Article 1, section 4, stipulated that only free white men of the age of twenty-one had the right to vote. These statutes are representative of most Southern states. See James, *Digest of the Laws of South Carolina*, 28. In 1818, Maryland's constitution allowed all free men, Black and white, to vote, stating, "All freeholders, freemen, and other persons qualified to give votes in the election of delegates, shall and are hereby obliged to be." However, by 1850, Maryland's constitution stated that "every free white male person . . . shall be entitled to vote." The same happened in North Carolina and Tennessee. See Maxcy, *Laws of Maryland*, 18; Hinkley, *Constitution of the*

State of Maryland, 18. On South Carolina's capitalization tax, see Edgar, *South Carolina*, 308; Myers, *Forging Freedom*, 80.

15. For more on how free people of color navigated their world, see Winch, *Between Slavery and Freedom*; Johnson and Roark, *No Chariot Let Down*; Stevenson, *Life in Black and White*, chap. 10.

16. On laws of coverture, see, for example, A. F. Scott, *Southern Lady*; Clinton, *Plantation Mistress*; Fox-Genovese, *Within the Plantation Household*; Glymph, *Out of the House of Bondage*; Jones-Rogers, *They Were Her Property*.

17. T. Morris, *Southern Slavery and the Law*, 263.

18. Baptist, "Absent Subject," 153.

19. Edward Baptist argues that white men attributed the qualities of weakness and dependence, whether justified or not, to Black people so that they could claim a position of authority over them. Forcing this condition of dependence and subordination on Black men was the ultimate key to white men's success. White men were able to create this subordination of Black manhood to white manhood by inflicting violence, making threats to separate families, and seizing wages and possessions. In other words, Black men subscribed to ideologies of manhood, manliness, and masculinity; however, white men systemically tried to subordinate Black masculinity and manhood to their own. Baptist, "Absent Subject," 136–38.

20. Jordan, *White over Black*, 24, 28, 34; J. Morgan, *Laboring Women*; D'Emilio and Freedman, *Intimate Matters*, 86.

21. With the increase in interracial sex between white men and African women, colonial leaders had to find a way to preserve the enslaved status of children who were claiming freedom as their birthright, given to them by their white fathers. This law set legalized, perpetual slavery into motion. For more, see E. Morgan, *American Slavery, American Freedom*, 327–38; K. Brown, *Good Wives*, 108–10; Fischer, *Suspect Relations*, 160–61.

22. Blassingame, *Slave Community*, 88.

23. Pennington, *Fugitive Blacksmith*, 2:549–50; McCurry, *Masters of Small Worlds*, 6, 14–15, 153; Baptist, "Absent Subject," 136–38, 142–43; Edwards, *Scarlett Doesn't Live Here Anymore*, 3.

24. William Ervin journal, vol. 2, 1846–1856, pp. 47–48, William Ethelbert Ervin Journals, 1839–1856, Southern Historical Collection (hereafter cited as SHC).

25. William Ervin journal, vol. 2, 1846–1856, pp. 47–48, William Ethelbert Ervin Journals, 1839–1856, SHC; Bibb, *Life and Adventures of Henry Bibb*, 2:367.

26. Dr. Richard Eppes diary, January 2, 1853, Dr. Richard Eppes Code of Laws, Section 69, Eppes Family Papers, 1722–1948, Virginia Museum of History and Culture.

27. Steward, *Twenty-Two Years a Slave*, 3:736–37.

28. H. Jacobs, *Incidents*, 44.

29. William Ward, interview, in Rawick, *AS*, 13.4 (Georgia), 133.

30. Clarke, "Leaves from a Slave's Journal of Life," 157.

31. Ishrael Massie, interview, in Perdue, Barden, and Phillips, *Weevils in the Wheat*, 207. Massie reported that he was eighty-eight years old at the time of the interview.

32. On large plantations with a significant enslaved population, certain Black men were selected to serve as drivers to assist owners and overseers with maintaining

order and maximizing productivity among the enslaved population. Drivers were frequently required to whip their fellow slaves, a task that most found excruciating. In other instances, drivers enjoyed their elevated place of authority, which created tension between them and other enslaved men *and* women. Mostly, slave drivers served as leaders within the slave quarters, serving as a buffer between the enslaved and overseers and owners. This illustrates that enslaved men were not completely void of authority, especially over one another. See Boles, *Black Southerners*, chap. 5.

33. Case of Peggy, Patrick, and Franky, Executive Papers, Pardon Papers, box 316, May–September 1830, Library of Virginia (hereafter cited as LVA); Bibb, *Life and Adventures of Henry Bibb*, 2:397.

34. Thomas Goodwater, interview, in Rawick, *AS*, 2.2 (South Carolina), 167.

35. On forced sexual reproduction among the enslaved population, see J. Morgan, *Laboring Women*; T. A. Foster, *Rethinking Rufus*. In *White Women, Black Men*, Hodes provides evidence of both coercive and consensual sexual relations between enslaved men and white women. See also Rothman, *Notorious in the Neighborhood*, for more on coercive and consensual sex across the color line.

36. Sam and Louisa Everett, interview, in Rawick, *AS*, 17.1 (Florida), 127–28. When Sam and Louisa Everett were interviewed, the interviewer combined and summarized most of their reflections. Louisa is the only one whom the interviewer quoted directly.

37. John Cole, interview, in Rawick, *AS*, 12.1 (Georgia), 228. Doddington, *Contesting Slave Masculinity*, 127, 131–32, 146; T. A. Foster, *Rethinking Rufus*, 63.

38. hooks, *Black Looks*, 90. In *We Real Cool*, bell hooks argues that there was a stark difference between the notions of masculinity that African men brought with them to the New World and the notions of masculinity and patriarchy that they were inundated with under the mastery of white men. For white men, mastery over women and the enslaved was an essential element of masculinity. Although African men were part of communities that valued gender roles and placed men at a higher status than women, that status did not equate to the domination of women. She argues that over the course of slavery, Black men unfortunately learned to mimic white men's dominance over women, which proved detrimental in the post–Civil War era (3–5). "When slavery ended these black men often used violence to dominate black women, which was a repetition of the strategies of control white slave-masters used" (4). For more of hooks's analysis on enslaved men, masculinity, and patriarchy, see hooks, *We Real Cool*, chap. 1.

39. Bibb, *Life and Adventures of Henry Bibb*, 2:356.

40. Black, *Black Male Concept of Manhood*, 143. See also Black, *Dismantling Black Manhood*.

41. Rediker, Amistad *Rebellion*, 25–26.

42. Historians have long debated the continuity or severance of African culture once enslaved Africans landed in the New World. For more on African American culture as a creolization of African and European/New World traditions, see Mintz and Price, *Birth of African-American Culture*. Stephanie Smallwood presents a compelling argument regarding the social transformation enslaved Africans experienced and the rebuilding of culture within the enslaved experience. Smallwood, *Saltwater Slavery*.

43. Black, *Dismantling Black Manhood*, 11–12, 29–31.

44. Bibb, *Life and Adventures of Henry Bibb*, 2:366.

45. Bibb, *Life and Adventures of Henry Bibb*, 2:391–94.

46. Craft, *Running a Thousand Miles for Freedom*, 3:899.

47. Steward, *Twenty-Two Years a Slave*, 3:702.

48. Henson, *Truth Stranger Than Fiction*.

49. Robert Smalls, interview, in Blassingame, *Slave Testimony*, 376.

50. Clarke, "Leaves from a Slave's Journal of Life," 157.

51. H. B. Brown, *Narrative of Henry Box Brown*, 2:457–58.

52. Brown, *Narrative of Henry Box Brown*, 2:457–58, 471–72; Lewis and Milton Clarke, *Narratives of the Suffering of Lewis and Milton Clarke*, 1:173.

53. Bibb, *Life and Adventures of Henry Bibb*, 2:367.

54. Great efforts were made to ensure the survival of slavery. The enslaved were conditioned, mostly through violence, to not question or attempt to usurp their owners' authority. The idea of the enslaved revolting against the establishment frightened slave owners beyond belief, and they did all they could to make sure that enslaved people did not attempt to chip away at the control they had established. Yet despite their efforts, enslaved people found ways to resist and rebel. On resistance and rebellion, see, for example, Franklin and Schweninger, *Runaway Slaves*; Camp, *Closer to Freedom*; Holden, *Surviving Southampton*.

55. Hayden, *Narrative of William Hayden*, 1:239.

56. Alfred (a slave) v. State, 37 Miss. 296 (1859). See also Catterall, *Judicial Cases concerning American Slavery*, 3:362.

57. For example, the 1831 North Carolina General Assembly's Act concerning Slaves and Free Persons of Color did not have to specifically prohibit the intermarriage of the enslaved because previous statutes deemed them chattel property, unable to enter into contracts—of which marriage is one. The 1831 act did, however, specifically forbid free persons of color, who had marriage rights, from intermarrying with slaves. See An Act concerning Slaves and Free Persons of Color, N.C. Rev. Code 105 (1831).

58. *Alfred (a slave) v. State*.

59. In addition to being a businessman, attorney, jurist, and member of the North Carolina House of Commons, Chief Justice Thomas Ruffin was a planter and slaveowner. By 1830, one year after being elected to the North Carolina Supreme Court, he owned thirty enslaved people and two plantations in Rockingham and Alamance Counties. In 1829, shortly after being elected to the court, he acquired a large plantation in Alamance County. Between this and other plantations in the piedmont region of North Carolina, Ruffin owned upwards of one hundred enslaved people. 1830 US Federal Census, Orange, North Carolina, Bureau of the Census, NARA.

60. State v. Samuel, 19 N.C. (2 Dev. & Bat.) 177 (1836).

61. Mississippi's High Court of Errors and Appeals was reconfigured by the state's 1869 constitution as the Supreme Court of Mississippi.

62. B. D. Jones, *Fathers of Conscience*, 99–101.

63. *Alfred (a slave) v. State*. See V. Morgan, *Laboring Women*. In an interview, Rose Williams said her former owner partnered her with Rufus because they were both

"portly," and he anticipated they would produce portly children. Rose Williams, interview, in Boykin, *Lay My Burden Down*, 160–62.

64. *Alfred (a slave) v. State*.

65. *Alfred (a slave) v. State*.

66. "Tryal of Ware's Ben," in Thomas Watkins to James Monroe, Executive Papers, Letters Received, box 116, January–March 1801, LVA. Ben's murder trial shows that even though some enslaved men were not afraid to act outside the parameters set for them by society and the law to protect women, the power slave owners wielded was formidable. Even when enslaved men wanted to react and operate according to their own devices, the grip of their owners' will was often inescapable. For more analysis on Ben's trial, see Rothman, *Notorious in the Neighborhood*, 145–49.

67. Because Ben's actions were instigated by Bass, even his efforts to assume authority over his wife were subject to a slave owner's authority.

68. "Tryal of Ware's Ben," in Thomas Watkins to James Monroe, Executive Papers, Letters Received, box 116, January–March 1801, LVA.

69. Case of Peggy, Patrick, and Franky, Executive Papers, Pardon Papers, box 316, May–September 1830, LVA. For more analysis on this case, see Johnston, *Race Relations in Virginia*, 307–8; Rothman, *Notorious in the Neighborhood*, 149–63; Nunley, *The Demands of Justice*, 145–48.

70. Case of Peggy, Patrick, and Franky, Executive Papers, Pardon Papers, box 316, May–September 1830, LVA.

71. Ball, *Fifty Years in Chains*.

72. Ball, *Fifty Years in Chains*.

73. Ball, *Fifty Years in Chains*.

74. Henson, *Life of Josiah Henson*, 2:506.

75. Henson, *Life of Josiah Henson*, 2:506.

Chapter Four

1. The title of this chapter is a quote from Henry Box Brown, *Narrative of Henry Box Brown*, 2:457; Robert Hamilton to Helen Brooke, January 15, 1843, in Helen Hamilton divorce petition, December 14, 1846, Richmond, Virginia, Legislative Petitions, Library of Virginia (hereafter cited as LVA).

2. Glover, *Southern Sons*, 126.

3. Robert Hamilton to Helen Brooke, January 15, 1843, in Helen Hamilton divorce petition, December 14, 1846, Legislative Petitions, LVA.

4. Robert Hamilton to Helen Brooke, January 15, 1843, in Helen Hamilton divorce petition, December 14, 1846, Legislative Petitions, LVA.

5. According to the 1820 census, Brooke owned sixty enslaved people between two properties, including St. Julien in Spotsylvania County. 1820 US Federal Census, Spotsylvania, Virginia, Bureau of the Census, National Archives and Records Administration (hereafter cited as NARA).

6. Mary Champe Brooke deposition, Helen Hamilton divorce petition, December 14, 1846, Legislative Petitions, LVA.

7. Mary Champe Brooke deposition, Helen Hamilton divorce petition, December 14, 1846, Legislative Petitions, LVA.

8. White, *Ar'n't I a Woman?*, 28–29.

9. Ebenezer Appleton to Moody Kent, April 7, 1804, Ebenezer Appleton Papers, South Caroliniana Library (hereafter cited as SCL).

10. Jack and Rosa Maddox, interview, in Rawick, *AS*, suppl. ser. 2, 7.6 (Texas), 2531.

11. Walton, interview, in Perdue, Barden, and Phillips, *Weevils in the Wheat*, 301.

12. Bardaglio, *Reconstructing the Household*, 55; D'Emilio and Freedman, *Intimate Matters*, 94.

13. Chancellor Harper, "Harper on Slavery," 44–45.

14. Mary Champe Brooke deposition, Helen Hamilton divorce petition, December 14, 1846, Legislative Petitions, LVA.

15. Mary Champe Brooke deposition and Martin Burton deposition, Helen Hamilton divorce petition, December 14, 1846, Legislative Petitions, LVA.

16. Francis Brooke deposition, Helen Hamilton divorce petition, December 14, 1846, Legislative Petitions, LVA.

17. According to historian Suzanne Lebsock, in the nineteenth century, women were considered the moral superiors of men. These notions of female virtue, the "cult of true womanhood" or the "cult of domesticity," created a discourse that allowed men to reference their flawed and inferior nature to explain intemperance, infidelity, and miscegenation. Lebsock, *Free Women of Petersburg*, 51.

18. William Kendall emancipation petition, December 15, 1813, King George County, Legislative Petitions, LVA; John Randolph to Henry Watkins, April 11, 1832, John Randolph Papers, Virginia Museum of History and Culture.

19. Bardaglio, *Reconstructing the Household*, 55; Thomas Jefferson to Edward Coles, in Rothman, *Notorious in the Neighborhood*, 46; James Henry Hammond, "Hammond's Letters on Slavery," 119; Rev. J. D. Long quote found in Clinton, *Plantation Mistress*, 210.

20. For more on Thomas Jefferson's long-term sexual relationship with Sally Hemings, see Gordon-Reed, *Thomas Jefferson and Sally Hemings*; Gordon-Reed, *Hemingses of Monticello*.

21. Clarke, *Narratives of the Suffering of Lewis*.

22. Paxton, *Letters on Slavery*, 129.

23. Paxton, *Letters on Slavery*, 129; Bible parable of the prodigal son, Luke 15: 11–32.

24. Diary entry, James Henry Hammond, December 15, 1850, in Hammond, *Secret and Sacred*, 212–13.

25. Bill of sale for Sally Johnson and daughter, January 12, 1839, Hammond-Bryan-Cumming Family Papers, SCL.

26. In a letter to his son Harry, Hammond acknowledged that he fathered children by both Sally Johnson and Louisa Johnson and asked Harry to provide for the children. He did not suggest that they be emancipated but that they remain the property of the Hammond family, presumably for their own protection. He said, "Sally says Henderson is my child. It is possible, but I do not believe it. Yet act on her's [*sic*]

rather than my opinion. Louisa's first child may be mine. I think not. Her second I believe is mine. Take care of her & her children who are both of your blood if not of mine & of Henderson." James Hammond to Harry Hammond, February 19, 1856, James Henry Hammond Papers, SCL. Full transcription of the letter can also be found in Faust, *James Henry Hammond and the Old South*, 87.

27. Carol Bleser, introduction, 9.

28. South Carolina law allowed male family members to draft premarital contracts that protected a woman's property and allowed it to remain in her name, even after marriage. See Myers, *Forging Freedom*, 140.

29. James and Catherine Hammond were married on June 23, 1831. Their first child, James Henry (Harry) Hammond II, was born approximately nine months later, on March 30, 1832. See Faust, *James Henry Hammond and the Old South*, 139.

30. It is unclear whether Catherine Hammond was particularly bothered by Sarah and Louisa's familial ties, Louisa's young age, or both. Southerners considered ten years old to be the age of consent for sexual relations. At twelve, Louisa had passed that threshold. However, Catherine most likely still viewed her as a child, one who probably had not started or at least was still going through puberty. On age of consent in the antebellum South, see Sommerville, *Rape and Race*, 43.

31. James and Catherine had eight children. At the time of their separation, James Henry was eighteen and in college in Columbia, South Carolina; their second-born child, Christopher Fitzsimons, died in 1848, two years before the separation. Their third- and fourth-born children, Edward Spann and William, were away in college in Athens, Georgia. (William would die two years later in 1852 of typhoid fever.) Their fifth-born child, Charles, died in infancy. Paul, their sixth-born child, was away in boarding school in Augusta, Georgia. Catherine "Cattie" and Elizabeth "Betty" were their last two children and the only daughters. As they were only ten and one, respectively, they accompanied their mother to Charleston. See diary entry, Hammond, December 15, 1850, and December 31, 1850, in Hammond, *Secret and Sacred*, 212, 224.

32. Diary entry, Hammond, December 15, 1850, in Hammond, *Secret and Sacred*, 212–13.

33. Diary entry, Hammond, December 15, 1850, in Hammond, *Secret and Sacred*, 213.

34. Diary entries, Hammond, May 25, 1851, and December 15, 1850, in Hammond, *Secret and Sacred*, 231, 212.

35. Diary entry, Hammond, May 21, 1852, in Hammond, *Secret and Sacred*, 254.

36. Diary entry, Hammond, May 21, 1852, in Hammond, *Secret and Sacred*, 254.

37. Diary entries, Hammond, January 31, 1844, and December 9, 1846, in Hammond, *Secret and Sacred*, 120, 173.

38. Diary entries, Hammond, December 9, 1846; January 31, 1844; and December 9, 1846, in Hammond, *Secret and Sacred*, 120, 168, 170, 172–73.

39. Faust, *James Henry Hammond and the Old South*, 87. Hammond speaks of his reconciliation with Catherine Hammond and the purchase of their new residence, Redcliffe, where Hammond lived until his death. See diary entry, Hammond, May 12, 1855, in Hammond, *Secret and Sacred*, 266.

40. Evelina Roane petition, Evelina Roane divorce petition, King William County, Legislative Petitions, LVA.

41. Fendall Gregory affidavit, Evelina Roane divorce petition, King William County, Legislative Petitions, LVA.

42. 1820 US Federal Census, King William, Virginia, Bureau of the Census, NARA.

43. Evelina Roane petition, Evelina Roane divorce petition, King William County, Legislative Petitions, LVA.

44. A more detailed discussion on the strategies used by white women to secure divorce in response to white men's sexual relations with enslaved women can be found in chapter 6.

45. Thomas Gregory affidavit, Evelina Roane divorce petition, King William County, Legislative Petitions, LVA.

46. Mary Gregory affidavit, Thomas Gregory affidavit, Fendall Gregory affidavit, and Evelina Roane petition, Evelina Roane divorce petition, King William County, Legislative Petitions, LVA.

47. Catherine Carter deposition, Lucy Norman divorce petition, Henry County, Virginia, Legislative Petitions, LVA.

48. Lucy Burwell petition and Thomas Burwell deposition, Lucy Burwell divorce petition, Mecklenburg County, Legislative Petitions, LVA.

49. Eliza Prince alimony petition, Charleston District, Records of the Equity Court, South Carolina Department of Archives and History (hereafter cited as SCDAH); Alwyn Prince deposition, Master's Report and Recommendation, Thomas Wigfall petition, Charleston District, Records of the Equity Court, SCDAH.

Chapter Five

1. The title of this chapter is a quote from Solomon Northup, *Twelve Years a Slave*, 328. A slaveholder in his own right, Roswell King Jr. relished the responsibility of managing slaves, which was reflected in his sense of entitlement to the bodies of the enslaved women who fell under his charge. He and his father, Roswell King Sr., were both successful slaveholders. At the time of his death in 1854, Roswell King Jr. owned 127 slaves. For more on the Kings, see Bell, *Major Butler's Legacy*, 531–32.

2. Kemble, *Journal of a Residence*, xxii, 238.

3. Kemble, *Journal of a Residence*, 238, 269.

4. Kemble, *Journal of a Residence*, 269. For more on Julia Maxwell King's slave ownership, see Bell, *Major Butler's Legacy*, 532.

5. Kemble, *Journal of a Residence*, 269.

6. On patriarchy and white women's subordination to white men, see Scott, *Southern Lady*; Clinton, *Plantation Mistress*, 6, 36–38; Fox-Genovese, *Within the Plantation Household*; Stevenson, *Life in Black and White*, chap. 3; K. Brown, *Good Wives*, 4–5, 13–17, 127.

7. See Chesnut, *Private Mary Chesnut*. Chesnut complains of the burdens placed on slave-owning women. They must manage slaves and tolerate their husband's illicit sexual behavior. Historian Jacqueline Jones quotes that slave-owning women like

Chesnut saw themselves as "slaves of slaves." Elizabeth Fox-Genovese, however, argues that historians as well as plantation mistresses were often seduced into making this false comparison. Fox-Genovese, *Within the Plantation Household*, 47; J. Jones, *Labor or Love, Labor of Sorrow*, 23.

8. In the first three chapters of *Out of the House of Bondage*, Thavolia Glymph challenges the previous historiography that failed to see slave-owning women as figures of authority within the system of slavery. She argues that historians' overreliance on patriarchy to characterize power in the antebellum South has obscured our ability to recognize slave-owning women as managers not only of households but of enslaved laborers within those households. These women were afforded the same opportunities as slave-owning men to oversee slave labor and issue punishment as they saw fit. Glymph's work provided a new framework for understanding slave-owning and enslaved women's relations. Building on Glymph, Stephanie Jones-Rogers provides an in-depth analysis of white women as slave owners and their influence within the slave-market economy. For more on slave-owning women's agency, see Glymph, *Out of the House of Bondage*; Jones-Rogers, *They Were Her Property*.

9. Kemble, *Journal of a Residence*, 269.

10. White women frequently referred to sexual relations between white men and enslaved women as "illicit" in their personal correspondence, diaries, and even public documents. For example, when Anna Allen of Chester District, South Carolina, filed for divorce from her husband, John Allen, she charged him with "illicit and criminal intercourse with a negro wench, a slave of her said husband." Anna Allen bill of relief and Anna Allen divorce petition, Richland County, Records of the Equity Court, South Carolina Department of Archives and History.

11. Thomas, *Secret Eye*, 168; Chesnut, *Private Mary Chesnut*, 21, 42.

12. H. Jacobs, *Incidents*, 51–52.

13. Chesnut, *Private Mary Chesnut*, 42, 82.

14. H. Jacobs, *Incidents*, 51–52.

15. T. Morris, *Southern Slavery and the Law*, 302–6; Block, *Rape and Sexual Power*, 65–71; Clinton, "Southern Dishonor," 65; Getman, "Sexual Control in the Slaveholding South," 135.

16. Testimony of Virginia Wainscott, State of Missouri v. Celia, a Slave, #4496, Callaway County Circuit Court, Fulton (1855); McLaurin, *Celia, a Slave*, 8–9.

17. Celia told William Powell, one of Newsom's neighbors, that Newsom came to her cabin around 10:00 P.M. at bedtime. See testimony of William Powell, *State of Missouri v. Celia*; McLaurin, *Celia, a Slave*, 18.

18. Testimony of William Powell and testimony of Jeffery Jones, *State of Missouri v. Celia*; McLaurin, *Celia, a Slave*, 27–29. Celia gave birth to two children between 1850 and 1855. According to the trial testimony of Jefferson Jones, Celia's second child belonged to Newsom. McLaurin writes that Newsom fathered at least one of Celia's children, but there is a possibility that he fathered both children. McLaurin, *Celia, a Slave*, 24.

19. Unnamed interviewee in Rawick, *AS*, 13.4 (Georgia), 295. On slave-owning women's silence and fear of speaking out against interracial sex, see Stevenson, "What's Love Got to Do with It?," 172–73.

20. Virginia Hayes Shepherd, interview, in Perdue, Barden, and Phillips, *Weevils in the Wheat*, 257.

21. Annie Young, interview, in Rawick, *AS*, 7.1 (Oklahoma), 362; Jacob Manson, interview, in Rawick, *AS*, 15.2 (North Carolina), 97–98.

22. Testimony of William Powell, *State of Missouri v. Celia*. Although Celia claimed to have killed Newsom on her own, there is a possibility that she had help from her lover, George, another of Newsom's slaves. She testified that George demanded that she put a stop to Newsom's sexual assaults. Celia was pregnant at the time of the murder, likely in the second trimester, with a child that could have been either George's or Newsom's. Considering her pregnancy and size, Celia likely needed help moving Newsom's body to her fireplace and burning it. George had motive to kill Newsom or at least assist in the murder and disposal of Newsom's body.

23. Chesnut, *Mary Chesnut's Civil War*, 169. Historian Deborah Gray White argues that because white women were able to do very little to stop their husbands' sexual relations with female slaves, they feigned ignorance, especially in public. See White, *Ar'n't I a Woman?*, 41.

24. W. L. Bost, interview, in Rawick, *AS*, 14.1 (North Carolina), 142; Wyatt-Brown, *Southern Honor*, 166.

25. Mary Reynolds, interview, in Rawick, *AS*, suppl. ser. 2, 8.7 (Texas), 3292–94.

26. Reynolds, interview, 3292–94.

27. Reynolds, interview, 3292–94.

28. Reynolds, interview, 3292–94. On the fancy-girl trade and the fetishization of enslaved women of mixed race, see W. Johnson, *Soul by Soul*, 113–15, 154–55; Baptist, "'Cuffy,' 'Fancy Maids,' and 'One-Eyed Men,'" 1639, 1641–49; Clark, *Strange History of the American Quadroon*.

29. Mary Reynolds, interview, in Rawick, *AS*, suppl. ser. 2, 8.7 (Texas), 3292–94.

30. Mary Wood, interview, in Perdue, Barden, and Phillips, *Weevils in the Wheat*, 332.

31. On slave-owning women and the idealized household, see Clinton, *Plantation Mistress*; Fox-Genovese, *Within the Plantation Household*; Glymph, *Out of the House of Bondage*.

32. Henry Ferry, interview, in Perdue, Barden, and Phillips, *Weevils in the Wheat*, 91.

33. See chapter 6 for a discussion of how slave-owning women broached the public sphere regarding their husbands' interracial relations with enslaved women.

34. Isabella Kelly petition and Edwin Kelly deposition, Isabella Kelly divorce petition, Records of the Chancery Court, University of South Alabama Archives.

35. Chesnut, *Private Mary Chesnut*, 42. According to Chesnut, white women's acute awareness of white men's sexual relations with enslaved women, coupled with expectations of their silence and acceptance, created a need for them to develop passive yet satisfying ways to discuss the topic and communicate their frustration. Historian Kathleen Brown argues that because women were marginalized from the male worlds of taverns, courthouses, government, and muster, they participated actively in other venues of public life, conveying status through the company they kept (in their homes) and the clothes they wore. See K. Brown, *Good Wives*, 284–85, 307.

36. Laura Gresham to Henry Gresham, September 21, 1864, Gresham Family Papers, Virginia Museum of History and Culture (hereafter cited as VMHC).

37. Shepherd, *Statutes at Large of Virginia*, 252. The original 1806 statute required all emancipated slaves to leave the state of Virginia within a year or face re-enslavement. In 1837, the general assembly amended the statute, permitting emancipated slaves to petition local courts for permission to remain in the state.

38. Laura Gresham to Henry Gresham, September 21, 1864, Gresham Family Papers, VMHC.

39. Thomas, *Secret Eye*, 319–20.

40. Chesnut, *Private Mary Chesnut*, 42; Thomas, *Secret Eye*, 168. Mary Chesnut's diaries are the exception to the rule, because while she might have initially intended for them to remain private, she eventually adopted the hope that they would one day be published. In the 1880s, she heavily edited and revised portions of her journals for publication. Her vision would come to fruition in 1905, when her friend and confidant Isabella D. Martin arranged to have a truncated version of her memoir published. It was titled *A Diary from Dixie, as Written by Mary Boykin Chesnut*.

41. Kemble, *Journal of a Residence*, 10.

42. Kemble, *Journal of a Residence*, 201. Pierce Butler and Frances Kemble's disagreements over slavery played a major role in the deterioration of their marriage. Unable to reconcile, Kemble left the United States and returned to England. During that time, Butler filed for divorce. The couple's divorce was finalized in 1849, and as was customary, Butler retained primary custody of their two children. See Riley, *Divorce: An American Tradition*, 51.

43. Aaron, *Light and Truth of Slavery*; Savilla Burrell, interview, in Rawick, *AS*, 2.1 (South Carolina), 150.

44. Pickard, *Kidnapped and the Ransomed*.

45. Pickard, *Kidnapped and the Ransomed*.

46. Jones-Rogers, *They Were Her Property*, 61–62; Glymph, *Out of the House of Bondage*, 52; Fox-Genovese, *Within the Plantation Household*, 24, 29, 97.

47. Jones-Rogers, *They Were Her Property*, 81–100, 123–50; Glymph, *Out of the House of Bondage*, 5, 18–33, 66; J. Jones, *Labor of Love, Labor of Sorrow*, 23–24; Fox-Genovese, *Within the Plantation Household*, 24, 132. In an 1847 letter, Joseph James Pope of Charleston, South Carolina, told a friend about a mistress who brutally murdered one of her female slaves: "The act was very aggravated, and the aggravating circumstances here produced an impression on the people which I have never seen equaled by a similar circumstance." He even presumed that the female slaveholder would be tried for the murder of the female slave. See Joseph James Pope to James Morrow, January 18, 1847, Joseph James Pope Papers, South Caroliniana Library.

48. Northup, *Twelve Years a Slave*, 312–33. Per the 1850 US Federal Census and Slave Schedule, Edwin Epps was originally from North Carolina. In 1850, the Eppses owned eight enslaved people, including a nineteen-year-old female. This enslaved woman was likely Patsey. 1850 US Federal Census, Avoyelles, Louisiana, 1850 US Federal Census, Slave Schedules, Bureau of the Census, National Archives and Records Administration.

49. Northup, *Twelve Years a Slave*, 334, 328.

50. Albert, *House of Bondage*.

51. Roper, *Narrative of the Adventures and Escape of Moses Roper*, 1:7.

52. Henry Norrell divorce petition, Records of the Chancery Court, Tallapoosa County Courthouse Archive.

53. Bynum, *Unruly Women*, 37.

54. H. Jacobs, *Incidents*, 34.

55. Richard Macks, interview, in Rawick, *AS*, 16.3 (Maryland), 55, II. Jacobs, *Incidents*, 32–35.

56. H. Jacobs, *Incidents*, 34.

57. H. Jacobs, *Incidents*, 34.

58. J. Morgan, *Laboring Women*, 12–49; K. Brown, *Good Wives*, 108–10; White, *Ar'n't I a Woman?*, 15.

59. H. Jacobs, *Incidents*, 31–35.

60. H. Jacobs, *Incidents*, 28.

61. Harriet Jacobs runaway ad, *American Beacon and Virginia and North-Carolina Gazette* (Norfolk, VA), July 4, 1835, State Archives of North Carolina.

62. Former slave Virginia Hayes Shepherd described another enslaved woman, Diana Gaskins, saying, "Diana was a black beauty if there ever was one. She had this thin silk skin, a sharp nose, thin lips, a perfect set of white teeth and beautiful long coal-black hair. Diana was dignity personified, the prettiest black woman I ever saw." According to Shepherd, because of Diana's beauty, her owner "wanted his Diana in every sense of the word." Virginia Hayes Shepherd, interview, in Perdue, Barden, and Phillips, *Weevils in the Wheat*, 257.

63. Pierce Cody, interview, in Rawick, *AS*, 13.1 (Georgia), 198.

64. Jack and Rosa Maddox, interview, in Rawick, *AS*, suppl. ser. 2, 7.6 (Texas), 2531.

65. Rebecca Hooks, interview, in Rawick, *AS*, 17.1 (Florida), 172.

66. H. Jacobs, *Incidents*, 13–14.

67. H. Jacobs, *Incidents*, 32–34; Thomas, *Secret Eye*, 253–54.

68. Thomas, *Secret Eye*, 168–69.

Chapter Six

1. The title of this chapter is a quote from Bernard Laspeyre, the husband of a discontented wife. See Bernard Laspeyre petition, Sampson County, General Assembly Session Records, Divorce and Alimony Petitions, State Archives of North Carolina (hereafter cited as SANC). On divorce in the South during the colonial and antebellum periods, see, for example, Basch, *Framing American Divorce*; Buckley, *Great Catastrophe of My Life*; Censer, "'Smiling through Her Tears'"; Chused, *Private Acts in Public Places*; Riley, "Legislative Divorce in Virginia"; Rothman, *Notorious in the Neighborhood*, 169–98; Schweninger, *Families in Crisis in the Old South*.

2. Ellen Shields Dunlap divorce petition, Augusta County, Virginia, Legislative Petitions, Library of Virginia (hereafter cited as LVA).

3. 1810 US Federal Census, Augusta, County, Virginia, Bureau of the Census, National Archives and Records Administration (hereafter cited as NARA); Boogher,

Gleanings of Virginia History, 321–22; Waddell, *Annals of Augusta County*. Robert Doak's surname is sometimes spelled Doake.

4. Over generations, white men succeeded in generating anxieties around interracial sex and its threat to racial purity and establishing that interracial intercourse went against standards of morality and respectability, expressly for white women. However, their lip service did little to curtail sexual appetites or disincentivize white men from raping or threatening sexual violence to exact power over enslaved populations.

5. On interracial sex, marriage, and the law in the United States, see, for example, Bardaglio, *Reconstructing the Household*; Bardaglio, "Shameful Matches"; R. Kennedy, *Interracial Intimacies*; Pascoe, *What Comes Naturally*; Rothman, *Notorious in the Neighborhood*; Wallenstein, *Tell the Court I Love My Wife*; Schweninger, *Families in Crisis in the Old South*.

6. Ellen Shields Dunlap divorce petition, Augusta County, Virginia, Legislative Petitions, LVA.

7. James Shields and Thomas Shields affidavit, Peggy and Rachel Shields affidavit, and Ellen Shields Dunlap divorce petition, Augusta County, Virginia, Legislative Petitions, LVA.

8. Ellen Shields Dunlap divorce petition, Augusta County, Virginia, Legislative Petitions, LVA.

9. Most slave-owning women had been indoctrinated from childhood to tolerate or at least camouflage their disdain for white men's sexual relations with enslaved women within the walls of their households. There were some who launched verbal attacks against their husbands. Others chose to distract themselves from their own household problems by gossiping about the "illicit intercourse" taking place in other people's homes. Enslaved testimony reveals that some coped with their frustration by exploiting their authority to inflict harsh punishments, both physical and psychological, on the enslaved women with whom their husbands had sexual relations. (See chapter 5 for a more detailed discussion.) See also Chesnut, *Private Mary Chesnut*; Chesnut, *Mary Chesnut's Civil War*; Thomas, *Secret Eye*.

10. Buckley, *Great Catastrophe of My Life*, 7, 14, 32; Censer, "'Smiling through Her Tears,'" 27; Riley, "Legislative Divorce in Virginia," 52; Schweninger, *Families in Crisis in the Old South*, 2–11.

11. Censer, "'Smiling through Her Tears,'" 35–37; Buckley, *Great Catastrophe of My Life*, 6; Schweninger, *Families in Crisis in the Old South*, 9–11; Riley, "Legislative Divorce in Virginia," 56; McCurry, *Masters of Small Worlds*, 86–87; Frierson, "Divorce in South Carolina."

12. I was initially introduced to these divorce petitions through the Race and Slavery Petitions Project, a digital catalog of over seventeen thousand legislative and court petitions, curated under the direction of Dr. Loren Schweninger. Based on his exhaustive research of these petitions, Schweninger wrote *Families in Crisis in the Old South*. For this study, Schweninger collected a sampling of 610 divorce, separation, and alimony petitions filed by white women from every slaveholding state, covering most geographical regions within each state and spanning from the Revolutionary War to the end of the Civil War. The statistics I use to discuss the demographics of who filed divorce petitions, the outcomes of divorce petitions, and the grounds on which petitions were filed

were derived from Schweninger's sampling. On how Schweninger derived this sampling, see Schweninger, *Families in Crisis in the Old South*, xi.

13. McCurry, *Masters of Small Worlds*, 86; Buckley, *Great Catastrophe of My Life*, 5–6, 141; Censer, "'Smiling through Her Tears,'" 36–37, 46; Riley, "Legislative Divorce in Virginia," 60; Schweninger, *Families in Crisis in the Old South*, x.

14. Buckley, *Great Catastrophe of My Life*, 15; Censer, "'Smiling through Her Tears,'" 37, 46; Riley, "Legislative Divorce in Virginia," 60; Schweninger, *Families in Crisis in the Old South*, x–xi.

15. Schweninger, *Families in Crisis in the Old South*, 17–31; Hodes, *White Women, Black Men*; Buckley, *Great Catastrophe of My Life*, 139–40.

16. Schweninger, *Families in Crisis*, 17–31; Buckley, *Great Catastrophe of My Life*, 139–41.

17. Ellen Shields Dunlap divorce petition, Augusta County, Virginia, Legislative Petitions, LVA; Wyatt-Brown, *Southern Honor*, 308. In many ways, Southern society required that slave-owning men and women partake in the delicate dance between discretion, ignorance, and silence. Ideally, the slave-owning wife would never find out. At minimum, these women expected their husbands to be discreet and save them from the details. Discretion was tantamount to honorability according to the South's social contract of honor and respectability. Per historian Bertram Wyatt-Brown, "A mother's honor was to be protected from the grossness of manhood, the lustiness that was both deplored and celebrated by the men themselves." Wyatt-Brown, *Southern Honor*, 166.

18. Sarah Smith divorce petition, Talladega County, Alabama, Records of the Circuit Court, Talladega County Judicial Building; Eliza Prince divorce petition, Charleston District, Records of the Equity Court, South Carolina Department of Archives and History (hereafter cited as SCDAH); Alzonuth Whitehead divorce petition, Adams County, Mississippi, Records of the Vice Chancery Court, Adams County Courthouse; Caroline Dungan petition, Michael McGee deposition, and Joshua Goza deposition, Caroline Dungan divorce petition, Claiborne County, Mississippi, Records of the Chancery Court, Claiborne County Courthouse. A female complainant or petitioner was sometimes referred to as an "oratrix" in petitions and other court documents filed with courts of equity.

19. Lucy Burwell divorce petition, Mecklenburg County, Virginia, Legislative Petitions, LVA.

20. John Burwell response, Lucy Burwell divorce petition, Mecklenburg County, Virginia, Legislative Petitions, LVA.

21. Lucy Burwell petition and Charles G. Feild deposition, Lucy Burwell divorce petition, Mecklenburg County, Virginia, Legislative Petitions, LVA.

22. Thomas Burwell deposition, Armistead Burwell deposition, J. E. Burwell deposition, and John Burwell deposition, Lucy Burwell divorce petition, Mecklenburg County, Virginia, Legislative Petition, LVA.

23. Mary Garrett divorce petition, Guilford County, North Carolina, County Court Divorce Records, SANC.

24. Evelina Roane divorce petition, King William County, Virginia, Legislative Petitions, LVA. For an extensive examination of the Evelina Roane petition, see Thomas E. Buckley, "'Placed in the Power of Violence.'"

25. Mary Hassell divorce petition, Bertie County, North Carolina, General Assembly Session Records, Divorce and Alimony Petitions, SANC.

26. Sarah Strickland, Wake County, North Carolina, County Court Divorce Records, SANC.

27. Emily Manning divorce petition, Lowndes County, Alabama, Records of the Circuit Court, Lowndes County Courthouse.

28. Emily Manning divorce petition, Lowndes County Courthouse.

29. Fendall Gregory affidavit, Thomas Gregory affidavit, and Evelina Roane petition, Evelina Roane divorce petition, King William County, Virginia, Legislative Petitions, LVA.

30. Sarah Ann Simpson divorce petition, Fairfield District, South Carolina, Records of the Equity Court, SCDAH.

31. Mary Cole answer, Stephen Cole divorce petition, Richmond County, North Carolina, County Court Divorce Records, SANC; Ruthey Ann Hansley v. Samuel G. Hansley, 32 N.C. 506 (1849).

32. Lucy Norman divorce petition, Henry County, Virginia, Legislative Petitions, LVA.

33. Stephen Terry affidavit, Sopha Dobyns divorce petition, Bedford County, Virginia, Legislative Petitions, LVA.

34. Glover, *Southern Sons*, 15–16.

35. Harriet Laspeyre divorce petition, New Hanover County, North Carolina, General Assembly Session Records, Divorce and Alimony Petitions, SANC.

36. Evelina Roane petition and John Gregory to Evelina Roane, August 24, 1824, Evelina Roane divorce petition, King William County, Virginia, Legislative Petitions, LVA.

37. Eliza Prince divorce petition, Charleston District, Records of the Equity Court, SCDAH.

38. Bill of sale for Jemmima Jones, August 18, 1829, Charleston District, South Carolina Estate Inventories and Select Bills of Sale, 1732–1872, SCDAH; Eliza Prince divorce petition, Charleston District, Records of the Equity Court, SCDAH.

39. Eliza Prince divorce petition, Charleston District, Records of the Equity Court, SCDAH; 1830 US Federal Census, Charleston Ward 1, Charleston, South Carolina, Bureau of the Census, NARA.

40. Eliza Prince divorce petition, Charleston District, Records of the Equity Court, SCDAH.

41. Eliza Prince petition and report of assets by James Wray, Eliza Prince divorce petition, Charleston District, Records of the Equity Court, SCDAH.

42. Anna Allen divorce petition, Columbia District, South Carolina, Records of the Equity Court, SCDAH.

43. Anna Allen divorce petition, SCDAH.

44. *Hansley v. Hansley*.

45. Fox-Genovese, *Within the Plantation Household*, 44.

46. Buckley, *Great Catastrophe of My Life*, 148; Schweninger, *Families in Crisis in the Old South*, 112.

47. See Alexander, *Ambiguous Lives*; Myers, *Forging Freedom*.

48. Evelina Roane divorce petition, King William County, Virginia, Legislative Petitions, LVA.

49. Glymph, *Out of the House of Bondage*, 18–31.

50. Evelina Roane divorce petition, King William County, Virginia, Legislative Petitions, LVA.

51. Evelina Roane petition, Thomas Gregory affidavit, and Mary Gregory affidavit, Evelina Roane divorce petition, King William County, Virginia, Legislative Petitions, LVA.

52. Elizabeth Clubb petition, Elizabeth Clubb affidavit, and David Clubb answer, Elizabeth Clubb divorce petition, Lincoln County, North Carolina, County Court Divorce Records, SANC.

53. Evelina Roane divorce petition, King William County, Virginia, Legislative Petitions, LVA.

54. Mary Gregory affidavit, Evelina Roane divorce petition, King William County, Virginia, Legislative Petitions, LVA.

55. Sarah Carter divorce petition, Columbia District, South Carolina, Records of the Equity Court, SCDAH; Elizabeth Cline divorce petition, Haywood County, North Carolina, Records of the County Court, SANC.

56. Elizabeth Pannell deposition, Elizabeth Pannell divorce petition, King William County, Legislative Petitions, LVA; Anne Wilson divorce petition, Burke County, North Carolina, County Court Divorce Records, SANC.

57. Barbara Pettus petition and Charles Thomas affidavit, Barbara Pettus divorce petition, Louisa County, Virginia, Legislative Petitions, LVA.

58. Harriet Laspeyre divorce petition, New Hanover County, North Carolina, General Assembly Session Records, Divorce and Alimony Petitions, SANC.

59. Bernard Laspeyre petition, Sampson County, General Assembly Session Records, Divorce and Alimony Petitions, SANC.

Epilogue

1. Du Bois, *Black Reconstruction in America*, 79.

2. Burton, *Memories of Childhood's Slavery Days*.

3. Feimster, *Southern Horrors*, 52. See also Rosen, *Terror in the Heart of Freedom*; Clinton, "Bloody Terrain"; K. Williams, *I Saw Death Coming*.

4. Schwalm, *Hard Fight for We*, 111–12.

5. Schwalm, *Hard Fight for We*, 102.

6. Feimster, "Rape and Mutiny at Fort Jackson," 23.

7. Schwalm, *Hard Fight for We*, 141.

8. Feimster, *Southern Horrors*, 52.

9. Rosen, *Terror in the Heart of Freedom*, 61–83; Feimster, *Southern Horrors*, 44, 53–54.

10. Feimster, "'What If I Am a Woman'"; Feimster, "Rape and Mutiny at Fort Jackson," 11; Edwards, "Sexual Violence, Gender, Reconstruction," 237–40; Feimster, *Southern Horrors*, 53–54; Rosen, *Terror in the Heart of Freedom*, 77.

11. May Satterfield, interview, in Perdue, Barden, and Phillips, *Weevils in the Wheat*, 245.

12. Wells, *Southern Horrors*. For more on Ida B. Wells and her anti-lynching campaign, see Feimster, *Southern Horrors*.

Bibliography

Archives

Adams County Courthouse, Adams County, Mississippi
    Records of the Vice Chancery Court
Claiborne County Courthouse, Claiborne County, Mississippi
    Records of the Chancery Court
Columbiana, Alabama, County Courthouse
    Records of the Chancery Court
Jefferson County Courthouse, Fayette, Mississippi
    Records of the Chancery Court
Library of Virginia
    Chancery Court Papers
    Executive Papers, Letters Received
    Executive Papers, Pardon Papers
    Legislative Petitions
Lowndes County Courthouse, Lowndes County, Alabama
    Records of the Circuit Court
National Archives and Records Administration, Washington, DC
    Bureau of the Census
    Bureau of Pensions, National Archives
    Department of Veterans Affairs, Record Group 15
    Records of the Bureau of the Census, Record Group 29
    Records of the Court of Claims, Record Group 123
    Slave Schedules, Bureau of the Census
South Carolina Department of Archives and History
    Records of the Equity Court
    Records of the General Assembly
    South Carolina Estate Inventories and Select Bills of Sale, 1732–1872
South Carolina Historical Society
    Hagar Richardson Papers
South Caroliniana Library
    Ebenezer Appleton Papers
    Hammond-Bryan-Cumming Family Papers
    James Henry Hammond Papers
    Joseph James Pope Papers
Southern Historical Collection, Wilson Library, University of North Carolina at
    Chapel Hill
    Cameron Family Papers, 1757–1978

Elizabeth Amis Cameron Blanchard Papers, 1694–1954
Rice C. Ballard Papers, 1822–1888
William Ethelbert Ervin Journals, 1839–1856
State Archives of Florida
  Chancery Case Files
State Archives of North Carolina
  County Court Divorce Records
  General Assembly Session Records, Divorce and Alimony Petitions
  Records of the County Court
Talladega County Judicial Building, Talladega, Alabama
  Records of the Circuit Court
Tallapoosa County Courthouse Archive, Dadeville, Alabama
  Records of the Chancery Court
University of South Alabama Archives
  Records of the Chancery Court
Virginia Historical Society
  Blanton Family Papers
Virginia Museum of History and Culture
  Eppes Family Muniments, 1722–1948
  Gresham Family Papers, 1787–1938
  John Randolph Papers

Published Slave Narratives and Interviews

Aaron. *The Light and Truth of Slavery: Aaron's History*. Documenting the American South. University Library, University of North Carolina at Chapel Hill, 2000. http://docsouth.unc.edu/neh/aaron/aaron.html. First published 1845 by the author (Worcester, MA).

Albert, Octavia V. Rogers. *The House of Bondage, or Charlotte Brooks and Other Slaves, Original and Life Like, as They Appeared in Their Old Plantation and City Slave Life*. Documenting the American South. University Library, University of North Carolina at Chapel Hill, 2000. http://docsouth.unc.edu/neh/albert/albert.html. First published 1890 by Hunt & Eaton (New York).

Anderson, William. *Life and Narrative of William J. Anderson, Twenty-Four Years a Slave*. Documenting the American South. University Library, University of North Carolina at Chapel Hill, 2000. http://docsouth.unc.edu/neh/andersonw /andersonw.html. First published 1857 by Daily Tribune Book and Job Printing Office (Chicago).

Ball, Charles. *Fifty Years in Chains; or, The Life of an American Slave*. Documenting the American South. University Library, University of North Carolina at Chapel Hill, 1997. http://docsouth.unc.edu/fpn/ball/ball.html. First published 1858 by Dayton & Asher (New York).

Bibb, Henry. *The Life and Adventures of Henry Bibb: An American Slave*. In *African American Slave Narratives: An Anthology*. Vol. 2. Edited by Sterling Lecatur Bland Jr. Westport, CT: Greenwood Press, 2001.

Blassingame, John, ed. *Slave Testimony: Two Centuries of Letters, Speeches, Interviews, and Autobiographies*. Baton Rouge: Louisiana State University Press, 1977.

Boykin, B. A. *Lay My Burden Down: A Folk History of Slavery*. 2nd ed. Athens: University of Georgia Press, 1989.

Brown, Henry Box. *Narrative of Henry Box Brown, Who Escaped from Slavery Enclosed in a Box 3 Feet and 2 Wide*. In *African American Slave Narratives: An Anthology*. Vol. 2. Edited by Sterling Lecatur Bland Jr. Westport, CT: Greenwood Press, 2001.

Brown, John. *Slave Life in Georgia: A Narrative of the Life, Sufferings, and Escape of John Brown, a Fugitive Slave, Now in England*. Documenting the American South. University Library, University of North Carolina at Chapel Hill, 2001. https://docsouth.unc.edu/neh/jbrown/jbrown.html. First published 1855 by W. M. Watts (London).

Brown, Josephine. *Biography of an American Bondman, by His Daughter*. Documenting the American South. University Library, University of North Carolina at Chapel Hill, 2000. http://docsouth.unc.edu/neh/brownj/brownj .html. First published 1856 by R. F. Wallcut (Boston).

Brown, William Wells. *Narrative of William Wells Brown, a Fugitive Slave*. In *African American Slave Narratives: An Anthology*. Vol. 2. Edited by Sterling Lecatur Bland Jr. Westport, CT: Greenwood Press, 2001.

Burton, Annie L. *Memories of Childhood's Slavery Days*. Documenting the American South. University Library, University of North Carolina at Chapel Hill, 1996. http://docsouth.unc.edu/fpn/burton/burton.html. First published 1909 by Ross (Boston).

Campbell, Israel. *An Autobiography. Bond and Free; or, Yearnings for Freedom, from My Green Brier House. Being the Story of My Life in Bondage, and My Life in Freedom*. Documenting the American South. University Library, University of North Carolina at Chapel Hill, 2001. http://docsouth.unc.edu/neh/campbell/campbell .html. First published 1861 by C. E. P. Brinckloe (Philadelphia).

Clarke, Lewis. "Leaves from a Slave's Journal of Life." In *Slave Testimony: Two Centuries of Letters, Speeches, Interviews, and Autobiographies*, edited by John Blassingame, 151–64. Baton Rouge: Louisiana State University Press, 1977.

———. *Narratives of the Suffering of Lewis, during a Captivity of More Than Twenty-Five Years, among the Algerines of Kentucky, One of the So Called Christian States of America*. Documenting the American South. University Library, University of North Carolina at Chapel Hill, 1999. http://docsouth.unc.edu/neh/clarke/menu .html. First published 1845 by David H. Ela (Boston).

Coffin, Levi. *Reminiscences of Levi Coffin, The Reputed President of the Underground Railroad: Being a Brief History of the Labors of a Lifetime in Behalf of the Slave, with the Stories of Numerous Fugitives, Who Gained Their Freedom Through His Instrumentality, and Many Other Incidents*. Documenting the American South. University Library, University of North Carolina at Chapel Hill, 2000. http://docsouth.unc.edu/nc /coffin/coffin.html. First published 1880 by Robert Clarke (Cincinnati).

Craft, William. *Running a Thousand Miles for Freedom; or, The Escape of William and Ellen Craft from Freedom*. In *African American Slave Narratives: An Anthology*. Vol. 3. Edited by Sterling Lecatur Bland Jr. Westport, CT: Greenwood Press, 2001.

Douglass, Frederick. *My Bondage and My Freedom*. In *Douglass: Autobiographies*.
New York: Library of America, 1996.
————. *Narrative of the Life of Frederick Douglass, an American Slave*. In *Douglass:
Autobiographies*. New York: Library of America, 1996.
Hall, Samuel. *Samuel Hall: 47 Years a Slave; A Brief Story of His Life Before and After
Freedom Came to Him*. Documenting the American South. University Library,
University of North Carolina at Chapel Hill, 2003. http://docsouth.unc.edu/neh
/hall/hall.html. First published 1912 by Journal Print (Washington, IA).
Hayden, William. *Narrative of William Hayden, Containing a Faithful Account of His
Travels for a Number of Years, Whilst a Slave, in the South. Written by Himself*. In
African American Slave Narratives: An Anthology. Vol. 1. Edited by Sterling Lecatur
Bland Jr. Westport, CT: Greenwood Press, 2001.
Henson, Josiah. *The Life of Josiah Henson, Formerly a Slave, Now an Inhabitant of
Canada, as Narrated by Himself*. In *African American Slave Narratives: An Anthology*.
Vol. 2. Edited by Sterling Lecatur Bland Jr. Westport, CT: Greenwood Press, 2001.
————. *Truth Stranger Than Fiction: Father Henson's Story of His Own Life*.
Documenting the American South. University Library, University of North
Carolina at Chapel Hill, 2000. https://docsouth.unc.edu/neh/henson58/henson58
.html. First published 1858 by John P. Jewett (Boston).
Jacobs, Harriet. *Incidents in the Life of a Slave Girl: Written by Herself*. Edited by Jean
Fagan Yellin. Cambridge, MA: Harvard University Press, 2000.
Jacobs, John. "A True Tale of Slavery." In *Incidents in the Life of a Slave Girl: Written by
Herself*, edited by Jean Fagan Yellin, 206–28. Cambridge, MA: Harvard University
Press, 2000.
Keckley, Elizabeth. *Behind the Scenes; or, Thirty Years a Slave, and Four Years in the White
House*. Edited by Frances Smith Foster. Chicago: University of Illinois Press, 2001.
Loguen, Jermain Wesley. *The Rev. J. W. Loguen, as a Slave and as a Freeman. A
Narrative of Real Live*. Documenting the American South. University Library,
University of North Carolina at Chapel Hill, 1999. https://docsouth.unc.edu/neh
/loguen/loguen.html. First published 1859 by J. G. K. Truair & Co. (Syracuse).
Northup, Solomon. *Twelve Years a Slave: The Narrative of Solomon Northup*. In *Puttin'
On Ole Massa*. Edited by Gilbert Osofsky. New York: Harper and Row, 1969.
Pennington, James. *The Fugitive Blacksmith; or, Events in the History of James W. C.
Pennington, Pastor of a Presbyterian Church, New York, Formerly a Slave in the State of
Maryland, United States*. In *African American Slave Narratives: An Anthology*. Vol. 2.
Edited by Sterling Lecatur Bland Jr. Westport, CT: Greenwood Press, 2001.
Perdue, Charles L., Jr., Thomas E. Barden, and Robert K. Phillips, ed. *Weevils in the
Wheat: Interviews with Virginia Ex-Slaves*. Charlottesville: University Press of
Virginia, 1976.
Pickard, Kate E. R. *The Kidnapped and the Ransomed. Being the Personal Recollections of
Peter Still and His Wife "Vina," After Forty Years of Slavery*. Documenting the
American South. University Library, University of North Carolina at Chapel Hill,
1999. http://docsouth.unc.edu/neh/pickard/pickard.html. First published 1856
by William T. Hamilton (Syracuse).

Picquet, Louisa, and Hiram Mattison. *Louisa Picquet, the Octoroon; or, Inside Views of Southern Domestic Life*. Documenting the American South. University Library, University of North Carolina at Chapel Hill, 2003. http://docsouth.unc.edu/neh /picquet/picquet.html. First published 1861 by the author (New York).

Randolph, Peter. *From Slave Cabin to the Pulpit. The Autobiography of Rev. Peter Randolph: The Southern Question Illustrated and sketches of Slaves Life*. Documenting the American South. University Library, University of North Carolina at Chapel Hill, 2000. http://docsouth.unc.edu/neh/randolph/randolph.html. First published 1893 by James H. Earle (Boston).

Rawick, George, ed. *The American Slave: A Composite Autobiography*. 19 vols. Westport, CT: Greenwood, 1972.

———, ed. *The American Slave: A Composite Autobiography*. Supplement, Series 1. 12 vols. Westport, CT: Greenwood, 1977.

———, ed. *The American Slave: A Composite Autobiography*. Supplement, Series 2. 10 vols. Westport, CT: Greenwood, 1979.

Roper, Moses. *A Narrative of the Adventures and Escape of Moses Roper, from American Slavery*. In *African American Slave Narratives*. Vol. 1. Edited by Sterling Lecatur Bland Jr. Westport, CT: Greenwood Press, 2001.

Steward, Austin. *Twenty-Two Years a Slave and Forty Years a Freeman*. In *African American Slave Narratives*. Vol. 3. Edited by Sterling Lecatur Bland Jr. Westport, CT: Greenwood Press, 2001.

Stroyer, Jacob. *My Life in the South*. Documenting the American South. University Library, University of North Carolina at Chapel Hill, 2001. http://docsouth.unc .edu/neh/stroyer85/stroyer85.html. First published 1885 by Observer Book and Job Print (Salem, MA).

Veney, Bethany. *The Narrative of Bethany Veney: A Slave Woman*. Documenting the American South. University Library, University of North Carolina at Chapel Hill, 1997. http://docsouth.unc.edu/fpn/veney/veney.html. First published 1889 by George H. Ellis (Worcester, MA).

Published Primary Sources

Chesnut, Mary Boykin Miller. *Mary Chesnut's Civil War*. Edited by C. Vann Woodward. New Haven, CT: Yale University Press, 1981.

———. *The Private Mary Chesnut: The Unpublished Civil War Diaries*. New York: Oxford University Press, 1984.

Clayton, Augustin. *A Compilation of the Laws of the State of Georgia, Passed by the Legislature since the Political Year 1800, to the Year 1810*. Augusta: Adams & Duyckinck, 1813.

Cooper, Thomas, and David McCord, eds. *The Statutes at Large of South Carolina*. 10 vols. Columbia: A. S. Johnston, 1836–41.

Hammond, James Henry. "Hammond's Letters on Slavery." In *The Pro-Slavery Argument, as Maintained by the Most Distinguished Writers of the Southern States*, 99–174. Philadelphia: Lippincott, Grambo, 1853.

————. *Secret and Sacred: The Diaries of James Henry Hammond, A Southern Slaveholder*. Edited by Carol Bleser. Oxford: Oxford University Press, 1988.

Harper, Chancellor. "Harper on Slavery." In *The Pro-Slavery Argument, as Maintained by the Most Distinguished Writers of the Southern States*, 1–98. Philadelphia: Lippincott, Grambo, 1853.

Hening, William Waller. *The Statues at Large: Being a Collection of all Laws of Virginia from the First Session of the Legislature, in the Year 1619*. Vol. 3. Richmond: R. & W. & G. Bartow, 1819.

Hinkley, Edward Otis, ed., *The Constitution of the State of Maryland: Reported and Adopted by the Convention of Delegates Assembled at the City of Annapolis, November 4th, 1850*. Baltimore: John Murphy, 1855.

Iredell, James, ed. *Reports of Cases at Law Argued and Determined in the Supreme Court of North Carolina, from August Term, 1849, to December Term, 1849, Both Inclusive*. Vol. 10. Raleigh, NC: Seaton Gales, 1850.

James, Benjamin. *A Digest of the Laws of South Carolina: Containing the Public Statute Law of the State, Down to the Year 1822*. Columbia: Telescope Press, 1822.

Kemble, Frances Anne. *Journal of a Residence on a Georgian Plantation in 1838–1839*. Edited by John A. Scott. New York: Knopf, 1961.

Lamar, Lucius Q. C. *A Compilation of the Laws of the State of Georgia, Passed by the Legislature since the Year 1810 to the Year 1819*. August: T. S. Hannon, 1821.

Laws of the State of Mississippi Passed at a Called Session of the Mississippi Legislature Held in the City of Jackson, October, November, and December 1865. Jackson: J. J. Shannon, 1866.

Maxcy, Virgil. *Laws of Maryland*. Baltimore: Philip H. Nicklin, 1811.

Olmsted, Frederick. *A Journey in the Seaboard Slave States, with Remarks on Their Economy*. New York: Mason Brothers, 1861.

Paxton, John D. *Letters on Slavery; Addressed to the Cumberland Congregation, Virginia by J.D. Paxton, Their Former Pastor*. Lexington, KY: Abraham T. Skillman, 1833.

The Pro-Slavery Arguments as Maintained by the Most Distinguished Writers of the Southern States. Philadelphia: Lippincott, Grambo, 1853.

Shepherd, Samuel. *Statutes at Large of Virginia, from October Session 1792, to December Session 1806, Inclusive, in Three Volumes, Being a Continuation of Hening*. Vol. 1. Richmond: Samuel Shepherd, 1835.

Swan, Joseph Rockwell. *Statutes of the State of Ohio, of a General Nature, in Force January 1st, 1854: With References to Prior Repealed Laws*. Cincinnati: H. W. Derby, 1854.

Thomas, Ella Gertrude Clanton. *The Secret Eye: The Journal of Ella Gertrude Clanton Thomas, 1848–1889*. Chapel Hill: University of North Carolina Press, 1990.

Weld, Theodore Dwight. *American Slavery as It Is: Testimony of a Thousand Witnesses*. New York: American Anti-Slavery Society, 1839.

Wells, Ida B. *Southern Horrors: Lynch Law in All Its Phases*. New York: New York Age Print, 1892.

Secondary Sources

Alexander, Adele Logan. *Ambiguous Lives: Free Women of Color in Rural Georgia, 1789-1879*. Fayetteville: University of Arkansas Press, 1992.

Anderson, Irina, and Kathy Doherty. *Accounting for Rape: Psychology, Feminism, and Discourse Analysis in the Study of Sexual Violence*. London: Routledge, 2008.

Anderson, Jean Bradley. *The Kirklands of Ayr Mount*. Chapel Hill: University of North Carolina Press, 1991.

Baptist, Edward E. "The Absent Subject: African American Masculinity and Forced Migration to the Antebellum Plantation Frontier." In *Southern Manhood: Perspectives on Masculinity in the Old South*, edited by Craig Thompson Friend and Lorri Glover, 136–73. Athens: University of Georgia Press, 2004.

———. "'Cuffy,' 'Fancy Maids,' and 'One-Eyed Men': Rape, Commodification, and the Domestic Slave Trade in the United States." *American Historical Review* 106, no. 5 (2001): 1619–50.

———. *The Half Has Never Been Told: Slavery and the Making of American Capitalism*. New York: Basic Books, 2016.

Bardaglio, Peter W. "Rape and the Law in the Old South: 'Calculated to Excited Indignation in Every Heart.'" *Journal of Southern History* 60, no. 4 (November 1994): 749–72.

———. *Reconstructing the Household: Families, Sex, and the Law in the Nineteenth-Century South*. Chapel Hill: University of North Carolina Press, 1995.

———. "'Shamefull Matches': The Regulation of Interracial Sex and Marriage in the South before 1900." In *Sex, Love, Race: Crossing Boundaries in North American History*, edited by Martha Hodes, 112–38. New York: New York University Press, 1999.

Basch, Norma. *Framing American Divorce: From the Revolutionary Generation to the Victorians*. Berkley: University of California Press, 1999.

Bell, Malcolm, Jr. *Major Butler's Legacy: Five Generations of a Slaveholding Family*. Athens: University of Georgia Press, 2004.

Berry, Daina Ramey, and Leslie M. Harris, eds. *Sexuality and Slavery: Reclaiming Intimate Histories in the Americas*. Athens: University of Georgia Press, 2018.

Black, Daniel. "The Black Male Concept of Manhood as Portrayed in Selected Slave and Free Narratives." PhD diss., Temple University, 1993.

———. *Dismantling Black Manhood: An Historical and Literary Analysis of the Legacy of Slavery*. New York: Garland, 1997.

Blassingame, John W. *The Slave Community: Plantation Life in the Antebellum South*. New York: Oxford University Press, 1972.

Bleser, Carol, and Henry Hammond, eds. Introduction to *Secret and Sacred: The Diaries of James Henry Hammond, a Southern Slaveholder*. Oxford: Oxford University Press, 1988.

Block, Sharon. *Rape and Sexual Power in Early America*. Chapel Hill: University of North Carolina Press, 2006.

Boles, John B. *Black Southerners, 1619-1869*. Lexington: University Press of Kentucky, 1984.

Boogher, William Fletcher. *Gleanings of Virginia History: An Historical and Genealogical Collection*. Washington DC: William Fletcher Boogher, 1903.

Brown, Elsa Barkley. "'What Has Happened Here': The Politics of Difference in Women's History and Feminist Politics." *Feminist Studies* 18, no. 2 (Summer 1992): 295–312.

Brown, Kathleen. *Good Wives, Nasty Wenches, and Anxious Patriarchs: Gender, Race, and Power in Colonial Virginia*. Chapel Hill: University of North Carolina Press, 1996.

Brown, Kimberly Juanita. *The Repeating Body: Slavery's Visual Resonance in the Contemporary*. Durham, NC: Duke University Press, 2015.

Brownmiller, Susan. *Against Our Will: Men, Women, and Rape*. New York: Bantam Books, 1976.

Buchwald, Emilie, Pamela Fletcher, and Martha Roth, eds. *Transforming a Rape Culture*. Minneapolis: Milkweed Editions, 2005.

Buckley, Thomas E. *The Great Catastrophe of My Life: Divorce in the Old Dominion*. Chapel Hill: University of North Carolina Press, 2002.

———. "'Placed in the Power of Violence': The Divorce Petition of Evelina Gregory Roane, 1824." *Virginia Magazine of History and Biography* 100, no. 1 (January 1992): 22–78.

Bynum, Victoria. *Unruly Women: The Politics of Social and Sexual Control in the Old South*. Chapel Hill: University of North Carolina Press, 1992.

Camp, Stephanie M. H. *Closer to Freedom: Enslaved Women and Everyday Resistance in the Plantation South*. Chapel Hill: University of North Carolina Press, 2004.

Catterall, Helen Tunnicliff, ed. *Judicial Cases concerning American Slavery and the Negro*. Vols. 1–3. Buffalo: William S. Hein, 1998.

Censer, Jane Turner. "'Smiling through Her Tears': Ante-Bellum Southern Women and Divorce." *American Journal of Legal History* 25, no. 1 (1981): 24–47.

Chused, Richard H. *Private Acts in Public Places: A Social History of Divorce in the Formative Era of American Family Law*. Philadelphia: University of Pennsylvania Press, 1994.

Clark, Emily. *The Strange History of the American Quadroon: Free Women of Color in the Revolutionary Atlantic World*. Chapel Hill: University of North Carolina Press, 2013.

Clinton, Catherine. "Bloody Terrain: Freedwomen, Sexuality, and Violence during Reconstruction." *Georgia Historical Quarterly* 76, no. 2 (Summer 1992): 313–32.

———. "Caught in the Web of the Big House: Women and Slavery." In *The Web of Southern Social Relations: Women, Family and Education*, edited by Walter Fraser Jr., R. Frank Saunders Jr., and Jon L. Wakelyn, 19–34. Athens: University of Georgia Press, 1985.

———. *The Plantation Mistress: Woman's World in the Old South*. New York: Pantheon Books, 1982.

———. "Southern Dishonor: Flesh, Blood, Race, and Bondage." In *In Joy and in Sorrow: Women, Family, and Marriage in the Victorian South, 1830-1990*, edited by Carol Bleser, 52–68. New York: Oxford University Press, 1991.

Clinton, Catherine, and Michele Gillespie, eds. *The Devil's Lane: Sex and Race in the Early South*. New York: Oxford University Press, 1997.

Collins, Patricia. *Black Sexual Politics: African Americans, Gender, and the New Racism*. New York: Routledge, 2004.

Cooper Owens, Deirdre. *Medical Bondage: Race, Gender, and the Origins of American Gynecology*. Athens: University of Georgia Press, 2017.

Cott, Nancy F. *The Bonds of Womanhood: "Women's Sphere" in New England, 1780–1835*. 2nd ed. New Haven, CT: Yale University Press, 1997.

———. "Passionlessness: An Interpretation of Victorian Sexual Ideology, 1790–1850." *Signs* 4, no. 2 (Winter 1978), 219–36.

Davis, Adrienne D. "'Don't Let Nobody Bother Yo' Principle': The Sexual Economy of American Slavery." In *Sister Circle: Black Women and Work*, edited by Sharon Harley and the Black Women and Work Collective, 103–27. New Brunswick, NJ: Rutgers University Press, 2002.

———. "Slavery and the Roots of Sexual Harassment." In *Directions in Sexual Harassment Law*, edited by Catherine MacKinnon and Reva Siegel, 457–78. New Haven, CT: Yale University Press, 2003.

Davis, Angela Y. *Women, Race and Class*. New York: Random House, 1981.

Davis, Thadious M. *Games of Property: Law, Race, Gender, and Faulkner's "Go Down, Moses."* Durham, NC: Duke University Press, 2003.

D'Emilio, John, and Estelle B. Freedman. *Intimate Matters: A History of Sexuality in America*. Chicago: University of Chicago Press, 1997.

Deyle, Steven. *Carry Me Back: The Domestic Slave Trade in American Life*. New York: Oxford University Press, 2005.

Doddington, David Stefan. *Contesting Slave Masculinity in the American South*. Cambridge: Cambridge University Press, 2018.

Du Bois, W. E. B. *Black Reconstruction in America: An Essay toward a History of the Part Which Black Folk Played in the Attempt to Reconstruct Democracy in America, 1860–1880*. New York: Taylor and Francis Group, 2013.

Dunaway, Wilma A. *The African-American Family in Slavery and Emancipation*. Cambridge: Cambridge University Press, 2003.

Edgar, Walter. *South Carolina: A History*. Columbia: University of South Carolina Press, 1998.

Edwards, Laura. *Gendered Strife and Confusion: The Political Culture of Reconstruction*. Urbana: University of Illinois Press, 1997.

———. "Law, Domestic Violence, and the Limits of Patriarchal Authority in the Antebellum South." *Journal of Southern History* 65, no. 4 (1999): 733–70.

———. *Scarlett Doesn't Live Here Anymore: Southern Women in the Civil War Era*. Urbana: University of Illinois Press, 2000.

———. "Sexual Violence, Gender, Reconstruction, and the Extension of Patriarchy in Granville County, North Carolina." *North Carolina Historical Review* 68, no. 3 (1991): 237–60.

Elkins, Stanley. *Slavery: A Problem in American Institutional and Intellectual Life*. 2nd ed. Chicago: University of Chicago Press, 1968.

Faust, Drew Gilpin. *James Henry Hammond and the Old South: A Design for Mastery*. Baton Rouge: Louisiana State University Press, 1982.

Feimster, Crystal. "Rape and Mutiny at Fort Jackson: Black Laundresses Testify in Civil War Louisiana." *Labor: Studies in Working-Class History of the Americas* 19, no. 1 (2022): 11–31.

———. *Southern Horrors: Women and the Politics of Rape and Lynching*. Cambridge, MA: Harvard University Press, 2009.

———. "'What If I Am a Woman': Black Women's Campaigns for Sexual Justice and Citizenship." In *The World the Civil War Made*, edited by Gregory P. Downs and Kate Masur, 249–68. Chapel Hill: University of North Carolina Press, 2015.

Fett, Sharla. *Working Cures: Healing, Health, and Power on Southern Slave Plantations*. Chapel Hill: University of North Carolina Press, 2002.

Finley, Alexandra. *An Intimate Economy: Enslaved Women, Work, and America's Domestic Slave Trade*. Chapel Hill: University of North Carolina Press, 2020.

Fischer, Kirsten. *Suspect Relations: Sex, Race, and Resistance in Colonial North Carolina*. Ithaca, NY: Cornell University Press, 2002.

Fleischner, Jennifer. *Mrs. Lincoln and Mrs. Keckly: The Remarkable Story of the Friendship between a First Lady and a Former Slave*. New York: Broadway Books, 2003.

Foner, Eric. *Reconstruction: America's Unfinished Revolution, 1863–1877*. New York: Harper & Row, 2002.

Ford, Lacy K. *Deliver Us from Evil: The Slavery Question in the Old South*. Oxford: Oxford University Press, 2009.

Foster, Frances S. "Ultimate Victims: Black Women in Slave Narratives." *Journal of American Culture* 1, no. 4 (Winter 1978): 845–54.

Foster, Thomas A. *Rethinking Rufus: Sexual Violations of Enslaved Men*. Athens: University of Georgia Press, 2019.

———. "The Sexual Abuse of Black Men under American Slavery." *Journal of the History of Sexuality* 20, no. 3 (2011): 445–64.

Foucault, Michel. *The History of Sexuality*. Vol. 1, *An Introduction*, translated by Robert Hurley. New York: 1978.

Fox-Genovese, Elizabeth. *Within the Plantation Household: Black and White Women in the Old South*. Chapel Hill: University of North Carolina Press, 1988.

Franklin, John Hope, and Loren Schweninger. *Runaway Slaves: Rebels on the Plantation*. New York: Oxford University Press, 1999.

Fraser, Rebecca. *Courtship and Love among the Enslaved in North Carolina*. Jackson: University Press of Mississippi, 2007.

Friend, Craig Thompson, and Lorri Glover. "Rethinking Southern Masculinity: An Introduction." In *Southern Manhood: Perspectives on Masculinity in the Old South*, edited by Craig Thompson Friend and Lorri Glover, vii–xvii. Athens: University of Georgia Press, 2004.

Frierson, Nelson J. "Divorce in South Carolina." *North Carolina Law Review* 9 (April 1931): 265–82.

Frye, Marilyn, and Carolyn M. Shafer. "Rape and Respect." In *Feminism and Philosophy*, edited by Mary Vetterling-Braggin, Frederick Elliston, and Jane English, 333–46. Totowa, NJ: Rowman and Littlefield, 1977.

Fuentes, Marisa. *Dispossessed Lives: Enslaved Women, Violence, and the Archive*. Philadelphia: University of Pennsylvania Press, 2016.

Gampel, Yolanda. "Reflections on the Prevalence of the Uncanny in Social Violence." In *Cultures under Siege: Collective Violence and Trauma*, edited by Antonius C. G. M. Robben and Marcelo M. Suárez-Orozco, 48–69. Cambridge: Cambridge University Press, 2000.

Gasper, David, and Darlene Clark Hine. *More Than Chattel: Black Women and Slavery in the Americas*. Bloomington: University of Indiana Press, 1996.

Genovese, Eugene. *Roll, Jordan, Roll: The World the Slaves Made*. New York: Pantheon Books, 1974.

Getman, Karen. "Sexual Control in the Slaveholding South: The Implementation and Maintenance of a Racial Caste System." *Harvard Women's Law Journal* 7, no. 1 (1984): 115–52.

Glover, Lorri. *Southern Sons: Becoming Men in the New Nation*. Baltimore: Johns Hopkins University Press, 2007.

Glymph, Thavolia. "African American Women in the Literary Imagination of Mary Boykin Chestnut." In *Slavery, Secession, and Southern History*, edited by Louis Ferlegher and Robert Paquette, 140–59. Charlottesville: University Press of Virginia, 2000.

———. *Out of the House of Bondage: The Transformation of the Plantation Household*. Cambridge: Cambridge University Press, 2008.

Gordon-Reed, Annette. *The Hemingses of Monticello: An American Family*. New York: W. W. Norton, 2008.

———. *Thomas Jefferson and Sally Hemings: An American Controversy*. Charlottesville: University Press of Virginia, 1997.

Greene, Sally. "*State v. Mann* Exhumed." *North Carolina Law Review* 87, no. 3 (2009): 702.

Griffin, Susan. "Rape: The All-American Crime." *Ramparts* 10, no. 3 (1971): 26–35.

———. *Rape: The Politics of Consciousness*. San Francisco: Harper & Row, 1986.

Gudmestad, Robert H. *A Troublesome Commerce: The Transformation of the Interstate Slave Trade*. Baton Rouge: Louisiana State University Press, 2003.

Gutman, Herbert. *The Black Family in Slavery and Freedom, 1750–1925*. New York: Pantheon Books, 1976.

Hartman, Saidiya. *Scenes of Subjection: Terror, Slavery, and Self-Making in Nineteenth-Century America*. New York: Oxford University Press, 1997.

Hine, Darlene Clark. "Rape and the Inner Lives of Black Women: Thoughts on the Culture of Dissemblance." In *Hine Sight: Black Women and the Re-construction of American History*, 37–47. Bloomington: Indiana University Press, 1997.

Hodes, Martha. *White Women, Black Men: Illicit Sex in the Nineteenth-Century South*. New Haven, CT: Yale University Press, 1997.

Holden, Vanessa M. *Surviving Southampton: African American Women and Resistance in Nat Turner's Community*. Urbana: University of Illinois Press, 2021.

hooks, bell. *Black Looks: Race and Representation*. Boston: South End Press, 1992.

———. *We Real Cool: Black Men and Masculinity*. New York: Routledge, 2004.

Hunter, Tera. *Bound in Wedlock: Slave and Free Black Marriage in the Nineteenth Century*. Cambridge, MA: Belknap Press of Harvard University Press, 2017.

Jennings, Thelma. "'Us Colored Women Had to Go though [sic] a Plenty': Sexual Exploitation of African-American Slave Women." *Journal of Women's History* 1, no. 3 (1990): 45–74.

Johnson, Michael P., and James L. Roark, eds. *No Chariot Let Down: Charleston's Free People of Color on the Eve of the Civil War*. Chapel Hill: University of North Carolina Press, 1984.

Johnson, Walter. *Soul by Soul: Life Inside the Antebellum Slave Market*. Cambridge, MA: Harvard University Press, 1999.

Johnston, James Hugo. *Race Relations in Virginia and Miscegenation in the South, 1776–1860*. Amherst: University of Massachusetts Press, 1970.

Jones, Bernie D. *Fathers of Conscience: Mixed-Race Inheritance in the Antebellum South*. Athens: University of Georgia Press, 2011.

Jones, Jacqueline. *Labor of Love, Labor of Sorrow: Black Women, Work, and the Family, from Slavery to the Present*. New York: Basic Books, 2010.

Jones, Norrece T. "Rape in Black and White: Sexual Violence in the Testimony of Enslaved and Free Americans." In *Slavery and the American South*, edited by Winthrop Jordan, 93–116. Jackson: University Press of Mississippi, 2003.

Jones-Rogers, Stephanie E. *They Were Her Property: White Women as Slave Owners in the American South*. New Haven, CT: Yale University Press, 2019.

Jordan, David K., and Marc J. Swartz. *Culture: The Anthropological Perspective*. New York: Wiley, 1980.

Jordan, Winthrop. *White over Black: American Attitudes toward the Negro, 1550–1812*. Chapel Hill: University of North Carolina Press, 1968.

Kaye, Anthony. *Joining Places: Slave Neighborhoods in the Old South*. Chapel Hill: University of North Carolina Press, 2007.

Kennedy, Cynthia. *Braided Relations, Entwined Lives: The Women of Charleston's Urban Slave Society*. Bloomington: Indiana University Press, 2005.

Kennedy, Randall. *Interracial Intimacies: Sex, Marriage, Identity, and Adoption*. New York: Pantheon Books, 2003.

King, Wilma. *The Essence of Liberty: Free Black Women during the Slave Era*. Columbia: University of Missouri Press, 2006.

———. "'Prematurely Knowing of Evil Things': The Sexual Abuse of African American Girls and Young Women in Slavery and Freedom." *Journal of African American History* 99, no. 3 (2014): 173–96.

Lebsock, Suzanne. *The Free Women of Petersburg: Status and Culture in a Southern Town, 1784–1860*. New York: Norton Press, 1984.

Lussana, Sergio. *My Brother Slaves: Friendship, Masculinity, and Resistance in the Antebellum South*. Lexington: University of Kentucky Press, 2016.

Lyons, Clare. *Sex among the Rabble: An Intimate History of Gender and Power in the Age of Revolution, Philadelphia, 1730–1830*. Chapel Hill: University of North Carolina Press, 2006.

McCurry, Stephanie. *Masters of Small Worlds: Yeoman Households, Gender Relations, and the Politics of the Antebellum South Carolina Low Country*. New York: Oxford University Press, 1995.

McKittrick, Katherine. *Demonic Ground: Black Women and the Cartographies of Struggle*. Minneapolis: University of Minnesota Press, 2006.

McLaurin, Melton A. *Celia, a Slave*. Athens: University of Georgia Press, 1991.

Millward, Jessica. *Finding Charity's Folk: Enslaved and Free Black Women in Maryland*. Athens: University of Georgia Press, 2015.

———. "Relics of Slavery": Interracial Sex and Manumission in the American South. *Frontiers: A Journal of Women Studies* 31, no. 3 (2010): 22–30.

Milteer, Warren, Jr. *Beyond Slavery's Shadow: Free People of Color in the South*. Chapel Hill: University of North Carolina Press, 2021.

———. *North Carolina's Free People of Color, 1715–1885*. Baton Rouge: Louisiana State University Press, 2020.

Mintz, Sydney, and Richard Price. *The Birth of African-American Culture: An Anthropological Perspective*. Boston: Beacon Press, 1992.

Morgan, Edmund. *American Slavery, American Freedom: The Ordeal of Colonial Virginia*. New York: W. W. Norton, 2003.

Morgan, Jennifer. *Laboring Women: Reproduction and Gender in New World Slavery*. Philadelphia: University of Pennsylvania Press, 2004.

Morris, Christopher. *Becoming Southern: The Evolution of a Way of Life, Warren County and Vicksburg, Mississippi, 1770–1860*. Oxford: Oxford University Press, 1995.

Morris, Thomas. *Southern Slavery and the Law, 1619–1860*. Chapel Hill: University of North Carolina Press, 1996.

Morrison, Toni. "Unspeakable Things Unspoken: The Afro-American Presence in American Literature." In *Within the Circle: An Anthology of African American Literary Criticism from the Harlem Renaissance to the Present*, edited by Angelyn Mitchell, 368–98. Durham, NC: Duke University Press, 1994.

Morton, Patricia, ed. *Discovering the Women in Slavery: Emancipating Perspectives on the American Past*. Athens: University of Georgia Press, 1996.

Myers, Amrita Chakrabarti. *Forging Freedom: Black Women and the Pursuit of Liberty in Antebellum Charleston*. Chapel Hill: University of North Carolina Press, 2011.

Nathans, Sydney. *To Free a Family: The Journey of Mary Walker*. Cambridge, MA: Harvard University Press, 2012.

Northen, William J., ed. *Men of Mark in Georgia: A Complete and Elaborate History of the State from Its Settlement to the Present Time, Chiefly Told in Biographies and Autobiographies of the Most Eminent Men of Each Period of Georgia's Progress and Development*. Atlanta: A.B. Caldwell, 1911.

Nunley, Tamika Y. *The Demands of Justice: Enslaved Women, Capital Crime, and Clemency in Early Virginia*. Chapel Hill: University of North Carolina Press, 2023.

———. *At the Threshold of Liberty: Women, Slavery, and Shifting Identities in Washington, D.C.* Chapel Hill: University of North Carolina Press, 2021.

Owens, Emily. *Consent in the Presence of Force: Sexual Violence and Black Women's Survival in Antebellum New Orleans*. Chapel Hill: University of North Carolina Press, 2023.

Painter, Nell Irvin. "Soul Murder and Slavery: Toward a Fully Loaded Cost Accounting." In *Southern History across the Color Line*, 15–39. Chapel Hill: University of North Carolina Press, 2002.

Parry, Tyler D. *Jumping the Broom: The Surprising Multicultural Origins of a Black Wedding Ritual*. Chapel Hill: University of North Carolina Press, 2020.

Pascoe, Peggy. *What Comes Naturally: Miscegenation Law and the Making of Race in America*. New York: Oxford University Press, 2009.

Phillips, Ulrich B. *American Negro Slavery: A Survey of the Supply, Employment, and Control of Negro Labor as Determined by the Plantation Regime*. New York: Appleton, 1918.

Preston, Dickson J. *Young Frederick Douglass: The Maryland Years*. Baltimore: Johns Hopkins University Press, 1980.

Rediker, Marcus. *The Amistad Rebellion: An Atlantic Odyssey of Slavery and Freedom*. New York: Viking Penguin, 2012.

Riley, Glenda. *Divorce: An American Tradition*. Lincoln: University of Nebraska Press, 1997.

———. "Legislative Divorce in Virginia, 1803–1850." *Journal of the Early Republic* 11, no. 1 (1991): 51–67.

Robben, Antonius C. G. M. "The Assault on Basic Trust: Disappearance, Protest, and Reburial in Argentina." In *Cultures under Siege: Collective Violence and Trauma*, edited by Antonius C. G. M. Robben and Marcelo M. Suárez-Orozco, 70–101. Cambridge: Cambridge University Press, 2000.

Rosen, Hannah. *Terror in the Heart of Freedom: Citizenship, Sexual Violence, and the Meaning of Race in the Postemancipation South*. Chapel Hill: University of North Carolina Press, 2009.

Rothman, Joshua. *The Ledger and the Chain: How Domestic Slave Traders Shaped America*. New York: Basic Books, 2021.

———. *Notorious in the Neighborhood: Sex and Families across the Color Line in Virginia, 1787–1861*. Chapel Hill: University of North Carolina Press, 2003.

Scarborough, William Kaufman. *Masters of the Big House: Elite Slaveholders of the Mid-Nineteenth Century South*. Baton Rouge: Louisiana State University Press, 2006.

Schermerhorn, Calvin. *Money over Mastery, Family over Freedom: Slavery in the Antebellum South*. Baltimore: Johns Hopkins University Press, 2011.

Schwalm, Leslie. *A Hard Fight for We: Women's Transition from Slavery to Freedom in South Carolina*. Urbana: University of Illinois Press, 1997.

Schwartz, Marie Jenkins. *Birthing a Slave: Motherhood and Medicine in the Antebellum South*. Cambridge, MA: Harvard University Press, 2006.

———. *Born in Bondage: Growing Up Enslaved in the Antebellum South*. Cambridge, MA: Harvard University Press, 2000.

Schweninger, Loren. *Families in Crisis in the Old South: Divorce, Slavery, and the Law*. Chapel Hill: University of North Carolina Press, 2012.

Scott, Anne Firor. *The Southern Lady: From Pedestal to Politics, 1830–1930*. Chicago: University of Chicago Press, 1970.

Scott, John A. Introduction to *Journal of a Residence on a Georgian Plantation in 1838–1839*, by Frances Anne Kemble, ix–lix. New York: Knopf, 1961.

Sides, Sudie Duncan. "Slave Weddings and Religion: Plantation Life in the Southern States before the American Civil War." *History Today* 24 (1974): 77–87.

Sirmans, M. Eugene. "The Legal Status of the Slave in South Carolina, 1670–1740." *Journal of Southern History* 28, no. 4 (1962): 462–73.

Smallwood, Stephanie. *Saltwater Slavery: A Middle Passage from Africa to American Diaspora*. Cambridge, MA: Harvard University Press, 2007.

Sommerville, Diane. *Rape and Race in the Nineteenth Century South*. Chapel Hill: University of North Carolina Press, 2004.

Spear, Jennifer M. *Race, Sex, and Social Order in Early New Orleans*. Baltimore: Johns Hopkins University Press, 2014.

Spelman, Elizabeth. *Inessential Women: Problems of Exclusion in Feminist Thought*. London: Women's Press, 1990.

Spillers, Hortense J. "Mama's Baby, Papa's Maybe: An American Grammar Book." *Diacritics* 17, no. 2 (Summer 1987): 65–81.

Starobin, Robert S., ed. *Blacks in Bondage: Letters of the American Slaves*. Princeton, NJ: Markus Wiener, 1994.

Stevenson, Brenda E. "Gender Convention, Ideals, and Identity among Antebellum Virginia Slave Women." In *More Than Chattel: Black Women and Slavery in the Americas*, edited by David Barry Gaspar and Darlene Clark Hine, 169–90. Bloomington: Indiana University Press, 1996.

———. *Life in Black and White: Family and Community in the Slave South*. New York: Oxford University Press, 1996.

———. "What's Love Got to Do with It? Concubinage and Enslaved Women and Girls in the Antebellum South." In *Sexuality and Slavery: Reclaiming Intimate Histories in the Americas*, edited by Daina Ramey Berry and Leslie M. Harris, 159–88. Athens: University of Georgia Press, 2018.

Tadman, Michael. *Speculators and Slaves: Masters, Traders, and Slaves in the Old South*. Madison: University of Wisconsin Press, 1996.

Waddell, Joseph A. *Annals of Augusta County, Virginia, with Reminiscences*. Richmond: J. W. Randolph & English, 1888.

Walker, Clarence. *Mongrel Nation: The America Begotten by Thomas Jefferson and Sally Hemings*. Charlottesville: University of Virginia Press, 2009.

Wallenstein, Peter. *Tell the Court I Love My Wife: Race, Marriage, and Law: An American History*. New York: St. Martin's Press, 2002.

Washington, John. *They Knew Lincoln*. New York: Dutton, 1942.

Welter, Barbara. "The Cult of True Womanhood." *American Quarterly* 18 (Summer 1966): 151–74.

West, Emily. *Chains of Love: Slave Couples in Antebellum South Carolina*. Urbana: University of Illinois Press, 2004.

White, Deborah Gray. *Ar'n't I a Woman? Female Slaves in the Plantation South*. 2nd ed. New York: Norton, 1999.

Williams, Heather A. *Help Me to Find My People: The African American Search for Family Lost in Slavery*. Chapel Hill: University of North Carolina Press, 2012.

Williams, Joyce E. "Secondary Victimization: Confronting Public Attitudes about Rape." *Victimology: An International Journal* 9, no. 1 (1984): 66–81.

Williams, Kidada. *I Saw Death Coming: A History of Terror and Survival in the War against Reconstruction*. New York: Bloomsbury, 2023.

Williamson, Joel. *New People: Miscegenation and Mulattoes in the United States*. Baton Rouge: Louisiana State University Press, 1995.

Winch, Julie. *Between Slavery and Freedom: Free People of Color in America from Settlement to the Civil War*. Lanham, MD: Rowman and Littlefield, 2014.

Wright, Nazera Sadiq. *Black Girlhood in the Nineteenth Century*. Urbana: University of Illinois Press, 2016.

Wyatt-Brown, Bertram. *Honor and Violence in the Old South*. New York: Oxford University Press, 1986.

———. *Southern Honor: Ethics and Behavior in the Old South*. 25th Anniversary ed. New York: Oxford University Press, 2007.

Yellin, Jean Fagan. *Harriet Jacobs: A Life*. New York: Basic Books, 2004.

Index

Page numbers in italics refer to illustrations.

Adeline, 48–53, *62*
adultery, 12, 65, 78, 124, 143–49, 153–54
agency, 4, 15, 42, 49–53, 57, 60, 62, 65,
    69–70, 124, 162; and consent, 36–37,
    52, 69, 89, 112
Albert, 90
Albert, Octavia, 131
alcohol (drinking), 22, 25, 37, 43, 54, 56,
    93, 129, 131, 149, 156, 170
Aldrich, Jacob, 27, 32–33
Alfred, 88–90, 94
Allen, Anna, 159–60, 166
Allen, John, 160
Alwyn, 111
American Freedmen's Inquiry
    Commission, 85, 170
Anderson, Andrew, 139
Anderson, William, 22; sons, Wash,
    Cliber, and Irvin, 22
Anthony, Aaron, 1–6, 23
Anthony, Andrew, 5
Anthony, Lucretia, 5
Appleton, Ebenezer, 99
Auld, Thomas, 5

Bailey, Pierce Jr., 48–53, *62*
Ball, Charles, 92–94
Ballard, Rice, 60–63
bargaining, 56, 120, 122, 141, 152
Bass, John, 90–91
Battle, Lawrence, 48–51
beauty, 2, 29–30, 38, 41, 54, 87, 118,
    129, 135–36
Ben, 90–91
Benford, Hugh, 33–34

Berry, 30, 54–55
Berry, Elisha, 42
Berry, Fannie, 8, 38
Bertram, John, 66
Betty, 73
Bibb, Henry, 27–28, 80, 83–84, 87
Big Jim, 81–82
Biney, 109–10, 151, 154, 157, 162–65
Black Codes, 63, 65
body (bodies): as archive of time, 20;
    autonomy, 42, 46, 59, 169–71;
    "beastly" Black bodies, 76; bodily
    rights and citizenship, 170–71;
    breasts, 19, 31, 76; and crime, 10, 17;
    as ideological landscape, 7; images of,
    20; and patriarchal privilege, 4, 17,
    51–54, 74, 130; in sale of enslaved
    peoples, 31–32; sexual maturation,
    19, 35–36; subjugation of, 10, 22.
    See also punishment
Body, Rias, 32
Bost, W.L., 120
Boyd, Samuel, 60–63
Boyd, Virginia, 60–62
breeding, 9, 31–32, 121
Bristow, George, 49
Brooke, Francis T., 98, 101
Brooke, Helen, 96–101
Brooke, Mary Champe, 98
Brooks, Jacob, 42
Brown, Ann, 68
Brown, Henry Box, 33, 86–87
Brown, Jack, 67
Brown, John, 21–23, 33
Brown, Thomas, 66–68

Brown, William Wells, 30, 44, 58–60
brutality, 2–7, 15, 21–22, 34, 71, 79, 86, 138
Bryant, Susan, 66–68
Bryant, William, 66–68
Burrell, Savilla, 128–29
Burton, Martin, 101
Burwell, Armistead and Thomas, 150
Burwell, John, 111, 149–51
Burwell, Lucy, 111, 149–51
Burwell, Robert and Anna, 16
Burwell, Thomas, 111, 150
businesses, 60, 87, 144, 170–71
Butler, Marshal, 32
Butler, Pierce, 34, 44, 73–74, 113, 128

Cameron, Duncan, 18, 20, 35
Cameron, Mildred, 18, 35
Campbell, Israel, 22
Caroline, 92
Carter, Benjamin, 165
Carter, Sarah, 165
Celia, 24–25, 49–41, 117–19
Charlotte, 88
Chesnut, Mary Cox, 116
Chesnut, James Jr., 116
Chesnut, Mary Boykin, 9, 12, 115–16, 120–24, 127, 142
Cheyney (Aunt), 121
churches, 16, 86, 170
Civil War, 44, 51, 63–69, 85, 108, 137, 143, 169–71. See also Confederacy; Union Army
Clarke, Delia, 30
Clarke, Lewis, 28, 30, 42–43, 79, 86–87, 102
class: planter, 116; and rape, 4; slave-owning, 9, 73, 118, 135, 143–48, 163, 166; women as oppressed, 42
Clay, Berry, 33
Cline, Daniel, 165
Cline, Elizabeth, 165
Clubb, David, 164
Clubb, Elizabeth, 164
Cody, Pierce, 136

Cofer, Willis, 32
Cole, John, 32, 82
Coleman, 88, 90
conception, 16, 28, 33, 44, 64
concubines, 9, 31, 38, 42, 49, 57, 65, 89, 115, 127, 157, 181n3. See also sexual servants
Confederacy, 35, 64, 85
Cook, David, 55–57
coverture, 75, 118, 144–45, 158
Craft, William, 29, 58, 84
Critty, 33–34
cruelty, 23, 30, 44, 60, 105, 129, 138, 143–46, 165–66
culture, defined, 9–10
Curry, James, 32
Curtis, Mattie, 26, 35, 41
Cynthia, 30, 58–60

David, 117
debt, 58, 90
Democratic Party, 64
Diana, 25, 28, 55, 57, 119
discretion, lack of, 10–12, 26, 63, 106, 120–23, 134–35, 140–41, 147–52
disobedience, 1, 55, 78–81, 88, 94, 166
divorce: for "acting like a wife," 147, 160–68; alimony, 144, 146, 157–59, 168; four prominent tropes, 147; and husbands' sexual liaisons with enslaved women, 12, 109–10, 123–24, 132–33, 138; for lack of discretion, 147–52, 156, 167–68, 197n17; legally accepted reasons for, 12, 143–49; for neglect of duty, 147, 150–51, 156–60, 164–68; and rape culture, 15, 139–48; self-divorce, 144; for withdrawal of affection, 147, 152–56
Doak, Robert, 139
Dobyns, Jonah, 155–56
Dobyns, Sopha, 155–56
Douglass, Frederick, 1–6, 23
Dred Scott v. Sandford, 74
Du Bois, W. E. B., 169
Duhon, Lucien, 28

Duhon, Victor, 28
Dungan, Caroline, 149
Dunlap, Ellen Shields, 139–42, 148
Dunlap, Robert, 139–41, 148
Dupuis, Euripa, 28
Dwight, William, 170

Eliza, 42
Ella, 131–32
emancipation, 35, 42, 44, 49–52, 57–58,
    63–64, 85, 101, 162; after Civil War, 169
emotion: as consciousness, 176n10; and
    enslaved family dynamics, 33–36, 45;
    and navigation of sexual violence, 11,
    23–24; and sexual servitude, 49; toll
    of sexual violence, 3, 72, 95, 140; and
    white masculinity, 107; and white
    women, 128, 133, 138, 153, 159–60, 166
enslaved children, 10, 12, 35, 60, 95,
    110, 115, 120–23, 126–27, 142, 149, 157
enslaved laborers: cooks, 24, 48, 55, 77,
    117, 161, 163, 165; domestic servants,
    24, 162, 171; field laborers, 17, 24–25,
    30–31, 42, 48–49, 53, 59, 71, 80–81,
    163–66; housekeepers, 24, 28–31, 39,
    48, 50–55, 59, 69, 92, 117, 171;
    housemaids, 31, 119; nursemaids, 24,
    55, 98, 134; seamstresses, 48, 54–55,
    104, 127, 136
enslaved men: eroticized, 31; experience
    sexual violence, 8, 14, 80–82; forced
    to punish others, 22–23, 80; hear
    enslaved women's sexual assault, 21,
    32, 73–74; and patriarchal authority,
    71–78, 82–83, 90, 95; and protection,
    27–28, 80–82; romantic relationships
    with enslaved women, 39, 48, 71–76,
    89; and same-sex relationships, 33;
    and sexual violence against enslaved
    women, 36, 80–82; and trauma, 86; in
    Union Army, 170; violence against,
    77–82, 94; violence perpetrated, 12,
    14, 87, 90–91
enslaved women: capacity for labor,
    31–32; constant threat of sexual

violence, 12–15, 18–28, 141, 162,
    169–73; many prefer death to rape,
    38; enslaved women as mistresses,
    28, 30, 54–59, 102, 109; as primary
    sexual assault victims in southern
    rape culture, 8–9; rape statutes do
    not protect, 17; systematic abuse of,
    3–4, 16; viewed themselves as agents,
    62; vulnerability of, 7, 14, 17, 36.
    See also enslaved laborers; interracial,
    sex; protection; reproductive
    exploitation; rape; sexual coercion;
    sexual servants; pregnancy; *and
    enslaved women by name*
Eppes, Richard, 78
Epps, Edwin and Mary, 131
Epsey, 153
Ervin, William Ethelbert, 77–78
estate, 31, 46, 51, 65, 109–10, 113,
    125–26, 151, 157
Ethel Mae, 27
Everett, Louisa, 81–82
Everett, Sam, 81–82
execution, 93

fancy-girls, 9, 29, 54, 57, 115, 121
Feild, Charles G., 150
Ferry, Henry, 123–24
Finney, Starling, 21
Fischer, L. C., 67
Fitzsimons family, 104–8
Flowers, Ignatius, 63–66, 69–70
Flowers, Susan, 63–70
Fondren, John D., 88
Frances, 84, 87, 92
Francis, John, 26–27, 80, 91–92
Frank, 73–75, 92–94
Franky, 92
Freedman's Bureau, 171
Fulkes, Minnie, 23, 36
Fungan, 149

Garrett, Edward, 150–51
Garrett, Mary, 150–51
Garrison, Madison, 84

Gaskins, 55, 119
Gatewood, William, 84
genitalia, 31, 76
Gooding, Joe, 91
Goodwater, Thomas, 81
gossip, 9, 12, 114, 124–25, 129, 138, 158
Grace, 165
Graves, Galespe, 23
Greene, Tom, 30, 54–55
Gregory, Fendall, 109, 154
Gregory, John, 157
Gregory, Mary, 163
Gregory, Thomas, 110, 163
Gregory, William, 109
Gresham, Henry, 125–26
Gresham, Laura Jones, 125–26

Hamilton, Robert, 96, 100–101, 105
Hammond, Catherine Fitzsimmons, 104–8
Hammond, James Henry, 102–8
Hampton, Wade, II, 107–8
Hampton, Ann Fitzsimmons, 107
Hansley, Ruthey Ann, 155, 160–63
Hansley, Samuel, 155, 160–63
Harper, Chancellor, 99
Harris, Shang, 22
Harris, William L., 89
Hassell, Benjamin, 152
Hassell, Mary, 152
Hayden, William, 87–88
Henson, Josiah, 71–72, 85, 94–95
Hester, 1–6, 15, 23
Hooks, Rebecca, 136
Hopper, George, 31
humiliation, 12, 38, 78, 101, 105–6, 140–42, 147, 150, 167–68

Indigenous peoples, 8
interracial: marriage, 65; relationships, 110; sex, 5–6, 10–11, 15, 26, 29, 97, 99, 102–3, 106, 113–16, 120, 123–27, 130, 133, 137–42, 145–49, 153, 159, 163, 167–68, 171. See also race

Jacobs, Harriet, 19–21, 25, 27, 29, 45–46, 79, 115–16, 131–36
Jacobs, John, 22
James, 38
James, Dr. 88
James, Jepsey, 22–23
James, Thomas, 23
jealousy, 10, 12, 20, 91, 97, 117, 129–38, 141, 167
Jefferson, Thomas, 102
Jerry, 45
Jesse, 26, 80, 91
Jim, 123
Johns, Thomas, 37
Johnson, William, 166
Jones, Jefferson, 39–40
Jones, Jemmima, 111, 157; Edward and Sam, 159
Judy, 113–14
judicial system: documents, 11–12, 97; enslaved peoples cannot testify in, 75; Georgia Supreme Court, 48, 51; judges, 18, 29, 60, 89, 136, 146, 153, 159, 166, 168; juries, 40, 88–89, 93, 146, 153, 166; jurists, 89–90, 98, 143, 145; King George County Court, 101; lawyers, 46, 50, 144; Mississippi's High Court of Errors and Appeals, 89; New Kent County Court, 92; North Carolina Supreme Court, 89; process of, 74; and white women, 143; US Supreme Court, 74; Virginia Court of Appeals, 98. See also Celia; divorce; law (legal)

Keckley, Elizabeth, 16–17, 37
Keckley, George, 16, 37–38
Kelly, Edwin, 124
Kelly, Isabella, 123
Kemble, Frances, 34, 73–74, 113–15, 128–31
Kendall, William, 101
killings, 12, 38–40, 71, 79–80, 87–93, 100, 110, 116, 119, 131–32, 171; infanticide, 37; murder, 27, 40–41, 79, 88–93

Kilpatrick, Andrew R., 120–22
King, Julia Maxwell, 113–14
King, Roswell, Jr., 73–75, 113, 128
King, Roswell, Sr., 73, 128
Kirkland, Alexander, 16, 37–38
knowledge (generational), 5, 18–24, 28, 34

labor: Black women's supposed capacity for hard labor, 7; mastery over, 74; reproductive, 8, 24, 31; sex as, 29, 41, 54, 58
land, 18, 31, 43, 74, 77, 104, 109, 118, 135, 144
Laspeyre, Bernard, 156, 167–68
Laspeyre, Harriet, 156, 166–68
Lavinia, 44
law (legal): abolition, 50; counsel, 143–46, 162, 168; enslaved people not protected by, 7, 17, 73–75, 112, 117, 127; enslaved women appeal to, 40; enslaved women as legal property, 58, 75; and inheritance, 63–69, 125; and marriage, 33, 44–45, 63, 70, 88–90; and rape culture, 8; and white women, 114, 118, 142–46, 152, 158, 162, 168; women's autonomy, 53. See also divorce; marriage
Leah and Rachel, 116
Lee, 86
legislators, 7, 139–46, 153, 156, 166–68
Lesley, Peter and Susan, 18–19, 35
Lessene, Joseph W., 152
Loguen, Jermain, 25
Long, J. D., 102
Louisa, 98–101, 104–8
lovers, 3–6, 23, 46, 92, 154
Lowe, William, 136
Lucretia, 111, 149–50
Lucy, 31, 92–93, 155, 160–62
lynching, 6, 172–73

Macks, Richard, 29–30
Maddox, Jack, 29, 54, 136
Maddox, Judge, 29, 136

Maddox, Rosa, 29
Malinda, 83–84
manhood, 71, 75–76, 82–83, 87–88, 107, 120, 185n19: as head of household, 77–78, 82, 123. See also patriarchy
Manning, Emily, 152–53
Manning, Moses, 152–53
Manson, Jacob, 9, 119
Margaret, 121–22
Maria, 41–43, 110, 129–30
marriage: contracts of, 75; of the enslaved, 14, 18, 32–35, 38, 42–46, 71, 86–91; extramarital affairs, 78, 105; forced sexual relationships between enslaved married people, 81; and inheritance, 63–69; interracial relationships abandoned for white wives, 28, 59; and patriarchal expectations of sexual access, 96–101, 104, 108–11, 113, 117–19; not performed, 65; "pseudo" marriages, 49; Rachel and Leah metaphor, 116; stability of white marriages threatened by sexual violence against enslaved women, 13, 122–23, 127, 130–35, 139–48; weddings, 45, 96, 152; white men who never married, 37, 48, 54, 58, 63. See also divorce
Martha, 123
Mary, 102
Massie, Ishrael, 27, 80
mastery, 4, 14, 23–27, 73–74, 83, 97, 106, 116, 138–39, 186n38
Matilda, 123
McCullough, Willie, 41, 57
McKiernan, 129–30
Memphis Race Massacre, 171–72
Meridian Mississippi Riot, 171
Milly, 139–42
morality, 11, 36, 46, 83, 90, 97, 101–2, 137, 142, 153, 169–70: immorality, 78, 124, 127, 135, 138, 155
Mordicia, Moses, 26, 41
Moss, Andrew, 31

Nancy, 86
Nathan, 87, 152
Newsom, Mary, 117–19
Newsom, Robert, 24–25, 39–40, 117–20
Newsom, Virginia, 117–19
Norcom, James, 19–21, 25, 27, 45–46, 134–35
Norcom, Mary, 133–35
Norman, James, 110, 155
Norman, Lucy, 110–11
Norrell, Delia, 132–33
Norrell, Henry, 132–33
Northrup, Solomon, 41–42, 131

obedience, 22, 55–57, 73, 80, 87, 93, 95, 147, 167
Odom, 37
Olmstead, Frederick, 37
overseers, 3, 21–23, 26–29, 38, 48, 52, 71–73, 79–80, 84, 88, 94, 113, 128, 170

Pannell, Edmund, 165
patriarchy: and enslaved men, 71, 73–78, 82–83, 94; and free Black men, 74; and juries, 89–90; in modern discourse, 173; and white familial organization, 103–4, 114; white patriarchal expectations of sexual access, 96–101, 104, 108–11, 113, 117–19; white patriarchal organization and race, 7, 10–15, 71–78, 89, 97, 140–43, 147, 151, 155, 168, 173; and white men's rape culture, 7–15, 74–78, 97, 108, 111–12, 127, 151, 155; and women's power, 138–43, 147, 155–56, 168
Patrick, 26–27, 80, 91–94
Patsey, 131
Paxton, John D., 103
Peggy, 26–27, 80, 91–92
Pennington, James, 9, 76
pensions, 66–69
Pettus, Barbara, 166
Pettus, Hugh, 166
Phillips, Simon, 32

Phyllis, 37
Picquet, Louisa, 54–57
pity, 21, 85, 124, 133, 136–37
Plummer, Rose, 170
Polly, 164
Powell, William, 39, 118
predators, 20–21, 24, 27–28, 38, 134, 151, 172
pregnancy, 9, 20, 22, 32–34, 37, 39, 62, 98, 101, 113, 121, 150
Presbyterians, 16, 86
Prince, Eliza, 111, 148, 157–59
Prince, John, 111, 157–59
Priscilla, 98
privacy (private): condemnations of interracial relationships, 15, 114, 123–24; difference from public life, 103; and divorce, 139–40, 143; and sexual violence, 25, 27, 55, 57, 80, 117, 121, 123, 135, 149, 162; space, 7, 14, 41–42, 46
privilege: and the enslaved, 41–43, 57–58, 71, 82, 86, 134; and rape culture, 5, 14, 25, 74, 97, 112, 139, 143; spousal, 89, 106, 157, 161–63; and white women, 75, 78, 134, 147, 157, 161–63, 166
property: compensation for war loss, 63–64; and enslaved people, 75, 131; and government power, 74; and inheritance, 58, 62, 65, 75, 83, 125; and marriage, 144, 156, 158, 167–68; and mastery, 52–53, 104; and sexual violence, 19, 33, 58; worth of, 50
protection: during the Civil War, 170; of enslaved marriages, 45; of enslaved women, 5–6, 11, 17, 19, 22, 35–37, 43, 46, 59, 71–74, 80–95, 117–20, 133–34, 169; following the Civil War, 171–72; and masculinity, 14; of one's self, 12; of reputation, 63, 106–8, 158; of white women and children, 27–28, 100, 111–12, 156, 165–68; of white women's economic interests, 142–47

punishment: for abstaining from sex, 36; for adultery, 78; flogging, 1–2, 12, 23, 44, 79–80–81, 94, 113–14; and mastery, 12, 77–80, 94; and protection of enslaved women, 73, 95; screams of pain, 1, 23, 71, 84; and separation from family, 113–14; and sexual jealousy, 1; for sexual violence, 101; by the state, 65; for violence against the enslaved, 151, 166–67; whip (whipping), 1–5, 21–23, 30, 43–44, 53–56, 72, 77, 81–84, 130–31; by white women, 129–32, 138

race: Blackness, 7, 75–76; Black women's power, 170–71; and definition of crime, 17; free people of color, 33, 43, 74–75, 91, 135; and hierarchy, 15, 64, 128, 161; light skin, 20, 26, 29, 34, 41, 58, 121, 123, 127, 135–36; mixed race, 10, 16, 29, 37, 43, 54, 101–2, 115, 118, 121, 123, 135, 141, 145; and mobility, 74; "Mulatto," 9, 29, 37, 54, 64, 99, 102–3, 115, 124–29, 135–37, 140, 151–54, 157, 164, 167; prescriptions, 13; racial difference, 7; racialized slavery, 15; racial power, 8; uplift, 172; white, 102–3; "yellow," 121–22, 125. *See also* interracial; white supremacy
Randolph, John, 101
rape: Black women as unrapable, 9; and class: 4; and divorce, 15, 139–48; enslaved women may sometimes prefer death to rape, 38; and privilege, 5, 14, 25, 74, 97, 112, 139, 143; rape statutes do not protect enslaved women, 17; as spectacle, 26–27, 140; systematic, 3–8, 11, 15–17, 135, 142, 169, 173; as tool of oppression, 173; as tool of power and pleasure, 14. *See also* enslaved laborers; interracial, sex; pregnancy; protection; reproductive exploitation; rape culture; sexual coercion; sexual servants; *and enslaved women by name*

rape culture, 5, 14, 25, 74, 97, 112, 139, 143; defined, 5–6; silence supports, 138; and social and economic advancement, 6, 62, 90, 167; and white men, 7–15, 74–78, 97, 108, 111–12, 127, 151, 155. *See also* rape
Reilly, 73
reproductive exploitation: 3, 7, 9, 17, 43, 71, 115, 142
Republican Party, 64–65, 171
respectability: Black politics of, 172; and honor, 120; marriage suitors, 96; and mastery, 77; and patriarchal expectations of sexual access, 25, 99–103; and white women, 99–100, 110, 118–23, 130, 140–42, 146, 150, 152, 160–61, 196n4
Reynolds, Mary, 120–22
Roane, Evelina, 108–10, 151, 154, 157, 162–65
Roane, Mary, 164–65
Roane, Newman, 108–10, 151, 154, 157, 162–65
Roberts, Edward, 1
Rogers, Hattie, 31
Roper, Moses, 132
Rose, 43–44
Ruffin, Thomas, 89–90
Rufus, 43–44
rural, 3, 10, 13, 144

Sally, 104–8
same-sex relationships, 33, 96
Satterfield, May, 24, 172
Sawyer, Samuel Tredwell, 46
Saxton, Rufus, 170
Scott, Anderson, 125–26
secrets, 13–14, 33, 67, 97, 107, 123, 131, 138–41
separation (sale) of enslaved people, 10, 31–34, 41–45, 54–55, 60–63, 71, 84, 90, 105, 115, 127, 130–33, 138, 144, 150
sex: double standard for men, 146; hypersexuality and promiscuity, 7, 9, 75–76, 99, 103, 127, 173; as labor, 29,

sex *(cont.)*
    41, 54, 58; in marital beds, 27, 147,
    153–55, 161; punishment: for
    abstaining from sex, 36; sexual
    jealousy, 1. *See also* interracial, sex;
    sexual servitude; sexual violence;
    sexual violence, sites of
sexual coercion: of enslaved women, 3,
    7, 9, 14, 16–20, 23–25, 28, 31–34,
    38–39, 42, 46–47, 52–53, 58, 69, 71,
    81–84, 99, 115, 117, 139, 141, 148,
    170; white women victims of, 8
sexual servants, 14, 48–62, 67–70,
    92–93, 115, 118, 121, 127, 147, 162,
    166. *See also* fancy girls
sexual violence, sites of: barns, 24–27, 55,
    80, 119, 166; bedrooms, 24, 27–28,
    55–56, 100, 111, 134–35, 149, 153, 155;
    cabins 24–27, 39–43, 46, 76, 79, 99, 101,
    117–21, 135, 153, 162, 169; cookhouses,
    24, 27; quarters, 9, 22, 26–27, 30, 32,
    41, 54, 57, 77, 80, 99, 111, 163; studies,
    24, 27; woods, 24, 27, 172
sexual violence: Black men seek to
    protect Black women from, 72;
    constant threat of, 12–15, 18–28, 141,
    162, 169–73; and the creation of rape
    culture, 6, 13–14; of forced sexual
    acts of the enslaved, 81; generational
    knowledge of, 35; of men and boys, 8;
    and patriarchal authority, 3–10, 114,
    117; prosecution for, 112; racialized,
    117. *See also* manhood; rape, rape
    culture; sexual coercion; trauma
Shackelford (Sister), 30, 54–57
shame, 10, 14, 21, 37, 41–42, 56, 82,
    97, 103, 116, 130, 140–42, 147, 151,
    154, 156
Shepherd, Virginia Hayes, 25, 28,
    55, 119
Sherman, Ellen, 137
Sherman, William Tecumseh, 35, 137
Shields, James and Thomas, 140
silence: in archives, 8–13, 16, 52,
    68, 114; expectations for women,

    12, 117–23, 153; supports rape
    culture, 138
Silva, 165–66
Simpson, Sarah Ann, 154
Sinclair, Ellen, 22
slave-owning men: and discretion, 120;
    incentives for remaining married to
    white women, 145; and interracial
    sex, 5; legal documents, 52; long-term
    relationships with enslaved, 14, 29,
    41, 43, 69, 85–87; and silence, 138;
    and terrorism of enslaved families,
    115; use sex as mastery, 14, 97,
    100–101, 108, 112. *See also* white men
    (southern)
slave-owning women: accuse husbands
    of adultery, 145–47; financial risk of
    divorce, 144; reactions to white men's
    sex with enslaved women, 114–33,
    138; sexual assault victims, 8; and
    white men's lack of discretion, 12;
    wield power, 155. *See also* divorce;
    jealousy; pity; silence; white women
    (southern)
slavery: chattel, 3, 7, 19, 19, 53, 76, 82,
    103, 144, 169; markets, 12, 15, 29, 42,
    53–54, 121; Middle Passage, 83;
    natural increase, 31, 81; patriarchy of
    enslaved men, 71, 73–78, 82–83, 94;
    and privilege, 41–43, 57–58, 71, 82,
    86, 134; slave-owning class, 9, 73,
    118, 135, 143–48, 163, 166; slave
    trade, 7, 21, 29, 33, 42, 54, 58, 60, 62,
    75–76, 84, 99, 121; South Carolina
    Slave Act (1690), 72. *See also* enslaved
    laborers; separation (sale) of enslaved
    people
Smalls, Robert, 85
Smith, Cotesworth P., 90
Smith, Sarah, 148
Snead, Ben, 122
Snead, Betty, 122
Southern Claims Commission (SCC),
    63–65, 69–70
Spratt, W.D., 65

Stanford, P. Thomas, 169
State v. Samuel, 89
Steed, J. B., 67–68
Steed, Jack, 68
Steed, Lee, 68
Stewart, Austin, 79
Still, Peter, 129
Stone, 87–88
Strickland, Sarah, 152
submission, 8, 26, 38, 42–43, 56, 74, 78, 81, 86, 91, 114, 119, 143

terrorism, 4, 19, 34, 78, 162, 171
Terry, Stephen, 155–56
Thomas, Ella Gertrude Clanton, 9, 115, 127, 131–32, 136–38, 142
Tolbert, 48–51
Tony, 34, 44
torture, 2, 22–23, 43, 79, 115, 129, 134, 151
trauma, 2–5, 10–11, 15–16, 21, 34, 46–47, 72, 80, 86, 94, 113–14, 142, 162
Trimble, B. F., 89–90
trust, 50–51, 62

Union Army, 35, 63–65, 85–86, 137, 170
urban, 3, 10, 13, 17, 29, 134, 144
US Army, 35, 63–64, 137, 170; Colored Infantry, 66. *See also* Union Army
US Bureau of Pensions, 66–68
US Congress, 64–65, 171
US Constitution, 169–70
US Senate, 107–8

venereal disease, 152, 164
Veney, Betheny, 36–37, 45
Venus, 154
Virginia House of Delegates, 139, 141, 148
vulnerability, 4–8, 13–14, 17–23, 35–36, 72, 84–85, 112, 115, 118, 171

Walker, Agnes, 18, 35, 169
Walker, Bryant, 18, 35
Walker, Frank, 18
Walker, Mary, 18–19, 35, 169
Walker, Mildred, 18

Walton, 99
Walton, Mrs. Bird, 27
Ward, William, 79
Ware, William, 90
Watkins, Henry, 101
Wells, Ida B., 172–73
West Africa, 15, 83
white supremacy, 8, 15, 89, 97, 103, 127, 142, 146, 156, 161–62, 167–70, 173
Whitehead, Alzonuth, 148–89
white men, southern: accuse wives of adultery, 145; and discretion, 12, 141–42; and divorce, 15; during the Civil War, 169–70; and enslaved men, 72–75, 79; enslaved women (seek to) resist, 24–27, 38, 120; erotic fantasies, 82; faced no legal repercussions for sex with enslaved women, 17, 19; incentivized to have sex with enslaved women, 9–10, 14, 51–53, 57; on juries, 139; long-term relationships with enslaved women, 14, 29, 41, 43, 69, 85–87; and mastery, 83; and patriarchal authority, 7, 10–15, 71–78, 89, 97, 140–43, 147, 151, 155, 168, 173; in Reconstruction, 171–73; and rights of patriarchy, 90, 140; sexual violence as privilege of, 7, 14–15, 51, 96, 99–103, 114–17, 124–25, 130–31, 146; silences surrounding interracial sex and, 11; viewed as prioritizing Black women's needs over their wives, 153, 161–62. *See also* interracial, sex
whiteness, 7, 75, 147, 161
white women, southern: and Black men's sexual access, 172; concerns about interracial sex, 11–12; and construction of rape culture, 10; and divorce petitions, 141–44, 155–56, 161–63, 166, 168; enslaved women accused of acting like, 147; erotic fantasies, 82; generational knowledge passed on, 116–17; jealousy, 133–36; and the judicial system, 143; labor as taxable, 7; limited rights, 75; and

white women, southern: *(cont.)*
  moral superiority, 153; and motherhood, 36; and power, 13, 15, 114; and
  the private sphere, 124, 127; and
  reproductive exploitation, 115; and
  self-pity, 137; and sexual violence, 8;
  and sexual virtue, 99–100, 145–46;
  and silence, 120
Whitfield, 35, 80–81

widows, 64, 66, 68, 117–18
wills, 31, 43, 48–52, 62, 65, 125
Wilson, Anne, 165–66
Wilson, William, 165–66
Winning, Lias, 81
womanhood: Black, 6, 18–20, 34–35,
  169; white, 99, 138, 161

Young, Annie, 119